On the Cutting Edge
of Globalization

On the Cutting Edge of Globalization

An Inquiry into American Elites

James N. Rosenau
David C. Earnest
Yale H. Ferguson
Ole R. Holsti

ROWMAN & LITTLEFIELD PUBLISHERS, INC.
Lanham • Boulder • New York • Toronto • Oxford

ROWMAN & LITTLEFIELD PUBLISHERS, INC.

Published in the United States of America
by Rowman & Littlefield Publishers, Inc.
A wholly owned subsidiary of The Rowman & Littlefield Publishing Group, Inc.
4501 Forbes Boulevard, Suite 200, Lanham, Maryland 20706
www.rowmanlittlefield.com

P.O. Box 317, Oxford OX2 9RU, UK

British Library Cataloguing in Publication Information Available

Library of Congress Cataloging-in-Publication Data

On the cutting edge of globalization : an inquiry into American elites /
    James N. Rosenau...[et al.].
        p.   cm.
    Includes bibliographical references and index.
    ISBN 0-7425-3975-X (cloth : alk. paper) — ISBN 0-7425-3976-8 (pbk. : alk. paper)
    1. Globalization—Political aspects.   2. Elite (Social sciences)—United States.
  3. Political leadership—United States.   4. United States—Foreign relations—2001–
  I. Rosenau James N.   II. Title.
    JZ1318.O52 2005
    303.48'2—dc22
                                                                    2005003659

Printed in the United States of America

♾™ The paper used in this publication meets the minimum requirements of American
National Standard for Information Sciences—Permanence of Paper for Printed Library
Materials, ANSI/NISO Z39.48–1992.

Contents

Contents

Preface

This book has had a long gestation. The idea of systematically assessing what moves the individuals who sustain and give direction to the processes of globalization has preoccupied us since globalizing dynamics began to accelerate in the early 1990s. But it was not an idea that was easily implemented. A method had to be developed; a research instrument had to be designed; funds had to be raised; data had to be generated; and techniques of incisive data analysis had to be fashioned. Thus, it was not until late in 1999 that we launched the empirical phase of our project. And even then a powerful event (the September 11, 2001, terrorist attacks on New York and Washington) compelled us to return to the field for an upgrade of our database. So it is with a sense of completion as well as more than a little satisfaction that we have reached closure and a bound volume.

Of course, closure is elusive. It never really happens. Like globalization, inquiries into its processes seem endlessly subject to alteration by the course of events, thus compelling an impulse to return to the field yet again (see chapter 11). All of this is to say that we welcome feedback as we ponder still another return to the field.[1]

A central challenge of a book such as this involves treading a fine line between presenting and analyzing systematic data on the one hand and constructing the book so that it can be read easily by those who are neither familiar with nor interested in statistical analysis. The former need to have the materials necessary to assess the accuracy of our substantive analyses, while the latter do not want to be bothered by all the bivariate and multivariate assessments of the data distributions and are thus inclined to accept that we are honorable scholars who would not knowingly distort the findings. We have met this challenge in two ways. Most important, while including the raw numbers and percentages in the books numerous tables as well as indicating which of the compared distributions are statistically significant, we have consigned the detailed statistical analysis of tabular data to a webpage that can be accessed by any reader who wants to dig deeper into the technical aspects and statistical foundations of the data: www.rowmanlittlefield.com/rl/books/rosenau. Second, for those readers who are dubious about any statistical enterprise, we have included a nontechnical dialogue among a "researcher" and two traveling companions who are skeptical about the meaning of the findings.

In addition to the pleasures that have accompanied our collaboration, we happily acknowledge the help and support of several individuals as well as our institutions. The former include Dawn L. Moncrief and Sally Montague, both of whom organized and implemented, at different times, our elaborate data-gathering procedures. This book would not exist without their efforts. Thanks, Dawn and Sally! Dan Foster provided a critical and helpful reaction to an early draft of the manuscript. William J. Kiamie, Einat Erlanger, and Christian Busche also provided valuable help in coding the data. We are also grateful to the members of Rosenau's seminar for conducting the interviews of people who gathered in the streets of Washington to protest the policies of the International Monetary Fund in April 2000. It is equally a pleasure to acknowledge the financial assistance of the National Science Foundation, the vice president for academic affairs at the George Washington University, the Research Council of Duke University, and the Rutgers University Research Council and Center for Global Change and Governance (Newark, New Jersey). Obviously, too, the project could not have been undertaken, much less completed, without the cooperation of the 1,719 leaders who responded to our questionnaires. Their identity is unknown to us, but we are enormously grateful for their cooperation. Finally, we have benefited from the creativity and guidance of our editor at Rowman & Littlefield, Jennifer Knerr, who is a first-rate person as well as a gifted editor.

NOTE

1. Write any or all of us at James N. Rosenau (jnr@gwu.edu), David C. Earnest (Dearnest@odu.edu), Yale H. Ferguson (yfergus@andromeda.rutgers.edu), and Ole R. Holsti (holsti@duke.edu).

1

On the Cutting Edge
of Globalization

For now, I like the feeling of being at home in a lot of places. I am rooted in myself, not in some place. I like the feeling that there are lots of places where I belong, that are familiar.... On New Year's Eve, my brother counted the stamps in my passport. There were 385. Since 1995. A lot of exotic ones like the Ukraine and Macedonia. There's a certain pride you take in the wealth of experience. That's kind of nice. That you belong all over the world rather than a little part. You're proud of the world, not just proud of your neighborhood. Proud to be part of it. It's not like you're saying, "Go Bronx." It's "Go World."

—Esther Dyson[1]

To have responsibilities that are worldwide in scope and that locate an individual on the cutting edge of globalization, as this epigraph suggests, is to undergo a transformation in one's orientations toward the world. It points to the evolution of new priorities, to new understandings of what is important and how one's identity evolves and adapts to globalizing dynamics. This possibility—that elite attitudes and loyalties undergo transformation in response to the tasks of leadership in a globalizing world—is a central concern of the ensuing pages.

* * *

Despite the temptation to conceive of globalization narrowly and exclusively in economic terms, here we employ a broad conception in which globalizing dynamics are conceived to be any processes that underlie the expansion of human activities beyond national boundaries on a scale that has the potential of becoming global in scope. The numerous processes that contribute to this expansivity consist of economic, social, cultural, religious, political, scientific, medical, and communications activities that result in flows of people, ideas, goods, money, pollution, disease, norms, authority, and practices across borders.

Complex as these processes are, however, the rapidly expanding literature on globalization has started to illuminate their dynamics.[2] But there remains at least one aspect of globalizing processes that remains elusive and unexplored as the focus of systematic inquiries: little is known about the leaders who give direction, structure, and meaning to—and set the limits of—the boundary-spanning dynamics and who can thus properly be described as operating on the cutting edge of globalization. How do Cutting-Edgers, as we call them, differ from other leaders in their fields of endeavor? Do they conceive of themselves as being located on the forefront of globalization? Do they interact often? Do they form coordinated networks, or do they mostly go their own way? Do they travel extensively and often, or do they conduct most of their boundary-spanning work electronically? Do they occupy positions to which expectations are attached that underlie their attitudes and actions with respect to globalizing dynamics? Does their participation in globalizing processes change their orientations toward their country of citizenship and the very world they are helping to transform? Do their lives on the cutting edge alter their attitudes toward the meaning of "home" and their local communities, toward change and charitable giving, toward the role of government and the rich–poor gap? Are they concerned about the downsides of globalization, about its possible cultural and environmental consequences and its effects on the stability of governments? Have the so-called battle of Seattle, wherein diverse groups marched to protest diverse globalization issues during a meeting of the World Trade Organization at the end of November 1999, and similar protests given them pause about the transnational activities in which they are involved? Did the September 11 terrorist attacks and the preemptive doctrine on which the war in Iraq was founded alter their orientations toward globalization?

Although answers to these questions require the collection and analysis of empirical data, they also depend on the theoretical perspectives that serve as the bases for gathering and analyzing the data. One such perspective involves the nature of leadership, how it is exercised, and the constraints within which it is limited. Second, the empirical questions cannot be probed without a theoretical perspective on the nature of globalization, its scope, its core processes, and its susceptibility to change. Before presenting our data, exploring our findings, and explicating the methodology we employed to trace the orientations and activities of Cutting-Edgers, we therefore need to set forth our conceptual understanding of what leadership entails with respect to globalization.

This understanding rests on the basic premise that globalization's powerful boundary-spanning processes are sustained by concrete and identifiable people—by public officials who frame issues, make choices, negotiate outcomes, and implement policies; by corporate executives who generate resources, sell products, and focus on market shares; by technological specialists who facilitate communications and the analysis of policy alternatives; by pundits who speak out on public issues; by entertainers, artists, and academics whose works are disseminated abroad and may express political support or dissent; by consumers who purchase goods and by the workers who produce them; by tourists and immigrants who travel extensively; by citizens who join protest marches; and by a host of other individuals who contribute to a vast diversity of transnational and international processes. To be sure, it is not possible to estimate with any exactitude the proportion of the myriad individuals caught up in globalizing dynamics who exercise leadership that gives direction to, or otherwise sustains, these dynamics. However, we are confident that our research instrument has yielded Cutting-Edgers—187 in 1999 and 167 in 2003 derived, respectively, from 889 and 830 larger samples of leaders—and that the orientations and actions they reported are, for better or worse, reflective of leadership on the cutting edge of globalization. As will be seen, the form and extent of their leadership varies considerably, but, taken together, their attitudes and activities provide insight into the processes that lie at the core of globalization.

NOTES

1. Quoted in Joel Garreau, "Home Is Where the Phone Is: Roaming Legion of High-Tech Nomads Takes Happily to Ancient Path," *Washington Post*, October 17, 2000, A1. Esther Dyson is an entrepreneur and a former chairwoman of the Internet Corporation for Assigned Names and Numbers.
2. See the 713 entries in the bibliography listed in Jan Aart Scholte, *Globalization: A Critical Introduction* (New York: St. Martin's Press, 2000), 318–48.

2

Theoretical Perspectives

While the nature and potential of leaders and leadership have long been a preoccupation of thoughtful observers and political activists, the complexity of present-day world affairs and the diverse ways in which globalizing dynamics appear to be lessening the authority of states have greatly intensified these preoccupations and significantly expanded the range and number of leadership positions that involve their occupants in globalizing activities. However, the very same complexity tends to encourage simplification and lead to analyses in which the course of events is all too easily ascribed to only the judgments, prejudices, and actions of the heads of states and international organizations, thus ignoring the multiplicity of leaders whose policies and actions contribute to the dynamics of globalization. Hence, political assessments and agendas today are crowded with issues that are often confined to the leadership exercised by political figures. But heads of state and their aides have to be territorial in their orientations, whereas Cutting-Edgers outside the political arena are able to look beyond territorial boundaries.

A theoretical approach to leaders who sustain globalization must thus be broad in scope and allow for clarity on a number of questions that are not likely to arise if only political leaders are of concern: to what extent are nonpolitical Cutting-Edgers mired in territorial orientations, or to what extent have their border-crossing activities freed them of such concerns? Should Cutting-Edgers be examined in terms of the values and traits they bring to their leadership positions? Are their conceptions of globalization shaped by salient experiences, ambitions, and commitments that evolved in earlier years? Or are Cutting-Edgers best understood as products of their time and cultures? In short, how do we go about probing the dynamics whereby Cutting-Edgers lead effectively, erratically, or minimally? Such questions ought to pervade an ever-growing literature, and they ought to do so for a good reason: given the large degree to which the course of events may hinge on the nature and exercise of leadership by those who occupy high positions in the institutions that sustain and give direction to globalization, probing inquiries are needed into how leaders cope with complexity and exercise their authority.

Our response to the foregoing questions is rooted in a long-standing notion that appropriate answers are best developed through explicating a multivariate conception, even a theory, of the nature of leadership in this period of late modernity marked by enormous complexity. Without an explicit approach to the subject, observers may rely on simplified analyses that either employ rational choice models to discount leaders as products of structural factors or that buy into intuitive assessments in which leaders are viewed as having brought the individual qualities they acquired in their early years to the leadership position they eventually occupy. Through explication, on the other hand, one can avoid both resorting to rational choice perspectives and downplaying the role of individual characteristics by locating Cutting-Edgers among domestic and globalizing dynamics that interactively shape and sustain the course of events. Here we approach the conceptualizing task by employing the following formula: Leadership = Extensive Expectations + Considerable Followership + Limited Discretion. None of the terms of the formula alone explains any single leader, but taken together they serve to account for how and why most leaders act as they do.

Before developing this formulation and applying it to the data on globalizing elites, we find it important to acknowledge that, as far as we know, our samples do not include anyone in the top leadership of the U.S. government. As implied, our conception of globalization is that its dynamics are to a large extent initiated and sustained by a broad range of leaders who occupy positions that do not require them to protect and advance the territorial integrity of their country. Obviously, however, there are important respects in which the nature and scope of globalization are shaped by top officials. Through their policies promoting trade and restricting immigration, for example, officials set boundaries within which globalizing processes play out. Likewise, the dynamics of globalization may be reconfigured during periods of high international tension when public officials focus on security issues, as has been the case since the attacks of September 11, 2001. Yet, notwithstanding the crucial role that governmental policies play in structuring the ways in which globalization unfolds at any moment in history, we regard these policies and the international conditions they seek to advance or offset as boundary conditions within which the orientations and activities of globalizing elites pursue their goals and make their decisions. Accordingly, our research instrument included variables that allow us to assess the impact of both domestic and international developments on Cutting-Edgers, but it does not treat these developments or the officials responsible for them as dimensions of globalization itself.

A THEORETICAL PERSPECTIVE ON LEADERSHIP

Underlying the analysis is a conception that posits all roles, both those of leaders and those of followers, as consisting of the expectations that the role occupants have of themselves as well as the expectations of them held by others—their role partners—with whom, for a variety of reasons, they have to interact.[1] Whatever their scope, all roles are composed of three realms: a realm that embraces the formal requirements or expectations embedded in a role, a realm that encompasses the informal requirements, and a discretionary realm that enables the occupant to employ his or her particular values, talents, and past experiences in order to perform in the role. The discretionary realm, in effect, provides leaders leeway to interpret the formal and informal requirements as they deem necessary. But there are limits to the discretion they can exercise that, in effect, trace the outer boundaries of the role beyond which the occupant is normally removed from the role. Starting with the collapse of Enron, the firing and prosecution of corrupt corporate executives in the United States form a quintessential example of how role limits can lead to the ouster of their occupants.

On those rare occasions when occupants are not removed from a role even though their conduct seems to exceed its outer limits, the role can be said to have undergone alteration along with the system in which it is located. For example, when students occupied the offices of university presidents in the 1960s, they were deemed to have exceeded the discretionary realm of their roles. Yet, after a period of turmoil and jailings, most universities, rather than ousting the students, agreed not to dismiss all those who were involved. Instead, the students were given seats on university committees and allowed to participate in their decision-making processes. In effect, the university system was altered rather the students being removed from their roles.

It follows that the distinction between the informal and discretionary realms in which any role is located is the difference between the known expectations attached to the role in the case of its informal requirements and the more ambiguous, often unarticulated limits set by the broad cultural or national system in which the role is located. Students had never been told not to occupy presidential offices, but both they and the presidents discovered that such behavior exceeded the student role.

Extensive Expectations

What follows applies both to leaders in organizations and to artists, writers, musicians, athletes, and others whose leadership status is based on individual talents and accomplishments. In both cases, extensive expectations attach to roles, but unlike nonorganizational leaders, those who occupy positions in organizations are subject to internal bureaucratic processes as well as limits imposed by their external environments. Irrespective of whether their leadership derives from individual accomplishments or from occupancy of top positions in political, governmental, business, academic, or any other type of organization, Cutting-Edgers have to minimally adhere to expectations that attach to their roles in order to remain effective in them. No matter how able, aggressive, or inspirational they may be, leaders whose conduct consistently falls short of the basic expectations embedded in their roles are eventually demoted, voted out of office, shunted aside, or otherwise removed from their positions. All the persons with whom a leader interacts in the performance of his or her role share the expectations, as do the role occupants themselves, or else the mismatch between the conduct of the former and that of the latter would become glaring and result in the leader's ouster.

By *expectations*, what is not meant are those transitory concerns linked to particular issues. Aside from illegal conduct or behavior that violates the fundamental norms of their organization or community, leaders can usually ride out any disaffection that may accompany particular actions in particular situations. It is when they continuously ignore, dismiss, or otherwise fall short of the basic expectations held by their followers that occupancy of their leadership positions become tenuous.

The formal expectations inherent in any organizational position are inscribed in constitutions, bylaws, court decisions, legislative regulations, or any other documented expectations. The formal expectations are neither subtle nor elaborate. They set forth the broad limits within which leaders are required to exercise the authority accorded to and embedded in their positions. On the other hand, the informal expectations that attach to roles are numerous and specific, but they are not recorded in writing. Nonetheless, they are no less firm than those set forth in written documents. Indeed, precisely because they are so extensive, the informal expectations can be rigorous and demanding, compelling leaders to conform even though they are not legally required to do so. Nothing in the constitution or legislative enactments of the United States, to cite an example from the world of politics, requires a secretary of state to testify before congressional committees; but all secretaries have, and it can be safely anticipated that all future secretaries will. That expectation is built into the organization's structure—the separation of powers—and is just as controlling as any that may be formally prescribed.

Likewise, expectations are not confined only to those with whom the role occupant personally and frequently interacts. In the case of political leaders and corporate executives, for example, they may be no less subject to the expectations of their societies and leaders abroad than they are to others in their organizations or counterparts among their competitors. Figure 2.1 uses an example from the world of politics to suggest the importance and complexity of this vast array of expectations. The president of the United States may be the most powerful leader in the world, but figure 2.1 clearly indicates that the position's occupant is deeply embedded in and confined by a myriad set of role relationships.

Much the same can be said about nonorganizational leaders. They are not subjected to the extensive formal expectations or bureaucratic pressures to which their organizational counterparts must be responsive, but nonetheless they cannot readily exceed the boundaries imposed by the norms of their professions or societies. In the case of performing artists, for example, they risk crossing a line of societal rejection and abandonment when they take issue with public policies during wartime. To take a recent example of many that could be cited, the Dixie Chicks, a popular Texan singing trio, suffered radio boycotts and public CD burnings after its lead singer told a London audience, "Just so you know, we're ashamed the president of the United States is from Texas." Indeed, within a week, the airplay of their music dropped 20 percent. Comparable consequences followed for actors Susan Sarandon, Martin Sheen, Sean Penn, and Janeane Garofalo, among others, when they publicly expressed opposition to the U.S. role in Iraq.[2] Or consider how artists fare under authoritarian regimes: during the communist period both Alexander Solzhenitsyn and Vaclav Havel paid the heavy price imposed on outspoken writers who violated the conformity norms of their systems.

Role Conflict

Given the multiplicity of diverse situations that leaders must address, and given the variety of actors internal and external to their organizations who have expectations of how the situations should be handled, a central problem for any leader arises whenever the various expectations are in conflict, whenever adhering to one set of expectations amounts to negating other sets. No leader can be all things to all those who constitute his or her circle of followers. Choices often have to be made, and those who are on the wrong side of the choices may readily be vociferous in their discontent over the leader's actions. In the example of the secretary of state's testifying before a congressional committee, he or she may have to choose between (1) supporting the demands of allies and offending key members of Congress and (2) pleasing the Congress and causing distress abroad, a role conflict

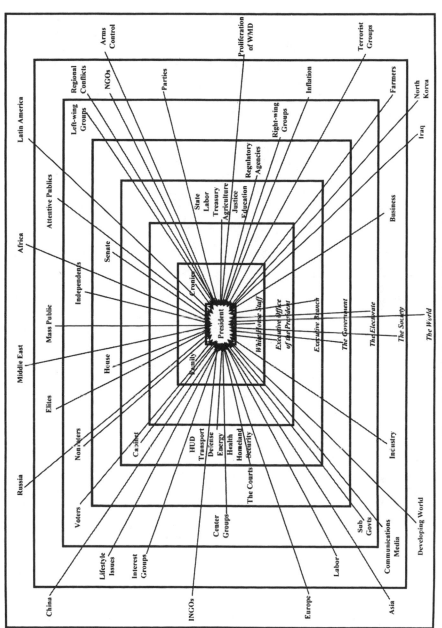

Figure 2.1   Role Partners of the U.S. President

that—to cite only but one of numerous examples that could be noted—former secretaries Dean Acheson and John Foster Dulles resolved quite differently, in good part because the latter sought to avoid the congressional hostility visited on the former.[3] In short, role conflicts are unavoidable, and effective leadership crucially depends on managing the conflicts in such a way that the losers on an issue do not opt out of the leader's followership.

Put differently, leadership never involves license for leaders to do whatever they please. Perforce, they must conduct their affairs in the context of many constraints. Even the most authoritarian leader is constrained, bounded by the limits of acceptability considered important by his peoples. It is dubious whether Stalin could have successfully required all men in the Soviet Union to grow beards, just as Hitler would probably not have remained in office long if he had ordered all German men to wear wigs. Several years ago, to cite an empirical example, the Chinese leadership ordered the dismantling of all satellite dishes, but a visitor to any city of China today will find the skyline dotted with satellite dishes.

Considerable Followership

Leadership is intimately and inextricably tied to followership. No leader can take his or her followers for granted. If the performances of Cutting-Edgers across time fall short of meeting the minimum expectations of their role partners, or if external circumstances change such that their performances fail to cope with the new situations, then the likelihood is that such leaders will lose favor and eventually be forced out of office. Some devotees and acolytes may remain faithful, but sound leadership requires considerable followership, a broad support among the relevant publics that can withstand the moments of unexpected downturn or acute crisis.

To be sure, in the case of authoritarian rulers, followership can be maintained through the threat and exercise of force. As the end of the Cold War has indicated, however, such followership can be fragile and hardly conducive to moving a society forward. Creative leadership requires a voluntary followership. The transformation of China's economy from communist to capitalist foundations is succeeding as much because the followership has become less ritualistic and more innovative as because the leadership has become less rigid.

But what about charismatic leaders, it might be asked. Are they not able to employ their charisma to overcome lethargic followership and any doubts about their leadership? The questions are profoundly misleading. They imply that charisma is inherent in a leader's personality and style, in character traits that the leader possesses. But charisma is not simply a possession. A leader's charisma is also deeply embedded in the orientations and needs of his or her followers. It can quickly dissipate, say, if a severe recession sets in, if corruption is uncovered, if a strike cripples an organization, or if a war is lost. Long is the list of so-called charismatic leaders, even those with police powers at their disposal, who were toppled when the charisma they "possessed" failed to maintain the compliance of their followers. If it means anything, in short, charisma is relational, a set of ties between leaders and those who are ready to follow their lead and comply with their urgings. It is rooted as much in the minds and emotions of followers as in the qualities of leaders.

Stated differently, followership today increasingly derives not from tradition but from how well leaders in both the public and the private sector perform in their roles. Indeed, in the present era, political legitimacy—that crucial foundation of viable societies—has undergone and is still undergoing a transformation in which traditional legitimacy has been replaced by performance legitimacy.[4] Publics are accepting of leaders if their conduct conforms, at least minimally, to the expectations built into their roles. Otherwise, as noted and as is readily evident in the recent histories of chief executive officer Michael Eisner of the Disney Corporation, president Hugo Chávez in Venezuela, former presidents Sanchez de Lozada of Bolivia and Jean-Bertrand Aristide of Haiti, and former governor Grey Davis of California, a leader's tenure is likely to be tumultuous and limited, perhaps even cut short of his or her prescribed term. The ouster and jailing of the leaders of Enron, Arthur Anderson, and other corporate heads when their corrupt practices became known provide a quintessential insight into the limits that expectations impose on leadership roles.

Limited Discretion

Is this to say that the personal qualities of leaders, their personalities, values, and talents, are irrelevant to how they conduct themselves and to the goals they do or do not achieve? No, it is not. Leaders are not prisoners of their roles. The unique qualities of any leader contribute to or detract from his or her successes. As noted, every leadership position can be seen to have a realm that entitles its occupant to pursue their values, express their personalities, and apply their prior experiences, thereby enabling them to exercise discretion in pursuit of their policies. And the higher the position in the organization, the greater the discretion accorded its occupant: a secretary of state who negotiates treaties has much more discretion than a secretary who types treaties. Furthermore, the way in which leaders use this discretionary power differentiates them from their predecessors and successors even as the formal and informal requirements of their roles account for the continuities that mark different leaders who occupy the same position through time.[5]

As for those whose leadership status does not derive from the occupancy of an organizational position, the better known they are, the wider their latitude to reframe issues and affirm unpopular perspectives. They achieve their status through unusual accomplishments that accord them freedom to advance causes that may run counter to the prevailing currents of public opinion. But there are limits to the discretion with which they can exercise this freedom. As we have noted, outspoken celebrities run the risk of suffering losses at the box office or reduced sales of their work because of their public statements. Jane Fonda's experience during the Vietnam War is a case in point. Today's celebrities, moreover, must cope with opposition mobilized through the Internet: "Web sites with names like Boycott-Hollywood.us and Famousidiot.com are spearheading e-mail and telephone campaigns against stars and, in the case of television performers, the companies that advertise on their shows."[6]

Put differently, in some ways the limits of discretion available to celebrities are more severe than those imposed on the ordinary person. Consider this excerpt from a letter by the president of the baseball Hall of Fame, Dale Petroskey, to actor Tim Robbins, one of the leads in the famous baseball movie *Bull Durham*, who criticized the United States for its role in the Iraq war. A weekend celebration of the movie's fifteenth anniversary was scheduled at the Hall of Fame, but Petroskey canceled it, explaining in the letter to Robbins the reason for the cancellation: "In a free country such as ours, every American has the right to his or her own opinions, and to express them. Public figures, such as you, have platforms much larger than the average American's, which provides you with an extraordinary opportunity to have your views heard—and an equally large obligation to act and speak responsibly."[7]

Another revealing example of both the range and the limits of discretion that attaches to nonorganizational leaders is that of George Soros. Both a financier and a philanthropist who has acquired a huge fortune in the former capacity even as he has given away huge amounts of money in the latter capacity, Soros has created a role for himself that is subjected to few formal and informal expectations and that allows him ample room to act on his personal commitments and values. He has broken the Bank of England and incurred the explicit enmity of a head of state (Mohammad Mahathir of Malaysia), but he is not tied down by an organization (other than the ones he created to manage his investments and charitable gifts) or by long residence in one country (he has four homes, three in the United States and one in the United Kingdom, though his strongest attachments appear to be to Eastern Europe and Hungary, where he was born and grew up). In effect, Soros pushes to an extreme our conception of how expectations are held by the role partners of leaders and by their own notion of what those expectations entail. As long as he does not engage in corrupt business operations or espouse ideas that are widely unacceptable, there are virtually no limits on his discretion nor expectations to which he is obliged to respond. The only limits on his discretion are the markets in which he invests, the goals to which he aspires, and the criticism to which his speculations give rise. While he has rarely been thwarted by markets, his goals have proved elusive, because of the popular perception that his philanthropy is inconsistent with his market speculations, since he desires nothing less than changing the world through his philanthropy and his writings. His vision for the future involves a "global open society,"[8] in which global capitalism is so unstable that it needs to be subjected to more international controls. He is deeply committed to globalization even as he warns against its excesses,[9] though his critics allege he is partly responsible for those excesses. In sum, the Soros example demonstrates that leadership is constrained by the nuanced expectations of followers.

It is worth noting that perhaps the most important set of discretionary decisions organizational leaders have to make are those in which they are subjected to contradictory pressures from their constituencies. As implied in figure 2.1, for political leaders such role conflicts are increasingly pervasive in this complex time, when the boundary between domestic and foreign affairs is increasingly porous.[10] Similarly, corporate executives are under continuous external pressure to improve the bottom line while resisting internal impulses to tamper with the annual figures. Indeed, in no leadership position are the role conflicts likely to be more excruciating than those in which the external demands are in sharp contrast with those emanating from within the organization.

On the other hand, in the case of the leaders sampled in our surveys, this conception of leadership as that stemming from the occupancy of roles highlights the important point that there is much more to leadership than the commitments, dedication, strengths, and weaknesses that Cutting-Edgers bring to their tasks. Indeed, as already indicated, the discretionary realm of any role is limited and not necessarily as wide as the realms composing its formal and informal requirements. Postwar American presidents, for example, differed considerably in their age, religion, education, party affiliations, philosophies, and prior experiences, but for the most part they pursued the same foreign policies.

Some might argue that the eleventh postwar U.S. president, George W. Bush, is an exception in this regard, that his withdrawal from several treaty commitments and his commitment to a policy of preemptive military strikes constitute a unilateral orientation that departs significantly from the multilateralism pursued by his ten postwar predecessors. But his unilateral orientations were jolted by the terrorist attacks of September 11, 2001, when it became clear that contesting terrorism necessitated working with allies abroad, with the result that he turned to the United Nations and yielded to other multilateral expectations built into the office that his predecessors had also honored. Then, when the UN Security Council rejected his proposal for military action against Iraq, Bush's unilateralist impulses surfaced once more and the war was launched, only to be quelled when the war was over and allies were again needed to help in the rebuilding of Iraq. Sharp fluctuations of this sort do not negate the power of role expectations; they only reaffirm the aforementioned point that the higher the position occupied by a leader, the wider the discretionary realm available to him or her.

Much the same can even be said about authoritarian leaders in the present period. They too feel obliged to respond to the informal external requirements of their role when an international organization or great power insists, say, that they admit inspectors to check whether they are developing weapons of mass destruction. Stated more generally, there are good reasons why even the most authoritarian of leaders hold periodic elections. Even though the elections may be rigged or they may have only the leader's name on the ballot and result in near 100 percent of the votes being recorded in his or her favor, authoritarians still experience a periodic need to affirm for themselves and their publics that they have met the domestic expectations of their position.

In short, while they are not prisoners of their roles, organizational leaders are not free to act as they please. To repeat, at the very least they must conform their actions and policies to the minimum expectations that attach to their positions. Put more assertively, whatever may be the discretionary realm available to them, to a large extent they are locked into positions that do not offer an unlimited capacity for bypassing the demands of their bureaucratic, domestic, and external constituencies.

Role Requirements and Change

Finally, if leaders are as locked into their positions as the foregoing formulation suggests, it might be wondered how meaningful change can occur. If the formal and informal requirements of leadership roles limit the extent to which their occupants can chart new goals and initiate new policies, how can anyone explain those moments of history when sharp breaks occur in the paths that organizations or societies follow through the course of time? The answer has multiple components. One component involves profound new developments within or external to an organization. A scandal, a depression, a war, or a technological breakthrough exemplifies the kind of event that so alters the informal expectations to which leaders must be sensitive that they are free—or, more accurately, required—to revise their priorities and alter the path down which they have been traveling. Then there are generational differences, those slowly evolving changes that lead to new values through which organizational lifestyles and markets are transformed and result in corresponding alterations in the expectations to which leaders had best respond. On rare occasions, too, forceful leaders may be able to overcome the restraints of their roles and successfully exercise discretion on behalf of values that their predecessors either did not contemplate or failed to realize. When this happens, the role can be said to have changed in key respects. A recent example is readily observable in the preemptive policies announced and pursued by President Bush in Iraq: the role partners noted in figure 2.1 have not changed, but the president's conduct in some of those relationships altered their substance.

In sum, for understandable reasons, it is possible to exaggerate the importance of leaders by downplaying the constraints with which they must cope. And it is easy to fail to appreciate that the course of events is sustained by the interactions that endlessly unfold between the attitudes and actions of people at the microlevel and the conduct of the leaders at the macrolevel.[11] As already noted, there can be no leadership without followership, and the importance of the latter is such that often it is not clear who is leading and who is following.

Role Expectations of Cutting-Edgers

The ensuing formulation of theoretical perspectives on globalization attaches considerable discretion to the roles of Cutting-Edgers. While there are more than a few positions that lock Cutting-Edgers into globalizing processes and require them to develop positive or negative orientations toward globalization—the executives of multinational corporations and labor unions are, respectively, illustrative of such roles—many other types of leadership roles offer their occupants leeway as to whether they are affirmative or resistant in their attitudes and actions toward globalizing dynamics. To cite an obvious example, media executives can hardly avoid participation in globalizing processes, but their jobs may allow them to adhere to a variety of favorable or opposing stances with respect to whether globalization should be encouraged or contested. For many Cutting-Edgers, in other words, globalization involves issues that may be only peripheral to the Cutting-Edgers' prime responsibilities, thus complicating the task of outlining a theoretical perspective on their likely conduct with respect to globalizing dynamics. More accurately, if economic processes are conceptualized as being only one of several dimensions of globalization (as we do in what follows), then the theoretical challenge is substantially greater.

A Theoretical Perspective on Globalization

Although globalization is viewed by many analysts as involving economic processes whereby trade and money flow freely around the world, we regard such a perspective as being much too narrow, as failing to account for the many other processes that have greatly reduced time and distance and thus rendered the world an increasingly smaller place. Accordingly, as indicated, here we offer a multivariate perspective on globalization. We are convinced that there are a multiplicity of globalizations, many globalizations that differ in the nature and kinds of activities they sustain even as they have one major quality in common: all of them are boundary-spanning processes. Whether the spanning processes involve ideas, norms, money, people, goods, practices, disease, terrorists, drugs, crime, pollution, or many other dimensions of modern life, they are not confined to the territorial space of conventional boundaries. Instead, as facilitated by the advent of microelectronic and other technologies, including the wide-body jet plane, virtually every dimension of life today has been touched by globalization. Indeed, our theoretical perspective treats the antiglobalization movement as a form of globalization. Being global in scope, it is one type of boundary-spanning process.

Our theoretical task is thus to develop a perspective that is sufficiently flexible to allow for the various processes and structures that constitute globalization. For example, a theory of information flows, such as those through the Internet and via global television, is needed to explore the technological aspects of globalizing dynamics, just as a theory of mobility is needed to probe the incentives and consequences through which tourists, business executives, immigrants, and other travelers shape and sustain globalization. The same theoretical imperatives could be listed with respect to the cultural, economic, monetary, environmental, political, and other major aspects of boundary-spanning flows. The enormity of these tasks raises difficult questions: Is a theory of globalization possible that allows for the derivation of hypotheses as to the attitudes and activities of Cutting-Edgers irrespective of the particular boundaries they span in their leadership roles? Did the battle of Seattle and subsequent skirmishes, the September 11 attacks, and the onset of a new terrorist/security climate curtail enthusiasm for globalization, heighten opposition to it, or otherwise redirect it? Has globalization thinking been shunted aside as the effects of tourism, trade, and other globalizing dynamics have lessened and the salience of the military power of states increased? How flexible are the expectations that attach to the roles of Cutting-Edgers? Have the expectations been altered by recent events? Indeed, what are the basic expectations of cutting-edge roles that prevail in all the realms wherein Cutting-Edgers are active? In short, is there an overarching set of theoretical premises that are relevant and applicable to both the diverse domains in which globalizing dynamics are operative and the consequences of unexpected shifts in the structures of world politics?

Our response to such queries is nuanced. Since each type of boundary-spanning activity can vary widely and thus require its own theoretical premises, generalizing about Cutting-Edgers is not easy. Perforce, our theorizing must be cast at a level that obtains for whatever fields of endeavor in which Cutting-Edgers may be engaged. This is another way of saying that, yes, we do envision an overarching set of theoretical hypotheses derived from a notion of what orientations and actions all cutting-edge roles expect of their occupants.

We start with the hypothesis that Cutting-Edgers, whatever their particular lines of work and irrespective of whether they favor or oppose globalization, are expected to establish and maintain contacts with counterparts beyond the boundaries of their home countries. Such expectations may require them to travel widely and to engage in electronic contacts with their role partners abroad. Built into their roles, in short, is a pervasive expectation that they be deeply involved in globalizing dynamics.

In addition to the activities to which their role expectations give rise, the same expectations are likely to encourage distinctive orientations on the part of Cutting-Edgers. Whether they are inclined to favor or oppose globalization, one consequence of their extensive involvement in globalizing processes is their appreciation of the contradictions and ambiguities of world affairs and the difficulties of bringing about change in the situations they are expected to address. Presumably, too, they perceive that the profound changes at work in the world infuse much greater complexity into global life and become increasingly central to the course of events at every level of community.[12] They may well be aware of the substantial evidence that rapid and pervasive boundary-spanning transformations are everywhere, as neoliberal economic policies, vast movements of people around the world, electronic and transportation technologies, and a host of other dynamics have led to the collapse of time and distance. It follows that individuals who are deeply involved in the economic, social, and political transformations have not simply absorbed the changes into their traditional behavior.[13] Rather, our social-scientific theoretical antennae tell us that all peoples—rich and poor, leaders and followers, Northerners and Southerners—are likely to have had significant aspects of their lives, outlooks, practices, and relationships effected by globalizing processes and the backlashes against them. More than that, we presume that some of the most extensive alterations have occurred in the lives of Cutting-Edgers in every line of endeavor who, for a variety of reasons, initiate or sustain the transformations presently underway. Unlike those who prefer existing or traditional institutions, Cutting-Edgers seem likely to seize the opportunities

afforded by the worlds they are creating and alter their long-standing practices and orientations to accommodate the dynamics of globalization. Such
reorientation may even involve a limited reaffirmation of the value of "the
local" in their own hyperglobal lives. Conceivably, Cutting-Edgers, not
least because of their often-rootless travel lifestyles, may be all the more
connected to "home." At the same time, given that they recognize the complexities inherent in globalizing processes, most Cutting-Edgers are likely
to be cautious about the prospects of achieving their goals.

But we do not see Cutting-Edgers as simply being those at the top of
their organizations, those with the highest salaries, or those who regu-
larly attend the annual meeting of the World Economic Forum at Davos,
Switzerland. Rather, we employ a complex and multifaceted conception
of Cutting-Edgers as being persons who configure the boundary-spanning
flows through extensive experience abroad, through networking or otherwise maintaining a growing acquaintanceship with counterparts in other
lands, and through recognition that their work entails responsibilities for
sustaining or reshaping the processes of globalization. In effect, Cutting-
Edgers are conceived as being persons highly involved in globalizing processes (or to put it in operational terms, as will be seen, as those who score
high on the Involvement Index).

Another dimension of the expectations that may attach to cutting-
edge roles concerns loyalties. It seems reasonable to anticipate that the
more Cutting-Edgers become enmeshed in the processes of globalization,
the more the priorities among their orientations toward their country, their
organization, and themselves are likely to change. At least in the case of
those who favor and benefit from such processes, it seems likely that their
expanded horizons will lead to a diminution of their national loyalties and
an increase in their sense of a more-encompassing world as an appropriate
focus for their allegiance—what is often comparable to the kind of cosmopolitanism expressed by Esther Dyson in the epigraph of chapter 1. But
can the same be said about leaders who are not on the cutting edge of
globalization? Are Other Leaders (as we shall call them) more or less likely
to face such loyalty conflicts than are Cutting-Edgers? Does involvement
in globalization induce Other Leaders to place their professional obligations above those that attach to their citizenship? Does globalization tend
to induce leaders to be more selfish or more altruistic?

To complicate matters further, there may be some leaders who are deeply
engaged in globalizing processes but whose orientations are not readily
viewed as being those of a cosmopolitan. Leaders of nongovernmental organizations (NGOs) are illustrative in this regard. The explosive growth
of their organizations across traditional boundaries may well induce them
to attach loyalties to collectivities other than the nation-state. These organizations may be worldwide in presence and scope—such as Amnesty

International or Greenpeace—or they may be so local in their perspective that their orientations and loyalties do not undergo substantial alterations. Consider the Zapatistas or other separatist movements. The reach and activities of their leaders may be global, but their orientations remain local as they struggle to achieve greater autonomy. In the case of the Zapatistas, their leaders have local orientations and objectives, but they rely on global communications and the ability to mobilize distant masses in order to compensate for their relatively meager resources.[14] In terms of leadership on the cutting edge, in short, the local–global distinction is hardly clear-cut.[15]

Furthermore, it is one thing to note the advent and significance of NGOs but quite another to argue that all or many of them are antistate or that many people will defy their governments either at the behest of an NGO with which they may identify or on their own initiative. Nevertheless, the antiglobalization movement that began in Seattle in 1999 and continues to this day demonstrates the degree to which some persons are ready to react to globalization as individuals or as followers of groups that are dramatically and even violently opposed to corporate policies or the positions espoused by the official representatives of their countries. Ironically, it is the antiglobalization movement that perhaps best exemplifies the willingness of people to place a transnational agenda above the interests of their nation-state even though their agendas may be essentially subnational or local in scope.

Cutting-Edgers, Other Leaders, and the Public at Large

While our inquiry focuses exclusively on Cutting-Edgers and Other Leaders, note needs to be taken of where ordinary citizens might fit in the globalizing dynamics that may be transforming orientations, identities, and loyalties. With one minor and unrepresentative exception (see tables 3.2 and 3.3), we have not surveyed members of the larger public who do not occupy positions of leadership. At best we can only speculate that while substantial segments of the public are aware that they live in an age of globalization, that jobs get outsourced, that it is possible and even easy to get information from distant places around the global, and that many of these places are accessible through the jet aircraft, the incentives for ordinary citizens to evolve new identities, to undergo a shift in their sense of territoriality, and to rethink their loyalties are not nearly so great as is the case for those in leadership echelons. Indeed, one observer perceives that "some people in American elite groups, business, financial, intellectual, professional, and even governmental, were becoming denationalized and developing transnational and cosmopolitan identities superseding their national ones," with the result being a "gap" that has "emerged between the primacy of national identity for most Americans and the growth of transnational identities among controllers of power, wealth, and knowledge in American society."[16] The extent to which such a gap has evolved cannot be deduced from the data and analyses presented in subsequent chapters, notwithstanding hints in the data that in some respects the gap may not be as wide as the foregoing comment suggests.[17]

SUMMARIZING HYPOTHESES

Several propositions that pertain to all the diverse types of globalization follow from the foregoing lines of reasoning. They may not add up to an overarching theory, but neither are they confined to particular types of Cutting-Edgers:

1. Since Cutting-Edgers are deeply immersed in globalizing processes, they are more likely than Other Leaders to look with favor on what they regard as being globalization.
2. Since Cutting-Edgers, whatever their particular lines of work, occupy roles that are extensively connected to the worlds beyond the borders of their countries, they presumably travel abroad more than Other Leaders do and are also more electronically connected to counterparts elsewhere.
3. The extensive involvement of Cutting-Edgers in leadership roles composed of expectations that they cope with or that extend globalizing processes is likely to shape their loyalties more than is the case for Other Leaders.
4. Cutting-Edgers are more likely to be sensitive to changing global circumstances than are Other Leaders.

These propositions are far from exhaustive. They do not subsume many of our findings, but they are singled out for explication because they underlie the original incentives to undertake the research presented in the ensuing chapters.

Furthermore, the propositions should not be interpreted as implying that the Other Leaders in our samples consist largely of individuals opposed to globalization. As seen in the next chapter, our procedures were designed to identify leaders on the cutting edge of globalization irrespective of whether they approved of its goals and practices. Largely because the antiglobalization movement did not gain momentum and prominence prior to the design and application of the first of two iterations of our research instrument, we did not attempt to compile a sample of persons sympathetic to this movement any more than we sought to survey those enthusiastic about the dynamism of globalization. Thus, while the Other Leaders in our samples were drawn from the same leadership compendia as the Cutting-Edgers, the former's orientations and activities as leaders were not so fully linked to the processes of globalization for them to record a sufficiently high score on the Involvement Index, used to identify the Cutting-Edgers. The compilation of the two samples, the construction of the Involvement Index, and the procedures used to differentiate the Cutting-Edgers from the Other Leaders constitute the focus of the next chapter.

NOTES

1. This section draws on James N. Rosenau, "Followership and Discretion: Assessing the Dynamics of Modern Leadership," *Harvard International Review* 26, no. 3 (Fall 2004), http://hir.harvard.edu/articles/index.html?id=1251 (accessed April 7, 2005).

2. Warren St. John, "The Backlash Grows against Celebrity Activists," *New York Times*, March 23, 2003, section 9, 1; Zev Singer, "Silence Doesn't Mean Defeat," *Ottawa Citizen*, April 29, 2003, A6; Nicholas Wapshott, "Anti-war Celebrities Count the Cost," *The Times* (London), May 10, 2003, 16; and Howard Kurtz, "No Kidding on Iraq," *Washington Post*, January 27, 2003, C1.

3. See, for example, James N. Rosenau, "Private Preferences and Political Responsibilities: The Relative Potency of Individual and Role Variables in the Behavior of U.S. Senators," in *Quantitative International Politics: Insights and Evidence*, ed. J. D. Singer (New York: Free Press, 1968), 17–50.

4. James N. Rosenau, *Turbulence in World Politics: A Theory of Change and Continuity* (Princeton, N.J.: Princeton University Press, 1990), 380–83.

5. The differential uses of these discretionary powers have long been the focus of complex psychological appraisals of the orientations and decision-making styles of leaders. One of the first efforts along this line can be found in Margaret G. Hermann and Thomas W. Milburn, eds., *A Psychological Examination of Political Leaders* (New York: Free Press, 1977). For a more recent inquiry, see Margaret G. Hermann and Juliet Kaarbo, "Leadership Styles of Prime Ministers: How Individual Differences Affect the Foreign Policymaking Process," *Leadership Quarterly* 9 (Fall 1998): 243–63.

6. St. John, "Backlash Grows," 1.

7. Ira Berkow, "The Hall of Fame Will Tolerate No Dissent," *New York Times*, April 11, 2003, S4. Perhaps the fact that twenty-eight thousand people called or sent critical e-mail messages in response to the letter further delineates the range of discretion inherent in the roles of outspoken celebrities.

8. George Soros, *George Soros on Globalization* (New York: PublicAffairs, 2002), 149–79.

9. George Soros, *Crisis of Global Capitalism: Open Society Endangered* (New York: PublicAffairs, 1998).

10. James N. Rosenau, *Along the Domestic-Foreign Frontier: Exploring Governance in a Turbulent World* (Cambridge: Cambridge University Press, 1997).

11. For a lengthy analysis of how micro- and macrointeractions sustain events, see James N. Rosenau, *Distant Proximities: Dynamics beyond Globalization* (Princeton, N.J.: Princeton University Press, 2003).

12. John Urry, *Global Complexity* (Cambridge: Polity Press, 2003).

13. For full discussions of the various transformations at work in the present era, see Rosenau, *Along the Domestic-Foreign Frontier*, and Yale H. Ferguson and Richard W. Mansbach, *Remapping Global Politics: History's Revenge and Future Shock* (Cambridge: Cambridge University Press, 2005).

14. Thomas Olesen, *International Zapatismo: The Construction of Solidarity in the Age of Globalization* (London: Zed Books, 2003).

15. The nexus between the local and the global is explored at length in Rosenau, *Distant Proximities*, chaps. 1–8.

16. Samuel P. Huntington, *Who Are We? The Challenges to America's National Identity* (New York: Simon & Schuster, 2004), 7–8.

17. See the data descriptive of the leaders' attachment to "home" set forth in chapter 5.

3

The 1999 and 2003 Surveys: Identifying the Cutting-Edgers

Imagine yourself on an airplane in November 1999 and again in January 2003. In both instances you strike up a three-way conversation with the persons sitting on either side of you. After first talking about the weather and the bumpiness of the flight, the discussion turns to the question of what each of the travelers does for a living. While one says that his family owns a business that he had joined years ago, the other speaks of having started as a therapist but of subsequently yielding to an impulse to be an artist. "And what do you do?" they exclaim almost in unison, turning to the narrator for an elaboration of his professional occupation. The response is clear-cut: "I'm a social scientist. I study why individuals and groups do what they do. At the moment I'm seeking to broaden understanding of leaders in the public arena, especially those who initiate and sustain the processes of globalization."

"Wow, that's interesting!" the businessman observes. "How are you going about it?"

Told that an elaborate mail questionnaire was involved, the artist seems agitated. "You mean you're going to quantify human experience!"

"Yes, we're going to try to find patterns in our welter of data."

"Why? For what purpose?"

"To advance comprehension of the complexities of globalization and the individuals who shape its processes."

But the artist is not satisfied. "You're implying that people engage in common behavior and have shared attitudes that form patterns. That strikes me as questionable!"

"I have doubts, too," the businessman chimes in. "In my experience people are marked by so much variability that patterns are elusive at best!"

"Yes, you're right, patterns are elusive," the social scientist replies. "It takes a lot of work to tease out meaning from great amounts of data. But we believe it can be done if you dig deep enough into the data. Let me put it this way: there's a story to be told in any systematically gathered data."

"What kind of story?" the artist asks skeptically.

"A story of hopes and fears, of differences and similarities, of changing loyalties, of cross-boundary activities, of how business people differ from those not in business, of how events like September 11 affect orientations and perceptions."

"Well, tell us the story!" the artist says challengingly.

"I can't do that without first recounting our procedures and methods."

"Don't be too technical," the businessman pleads.

"I won't. It's really not that complex."

* * *

The theoretical concerns and propositions set forth in the previous chapter are the subject of much speculation and unsubstantiated analysis,[1] but to our knowledge they have not been pursued in any available systematic surveys.[2] In subsequent chapters, we offer the empirical results of our efforts to reduce this important knowledge gap. We readily acknowledge, however, that these efforts are limited because our random samples of possible Cutting-Edgers consist entirely of individuals from the United States and persons listed in elite sources such as *Who's Who in America*. Our resources for the surveys are such that we were unable to administer our research instrument to those who are on the cutting edge in other countries, a limitation we recognize as being serious enough that we have sought to persuade colleagues elsewhere in the world to undertake similar inquiries that will facilitate cross-country analysis.[3]

THE SURVEYS

Here we outline the procedures that we employed to delineate Cutting-Edgers and compare their attitudes and orientations with those of Other Leaders. Our primary research instrument consisted of two extensive mailed questionnaires designed to assess the attitudes and actions of leaders on the cutting edge of globalization. The first was a 56-item, 173-subitem questionnaire mailed on November 17, 1999, to 3,338 persons randomly chosen from leadership compendia. More accurately, working on the assumption that persons in the economic realm predominate in globalizing processes, we compiled the list of recipients randomly in two broad occupational categories: one, those whose brief biographies indicated that they were business executives and, two, those lacking any indication that business was central to their accomplishments.[4] Of the 2,267 forming the business sample, 592, or 26 percent, returned the questionnaire, while the comparable figures for the 1,071 individuals in the nonbusiness sample were 297, or 28 percent. All the recipients were given an alternative of electronically answering the questionnaire or responding through the postal system with a postage-paid envelope. In sum, 5 percent chose to respond online, and 95 percent elected to return their questionnaire by mail. The total number of respondents, 889, is 27 percent of the original mailing.[5] Their responses are henceforth referred to as those of the 1999 sample.

Since the research instrument was prepared before the battle of Seattle, it did not include items that specifically probed for differences between Cutting-Edgers and those inclined to resist the momentum toward a globalized world. Indeed, since nearly half of the questionnaires were returned during the two weeks prior to the Seattle protests, it did not even allow for an inferential probing for resistance orientations.[6] However, in an effort to lessen this deficiency, we took advantage of the acceleration of the protest movement when it gathered in mid-April 2000, on the streets of Washington, D.C., during a board meeting of the International Monetary Fund to conduct street interviews among a random sample of those who marched.[7] Although this truncated oral survey took a different form than the mailed questionnaire, two questions used in the oral interviews were taken verbatim from the mailed questionnaire. While we cannot account for any possible bias resulting from the use of different research instruments, we can plausibly offer comparisons based on these two identical questions (discussed later).

More important, the original survey was conducted before the September 11, 2001, terrorist attacks on the World Trade Center towers and the Pentagon. This event, combined with the acceleration of antiglobalization protests subsequent to our first mailing, seemed so potentially relevant to the role of Cutting-Edgers that we sent out a revised questionnaire to the same original sample on January 15, 2003. To make room for several items that focused on the September 11 attacks and the antiglobalization protests, a corresponding number of items was dropped from the original questionnaire. All in all, 56 questions and 142 subquestions were included in the revised version, more than enough to compare changes across the two periods. The 2003 mailing was sent to 3,191 leaders, fewer than the first mailing because the original address list was shortened by 148 persons who had either died or whose envelope was returned for want of an accurate address. Of the 3,191 leaders in the 2003 sample (as we refer to it), 267 of their questionnaires proved to be undeliverable, leaving a total mailing of 2,924. Of these, 1,914 consisted of mailings to business leaders, of whom 543, or 28 percent, returned the questionnaire. The comparable figures for

Table 3.1   Comparison of the 1999 and 2003 Mailings

	Business leaders				Nonbusiness leaders				Overall totals			
	1999		2003		1999		2003		1999		2003	
	(n)	%	(n)	%	(n)	%	(n)	%	(n)	%	(n)	%
Questionnaires mailed and delivered*	(2,267)		(1,914)		(1,071)		(1,010)		(3,338)		(2,924)	
Questionnaires returned	(592)	26	(543)	28	(297)	28	(287)	28	(889)	27	(830)	28
Those returned by mail	(561)	95	(498)	92	(285)	96	(266)	93	(846)	95	(764)	92
Those returned electronically	(31)	5	(45)	8	(12)	4	(21)	7	(43)	5	(66)	8

* These figures do not include the questionnaires returned by the post office because of addressees' death or faulty addresses.

the 1,010 nonbusiness leaders were 287, or 28 percent. The overall response of the 2003 sample was 830, or 28 percent, a proportion virtually identical to the figure for the 1999 sample that replied and surely enough in both instances to allow for meaningful comparisons between the samples.

Table 3.1 presents a comparison of these parametric data for the 1999 and 2003 mailings. Two comparisons are particularly noteworthy. One is the absence of noticeable differences between the business and nonbusiness elites. Virtually the same proportions of both groups returned the questionnaires in each year. Second, compared to the 5 percent who replied online in 1999, the figure for the 2003 sample was 8 percent, as if the passage of time had generated greater comfort in the use of the Internet.

In sum, the total response to the two surveys yielded a database consisting of 1,719 respondents. However, since the two surveys were conducted anonymously, there is every reason to presume that the two samples do not consist of exactly the same individuals. But some leaders did send back both questionnaires. As can be seen in tables 3.2 and 3.3, which present the results of the two items in the 2003 survey that asked about the 1999 survey, presumably some respondents returned both questionnaires, but there is no sure way to accurately calculate the exact number who did so. Estimated conservatively on the basis of the two tables, somewhere between a quarter and a third of the respondents probably answered both questionnaires. In addition, despite firm assurances that the respondents were guaranteed anonymity and need not feel obliged to identify themselves, in 1999 eighty-four respondents identified themselves in one way or another, and eighty-three did so when they returned the 2003 questionnaire. Of these, only ten appear on both lists of self-identifiers.[8] Otherwise, as noted, there is no

Table 3.2   How Would You Characterize Your Recollection of Receiving the 1999 Version of the Questionnaire?

	(n)	%
I clearly remember receiving it	(144)	17
I vaguely remember seeing it	(233)	28
I do not remember receiving it	(430)	52
Other (kindly specify)	(7)	1
Did not answer the question	(16)	2
Total	(830)	100

sure way to calculate the proportion of persons who responded to both surveys.

In short, it is important to recall that any sum of the two surveys presented in the ensuing analysis is to some extent misleading in the sense that it includes some respondents who were counted twice. The same can be said for any comparisons between the two samples, though this distortion is offset by the probability that the leaders who answered both surveys did not necessarily respond identically to the same questions posed in both surveys.

It might well be asked whether our procedures allow us to assert with certainty that we identified and surveyed leaders on the cutting edge of globalization? A negative answer, of course, is in order. So much depends on assumptions and methodology that there can be no certainty in this respect. All we can do is reiterate that our sample was drawn from elite compendia and that our procedures, as outlined in the ensuing two paragraphs, differentiated Cutting-Edgers from Other Leaders in ways that reflect what we understand to be the core dimensions of globalization.

Identifying the Cutting-Edgers

While all the respondents had biographies in leadership compendia, we did not assume that they were all Cutting-Edgers. Rather, we presumed

Table 3.3   If You Did Receive the Questionnaire, Did You Complete and Return it?

	(n)	%
Yes	(307)	37
No	(35)	4
Not sure	(290)	35
Did not answer the question	(198)	24
Total	(830)	100

that some, perhaps many, were leaders in fields not encompassed by the dynamics of globalization. Accordingly, we used a series of procedures to identify those respondents in the 1999 and 2003 samples who could be classified as those active on the cutting edge. These procedures, elaborated in appendix A, culminated in the creation of the Involvement Index, based on fifteen questionnaire items reflective of one form or another of involvement. For the index to be regarded as being statistically reliable, it had to yield a Cronbach alpha score of over .70. Both the 1999 and the 2003 index met this test, with the score for the former being .73 while the 2003 score was .71. Further procedures, also detailed in appendix A, yielded 741 respondents in 1999 and 565 in 2003 who answered all fifteen items, which led to the presumption that the respondents whose scores were at or above a cutoff point of 75 percent (roughly the top quartile) could reasonably be assumed to be Cutting-Edgers. As a result, 187 respondents in 1999 and 167 in 2003 were so classified. We use the label of Other Leaders to designate the remaining 554 in 1999 and 398 in 2003 whose scores fell below the cutoff point (roughly the lowest three quartiles of the index).[9] In both cases, the sum of Cutting-Edgers and Other Leaders is less than the number who returned the questionnaire, because some respondents did not answer all the items constituting the Involvement Index.[10]

The Involvement Index

Responses to the fifteen items that form the Involvement Index are presented in table 3.4. Given a conviction that our data are sufficiently unique as to warrant a full presentation in the event others have occasion to make use of them, we err on the side of completeness by including in table 3.4 the responses of the Cutting-Edgers to each of the fifteen items in both 1999 and 2003. The same reasoning underlies the inclusion of the distributions for Other Leaders, even though the differences between them and the Cutting-Edgers on all the items are, by definition, bound to be sizable and thus not appropriately subjected to statistical comparisons. In no instance, for example, did the Other Leaders even come close to matching the proportion of Cutting-Edgers who responded to the high involvement alternatives of the fifteen items in each of the two surveys. In both years, for example, the proportion of Cutting-Edgers more than tripled that of the Other Leaders who "closely identified with professional associates abroad," and similar differences marked the proportion of the two groups in each year that reported studying abroad.

While table 3.4 must be interpreted cautiously, it clearly upholds our assumption that involvement in the processes of globalization is founded on a number of diverse factors—behavioral, attitudinal, and experiential. This presumption is amplified in the patterns uncovered in the many

Table 3.4 The Fifteen Components of the Involvement Index and Distribution of Responses to Them in 1999 and 2003

1. What are the bases for your contacts abroad? (check if applicable)

Your professional expertise is in demand

	Cutting-Edgers				Other Leaders			
	Check		No check		Check		No check	
	(n)	%	(n)	%	(n)	%	(n)	%
1999 survey	(161)	86	(26)	14	(247)	45	(307)	55
2003 survey	(117)	70	(50)	30	(141)	35	(257)	65

2. To what extent do you feel a sense of identity with professional associates abroad?

	Closely identified		Somewhat identified		Mildly identified		None	
	(n)	%	(n)	%	(n)	%	(n)	%
1999 Cutting-Edgers ($n = 187$)	(76)	41	(96)	51	(14)	7	(1)	1
1999 Other Leaders ($n = 554$)	(62)	11	(179)	32	(206)	37	(107)	19
2003 Cutting-Edgers ($n = 167$)	(60)	36	(84)	50	(21)	13	(2)	1
2003 Other Leaders ($n = 398$)	(40)	10	(131)	33	(128)	32	(99)	25

3. To what extent do you feel you have more in common with counterparts in your profession elsewhere in the world than with your fellow citizens in different lines of work? (check only one)

	Cutting-Edgers				Other Leaders			
	1999		2003		1999		2003	
	($n = 187$)	%	($n = 167$)	%	($n = 554$)	%	($n = 398$)	%
I have more in common with my fellow citizens than distant professional counterparts	(28)	15	(48)	29	(246)	44	(225)	57
I have more in common with professional counterparts abroad than with my fellow citizens	(59)	32	(35)	21	(86)	16	(51)	13
I feel equal commonality with both my fellow citizens and my professional counterparts abroad	(100)	53	(84)	50	(222)	40	(122)	31

Table 3.4   (continued)

4. Approximately how many times have you traveled abroad in the past two years for a vacation or other personal matters?

	Cutting-Edgers		Other Leaders	
	Average number of trips	(n)	Average number of trips	(n)
1999 survey	1.22	(187)	0.65	(554)
2003 survey	2.26	(167)	1.24	(398)

5. Is networking with others abroad important to you?

	Yes		No	
	(n)	%	(n)	%
1999 Cutting-Edgers ($n = 187$)	(176)	94	(11)	6
1999 Other Leaders ($n = 554$)	(334)	60	(220)	40
2003 Cutting-Edgers ($n = 167$)	(150)	90	(17)	10
2003 Other Leaders ($n = 398$)	(203)	51	(195)	49

6 and 7. Are you inclined to actively promote dialogue in your home or professional community about essential global issues? (check all that apply)

6. Yes, I feel a sense of responsibility in this regard

	Check		No check	
	(n)	%	(n)	%
1999 Cutting-Edgers ($n =187$)	(149)	80	(38)	20
1999 Other Leaders ($n =554$)	(354)	64	(200)	36
2003 Cutting-Edgers ($n =167$)	(141)	84	(26)	16
2003 Other Leaders ($n =398$)	(261)	66	(137)	34

7. No, my leadership responsibilities do not encompass these issues

1999 Cutting-Edgers ($n =187$)	(32)	17	(155)	83
1999 Other Leaders ($n =554$)	(163)	29	(391)	71
2003 Cutting-Edgers ($n =167$)	(16)	10	(151)	90
2003 Other Leaders ($n =398$)	(95)	24	(303)	76

Table 3.4   (continued)

8, 9, and 10. How would you characterize the relevance of your work with respect to the diverse processes of globalization?

	Cutting-Edgers				Other Leaders			
	1999		2003		1999		2003	
	(n = 187)	%	(n = 167)	%	(n = 554)	%	(n = 398)	%
8. Economic processes								
Continuously relevant	(143)	76	(112)	67	(252)	45	(124)	31
Occasionally relevant	(36)	19	(43)	26	(185)	33	(148)	37
Seldom relevant	(7)	4	(11)	7	(86)	16	(102)	26
Never relevant	(1)	1	(1)	1	(31)	6	(24)	6
9. Cultural processes								
Continuously relevant	(116)	62	(89)	53	(195)	35	(117)	29
Occasionally relevant	(59)	32	(65)	39	(223)	40	(159)	40
Seldom relevant	(12)	6	(10)	6	(108)	19	(98)	25
Never relevant	(0)	0	(3)	2	(28)	5	(24)	6
10. Political processes								
Continuously relevant	(101)	54	(78)	47	(129)	23	(81)	20
Occasionally relevant	(63)	34	(63)	38	(190)	34	(133)	33
Seldom relevant	(20)	11	(23)	14	(169)	31	(125)	31
Never relevant	(3)	2	(3)	2	(66)	12	(59)	15

11. Did you ever study abroad?[a]

	Yes		No	
	(n)	%	(n)	%
1999 Cutting-Edgers (n = 187)	(103)	55	(84)	45
1999 Other Leaders (n − 554)	(99)	18	(455)	82
2003 Cutting-Edgers (n = 167)	(99)	59	(68)	41
2003 Other Leaders (n = 398)	(49)	12	(349)	88

Table 3.4 (continued)

12. How many languages do you read or speak?[a]

	One		Two		Three		Four		Five or more	
	(n)	%	(n)	%	(n)	%	(n)	%	(n)	%
1999 Cutting-Edgers (n = 187)	(29)	16	(74)	40	(56)	30	(19)	10	(9)	5
1999 Other Leaders (n = 554)	(312)	56	(195)	35	(37)	7	(7)	1	(3)	1
2003 Cutting-Edgers (n = 167)	(39)	23	(62)	37	(39)	23	(15)	9	(12)	7
2003 Other Leaders (n = 398)	(241)	61	(121)	30	(24)	6	(5)	1	(7)	2

13, 14, and 15. Approximately how many times have you resided for more than six months outside the country in which you . . .

	Cutting-Edgers		Other Leaders	
	1999 (n = 187) Average number	2003 (n = 167) Average number	1999 (n = 554) Average number	2003 (n = 338) Average number
13 . . . were born?	1.16	1.63	0.22	0.25
14 . . . are a citizen?	1.09	1.52	0.19	0.24
15 . . . are employed?	0.84	1.27	0.12	0.18

[a] It is interesting to compare the Cutter-Edgers' data for study abroad and languages spoken or read with comparable figures for members of the U.S. Congress: nearly one-third of the members were reported to have studied or worked abroad, and one-fifth said they "speak a foreign language well enough to conduct business beyond America's borders." Eric Schmitt and Elizabeth Becker, "Insular Congress Appears to Be Myth," *New York Times*, November 4, 2000, A9.

non–Involvement Index items of the questionnaire presented in subsequent chapters.

* * *

"That's a lengthy table," the businessman says skeptically after poring over it. "Are you contending that on the basis of the answers to those fifteen items you can draw meaningful inferences about the differences between those of us who are Cutting-Edgers from those who are Other Leaders? That strikes me as a big stretch. People are too complicated to allow for an index, even one as comprehensive as yours, to differentiate the two types of leaders."

"I agree," says the artist. "How do you know that the Cronbach alpha scores are reliable? Perhaps chance factors account for the fact that they exceeded the .70 cutoff point."

The social scientist struggles to maintain his patience. "You have to accept the rules of the statistics game," he responds. "More than that, if you want to grasp the importance of our findings in later chapters, you have to take the Involvement Index in table 3.4 seriously. It serves the need to compare Cutting-Edgers and Other Leaders reliably and systematically. There may be a variety of explanations for the distributions we turned up, but the significant differences on certain questions have to be treated as meaningful in some way. I'd welcome your intervening as we go along and indicating where you think another interpretation is more reasonable, but simply to discount the differences because you have trouble playing by the rules of the statistics game is to miss the point. Go back and compare carefully the differences between the Cutting-Edgers and the Other Leaders in table 3.4. All of them are huge. They are not trivial differences. They don't just happen. They happen for systematic reasons. And the explanation of them seems clear: due to the way in which we constructed the Involvement Index, our procedures were such that the differences reflect a greater involvement in the processes of globalization on the part of the Cutting-Edgers than is the case for the Other Leaders. In addition to the differences already indicated, note how much more the expertise of the Cutting-Edgers was in demand abroad; how much more they traveled and networked abroad; how much more relevant their work was to the economic, political, and cultural dynamics of globalization; how many more languages they spoke; or how much less they felt a commonality with their fellow citizens when compared to professional counterparts elsewhere in the world."

He pauses to let his argument sink in. Seeing that it is having an effect, he adds what he considers to be the clincher. "Let me put it differently. Statistical theory presumes that everything regresses to the mean, that significant differences will not be uncovered in the absence of systematic factors. And that was true in the case of our surveys. As you'll see, the number of comparisons between the Cutting-Edgers and the Other Leaders that fell short of statistical significance were far more numerous than those that were significant. In other words, both the Cutting-Edgers and the Other Leaders occupied leadership positions, but the greater involvement of the former in globalizing processes led to noteworthy differences in their activities and orientations. And therein lies the core motive for our investigation: In what ways do they differ?

"Are we saying that the Cutting-Edgers really exist? No, that is not even close to what we are saying. We are only claiming that our methods and the Involvement Index have identified Americans drawn from leadership compendia who scored in the top quartile of the index. In effect, we have created the category of 'Cutting-Edgers' and the distinction between their practices and orientations and those of the Other Leaders. But in so doing we have facilitated an opportunity to explore how leaders have affected the processes of globalization. As will be seen, the distributions of the data based on the distinction are such as to delineate through statistical tests behavioral and attitudinal differences that lend considerable credence to our probes into the ways in which the dynamics of leadership sustain and shape globalization.[11] More specifically, throughout our analysis of the data distributions, we employ both bivariate and multivariate tests of statistical significance to differentiate those that could well have resulted from chance factors from those that are likely to be due to systematic differences between the compared groups."[12]

The businessman is quick to interrupt. "I took an introductory statistics course in college. So I know what bivariate and multivariate tests involve, but I can't recall what the analyst does when the results of the two kinds of tests are discrepant, when one yields significance and the other does not. How do you handle that problem?"

The researcher quickly abandons his impatience and calmly explains the procedures used to interpret discrepant results. "It is not as complicated as it may sound. There are four possible outcomes in any comparison: first, both the bivariate and the multivariate test yield significant differences; second, both tests yield no significance; third, the two yield different results, with the bivariate test finding a significant effect but with the multivariate test finding a nonsignificant effect; and, fourth, the multivariate test yields significance, and the bivariate does not. In the case of the first result, when both tests find a significant effect of the Cutting-Edger–Other Leader distinction, we attribute greater confidence to our inferences. That is to say, the effect of the Cutting-Edger–Other Leader distinction obtains even after we control for a respondent's profession, gender, education, minority status, and political orientation. We therefore conclude that the Cutting-Edge–Other Leader variable has significant effects independent of other demographic and attitudinal factors. By contrast, in the case of the second result, when both tests find no significance, we conclude with greater confidence that there are no demographic or orientation effects that are confounding the relationship between a subject's response and his or her status as a Cutting-Edger or Other Leader. In the case of both the third and the fourth result, we lend greater inferential weight to the multivariate tests. When the multivariate test finds no significant effects even though the bivariate test does, we conclude that a respondent's gender, education, profession, minority status, or political orientation explains the significant difference in the bivariate test, not the Cutting-Edger–Other Leader distinction. Contrariwise, when the multivariate test proves significant and the bivariate test does not, we interpret the former as being meaningful because one of the control variables confounded the relationship between the Cutting-Edger–Other Leader variable and the subject's response. That is to say, when we controlled for the demographic and political orientation variables in the multivariate test, we corrected this confounding relationship and uncovered a significant difference between Cutting-Edgers and

Other Leaders. In short, whenever the bivariate and multivariate tests disagree about the significance of our Cutting-Edger–Other Leader distinction, we emphasize the multivariate findings in our inferences."

Both traveling companions become silent for a moment, as if trying to absorb the four distinctions and perhaps still remaining eager to find alternative explanations that defy the statistical game. Finally, the artist speaks up, more than a little triumphantly: "But in neither the first nor the fourth case can you say for sure that involvement in globalizing processes explains the differences."

"Well, okay, how would you explain them?" the researcher replies. Again, silence sets in, only to be broken by the flight attendant asking if they would like a drink before the movie begins.

"I'd like a beer," the businessman replies, relieved to postpone answering the question.

"Me too," echoes the artist, no less relieved.

The social scientist also welcomes a break and seeks to lighten the burden of his argument by acknowledging that certain initial findings are less rigorous and not organized in terms of the Involvement Index.

Some Initial Findings

To give an initial sense of the richness and subtlety of the materials analyzed in subsequent chapters, we find it useful to record a brief straightforward comparison of the two items that were identical in both the 1999 leadership questionnaire and the aforementioned oral survey of 149 protesters in the streets surrounding the International Monetary Fund headquarters in April 2000. One question common to both research instruments concerns the respondents' orientation toward a globalized future. It consists of identical wording about the degree to which change is perceived as being controllable. As can be seen in table 3.5, the protesters, in all likelihood

Table 3.5   In General, Do You Feel You That You Control Change, or Does Change Control You?

	1999 Leadership sample		Protest sample	
	(n = 889)	%	(n = 147)	%
I control change	(295)	33	(100)	68
Change controls me	(232)	26	(11)	7
Not sure	(190)	21	(10)	7
Other	(172)	19	(26)	18

Note: This comparison was significant at the .001 level. Percentages may not sum to 100 owing to rounding.

Table 3.6   Would You Say Patriotism Is . . . (Check All that Apply)

	Check		No check	
	(n)	*%*	*(n)*	*%*
. . . an increasingly obsolete sentiment?[a]				
1999 Leadership sample (*n* = 878)	(136)	15	(742)	85
Protest sample (*n* = 132)	(29)	22	(103)	78
. . . of continuing major importance?[b]				
1999 Leadership sample (*n* = 878)	(570)	65	(308)	35
Protest sample (*n* = 132)	(25)	19	(107)	81
. . . of largely symbolic or psychological significance?[a]				
1999 Leadership sample (*n* = 878)	(322)	37	(556)	63
Protest sample (*n* = 132)	(55)	42	(77)	58
. . . no longer relevant to the course of events?[b]				
1999 Leadership sample (*n* = 878)	(29)	3	(849)	97
Protest sample (*n* = 132)	(33)	25	(99)	75

[a] This comparison was not significant.
[b] This comparison was significant at the .001 level.

because they were surveyed while acting in the service of their own values, were significantly more inclined to believe that they could control change than were those in the 1999 leadership sample.

The second item offers the option of choosing among five characterizations of patriotism. Inclusion of this item is based on the proposition that the processes of globalization can loosen up a person's attachment to the country and community in which one grew up. Such reasoning, however, is not held up by the responses. The comparison presented in table 3.6 reveals that the protest sample is more dubious about the importance and relevance of patriotism, a finding possibly suggesting awareness that their actions are unlikely to be viewed as being patriotic even as the leaders may have viewed such sentiments as undermining sound policymaking on behalf of globalization.

It bears repeating that the protest sample was anything but systematic and cannot be taken as seriously as the more thorough and elaborate comparisons and data generated by the questionnaires. And while the latter are surely not the last word on the ways in which leadership is exercised in the realm of globalization, they do offer systematic data that portray complex patterns and provocative insights. The chapters that follow undertake to present these materials and highlight the significant findings and trends they reflect.

＊

"In contrast to the lengthy and cumbersome table depicting the components of the Involvement Index," the businessman says, "these last two are truly impressive. The different attitudes toward controlling change between the protesters and the leaders are startling. Perhaps it reflects the idealism of youth, especially those who are active in politics."

"But remember," the researcher replies, "the interview data are far from reliable."

"I know, you said that quite clearly. Still, I regard the data in table 3.5 as remarkable despite the unsystematic and crude nature of the methodology." The businessman pauses, then adds, "I look forward to seeing more."

NOTES

1. See, for example, Peter L. Berger, "Four Faces of Global Culture," *National Interest*, no. 49 (Fall 1997): 23–29; Geoffrey Garten, *The Mind of the CEO* (New York: Perseus, 2001); Ulf Hannerz, "Cosmopolitans and Locals in World Culture," in *Global Culture: Nationalism. Globalization and Modernity*, ed. Mike Featherstone (London: Sage, 1990), 237–52; Christopher Lasch, *The Revolt of the Elites and the Betrayal of Democracy* (New York: Norton, 1995); Robert Reich, *The Work of Nations: Preparing Ourselves for 21st-Century Capitalism* (New York: Knopf, 1991).

2. While one inquiry closely approximates the substantive concerns and scope of our study, it is based on a different methodology (interviews), one that involved a much smaller sample of elites than we surveyed—namely, "the senior management and executives of twenty-three transnational organizations and corporations." See James Davison Hunter and Joshua Yates, "In the Vanguard of Globalization: The World of American Globalizers," in *Many Globalizations: Cultural Diversity in the Contemporary World*, ed. Peter L. Berger and Samuel P. Huntington (New York: Oxford University Press, 2002), chap. 10 (quote on 356). For a narrow and partially available survey, see PricewaterhouseCoopers, *Inside the Mind of the CEO: The 2000 Global Survey Report* (New York: PricewaterhouseCoopers, 2000). Pricewaterhouse-Coopers, which designed and carried out the survey with the support of the World Economic Forum, has conducted several surveys of business people, but its latest inquiry was confined to 1,020 chief executive officers worldwide, whereas our inquiry was not confined to a single occupation or to a narrow set of questions about business. For another study confined to business people but employing a different methodology than the one used here, see Leslie Sklair, "Who Are the Globalisers? A Study of Key Globalisers in Australia," *Journal of Australian Political Economy*, no. 38 (December 1996): 1–30.

3. Cross-country surveys present innumerable problems in terms of language and comparable samples, but colleagues in Belgium and Turkey have indicated a readiness to pursue such a collaboration, assuming the methodological hurdles can be surmounted.

4. From an initial batch of 4,359 business leaders selected from the compendia, we used a pseudo-random-number generator to pare this sample down to 2,267 individuals, who received copies of the questionnaire in the mail. Likewise, from an initial sample of 13,041 individuals identified as being in the nonbusiness community, we used a pseudo-random-number generator to select 1,071 individuals, who received mailed copies of the questionnaire.

5. Following the initial mailing of the questionnaire in November 1999, a follow-up was sent in December 1999. The first wave evoked 93 percent of the total responses; the second wave, 7 percent.

6. We did record the date when we received each respondent's survey, allowing us to compare broadly the responses of those we received before the protests on November 30, 1999, to those we received afterward. We conducted statistical tests to determine whether the respondents who replied before the protests scored higher on either our Involvement Index or an index of orientations (positive/negative) toward globalization. To account for a possible lag in reporting, we tested two separate groups: those who returned their survey before November 30, 1999, and those who returned it before December 7, 1999. The tests show that those respondents returning their survey before the protests did not score significantly higher on either index. We thus concluded that the occurrence of the protests in Seattle did not bias the results of our 1999 survey.

7. For an analysis of the responses of 243 persons interviewed during a protest rally against international financial institutions in April 2002, see Glenn Adler and James H. Mittelman, "Who Is Protesting Globalization, Why, and What Are They For?" reproduced in James H. Mittelman, *Whither Globalization? The Vortex of Knowledge and Ideology* (London: Routledge, 2004), chap. 6. This survey suggests that it is erroneous to characterize such protests as being expressive of an "antiglobalization movement," that the findings did not depict "a complete rejection—'antiglobalization'—but a selective rejection of aspects of globalization, especially neo-liberal policies and institutions that seek to universalize them" (73).

8. Although these ten respondents are too few to allow for reliable statistical testing of the differences in their responses to the two surveys, where appropriate in subsequent chapters we take anecdotal note in those cases where their 2003 responses differed from their earlier replies.

9. The word *roughly* is included parenthetically in this and the earlier sentence because the Cutting-Edgers in 2003 form slightly more than 25 percent of the leaders who received index scores. This arises from our method of handling those leaders whose scores fell exactly on the seventy-fifth-percentile divide. In 1999, we included these individuals among the Cutting-Edgers, which gave us 187 Cutting-Edgers out of the 741 who received scores, or approximately 25 percent. (If we had included these individuals with the Other Leaders, by contrast, the Cutting-Edgers would form approximately 20 percent of the leaders.) To be consistent, we replicated this method for the 2003 sample, thus resulting in 167 Cutting Edgers out of 565 scorers, or approximately 30 percent of the total number of leaders receiving a score in 2003. The inclusion of these borderline leaders among the Cutting-Edgers arguably biases statistical tests toward findings of no significance, since by construction these borderline leaders are closer to the mean index score.

10. In 1999, 148 respondents did not provide enough data to calculate a score on the index, and the comparable figure for 2003 was 265. There is no reason to believe, however, that the inclusion of the nonscorers would have materially altered our findings. Of 170 comparisons between the responses of the omitted 148 and the 741 who recorded an index score in 1999, in only eleven instances did the scorers and nonscorers differ significantly, and only one of these was significant at the $p < .001$ level (at that level, the nonscorers were more inclined to specify that "certain individuals" constituted "a threat to your well-being" than were the scorers—a finding that eludes interpretation and seems essentially random). In 2003, of the 189 possible comparisons between those leaders who received scores and those who did not, in only five cases were the differences between the scorers and nonscorers significant at the $p < .001$ level. We concluded that in only these five instances did the nonscorers possibly alter the findings presented in subsequent chapters.

11. Throughout chi-square and t tests are employed so as to identify those comparisons that are statistically significant (i.e., the likelihood of their occurring by chance is very small). To serve readers who might find the statistical tests intrusive and confounding, we have limited the tables in the chapters to only the distribution of responses to the various questionnaire items, along with table notes for each comparison of the responses of the Cutting-Edgers and Other Leaders that indicate whether the comparison involves a significant difference and, if so, at what level of significance. For those readers who require data on the statistical tests to confidently assess the distributions, the tables are reproduced on the publisher's webpage at www.rowmanlittlefield.com/ri/books/rosenau.

12. The tables of data in the publisher's webpage (www.rowmanlittlefield .com/ri/books/rosenau) contain results from bivariate chi-square tests or t tests in the "bivariate model" columns and from multivariate probit or ordered probit results in the "multivariate model" columns. All multivariate tests of significance control for a respondent's profession, gender, education, minority status, and political orientation. For economy of presentation, we present only the findings for the Cutting-Edger–Other Leader variable (and for the year of sample, in chapter 9). It is important to note that although all the comparisons are reported in tabular form, the analysis focuses on those differences that are at the .05, .01 and .001 levels of probability. While we utilize these conventional levels of significance, we focus mainly on those that meet the most stringent level, .001. Differences at the more conventional but less rigorous .05 and .01 levels are noted but regarded as being only marginally significant. In the case of those items that required the calculation of mean scores to employ a t test for significance—such as the respondents' reported number of trips abroad in the last two years—we recoded unusually large values in the direction of a finding of *no significance*. For example, for the 166 respondents in 2003 who specified more than four trips abroad in the last two years, we recoded their reported value as a "4" in order to avoid a few scores unduly skewing the t value in the direction of significance.

4

How Do You Know a Cutting-Edger When You Encounter One?

The researcher cannot help wondering whether his traveling companions are representative of the Cutting-Edgers and the Other Leaders. How would one know a member of either group if one encountered them? The question quickly leads to a more specific puzzle: How would one know whether the Cutting-Edgers among them shared the perspectives articulated by Esther Dyson in the epigraph of chapter 1? Our findings suggest complex answers to these questions. Not all our respondents live as fully on the cutting edge of globalization as does Dyson.

Indeed, irrespective of the extent of their involvement in globalizing processes, the two groups of leaders have much in common. On any flight, any of your traveling companions may be either a Cutting-Edger or an Other Leader. Each is likely to be nearly sixty years old, having been born before 1945. Each is also much more likely to be a man than a woman, as well as somewhat more likely to be a Republican than a Democrat or an Independent, with political orientations that are not extreme in either a Left or Right direction but lean more toward moderate or somewhat conservative perspectives than somewhat liberal outlooks.

When problems arise with the movie projector, the researcher quickly inquires into the amount of education his companions have had. "Boy, you're relentless," the artist observes.

"We have to be," the researcher responds, "else we'll not be able to tell our story."

The resumed conversation yields hints that one of the travelers is an Other Leader while the other is a Cutting-Edger. In 1999 our companions were likely to have had the same degree of education, but in 2003 the Other Leader had slightly less education than that of the Cutting-Edger, with the former being less likely than the latter to have studied after obtaining a college degree. In both years, they were equally likely to obtain business, law, and medical degrees, but the Cutting-Edger was more likely than the Other Leader to have obtained a doctorate.

More pronounced differences between the two travelers begin to come out when the discussion shifts to experiences and, somehow, to earned income. On both flights (1999 and 2003), the Cutting Edger had a significantly higher income than that of the Other Leader. Interestingly, however, the former was no more likely than the latter to hold a position in the world of business. Despite the widespread presumption that the leadership of globalizing processes is carried out predominantly by businessmen and businesswomen, our traveling companions were as likely as not to occupy leadership positions in fields outside the business community.

But it is when the talk turns to parents, childhood, language skills, and encounters with foreign cultures that the differences between the two passengers become so unmistakable as to suggest that some of the roots of life on the cutting edge of globalization are planted at a young age. The Other Leader acknowledges many fewer contacts with distant cultures than those described by the Cutting-Edger. Not only does the latter indicate more extensive language skills than those of the former, but when they compare notes on the extent of time they spent residing and studying abroad as children and teenagers, it becomes clear that the Cutting-Edger spent much more time in foreign lands than did the Other Leader. More than that, the Cutting-Edger is more likely to have been a citizen of more than one country and to have lived for less time in his present country of residence. In addition, he is more likely to have parents who came from a country other than the United States, who spoke languages in addition to English, who traveled extensively, and who took him with them on their travels.

By the time the movie comes on and brings the conversation temporarily to a close, it becomes clear that while there are surely a number of reasons (noted in subsequent chapters) why a Cutting-Edger gets more caught up in globalizing processes than does an Other Leader, his or her considerable immersion in distant cultures early in life at least partially accounts for both his or her different orientations toward globalization and his or her activities on a global scale as an adult.

FROM ANECDOTAL INTERPRETATIONS TO SYSTEMATIC DATA

This anecdotal summary of the socioeconomic background of the respondents to the two questionnaires is derived from the data and distributions presented in tables 4.1, 4.2, 4.3, and 4.4, which offer more precise

Table 4.1 Socioeconomic Backgrounds of the Cutting-Edgers and Other Leaders in 1999 and 2003

	1999				2003			
	Cutting-Edgers		Other Leaders		Cutting-Edgers		Other Leader	
	(n)	%	(n)	%	(n)	%	(n)	%
Gender[a]								
Women	(30)	16	(124)	22	(30)	18	(73)	18
Men	(157)	84	(429)	78	(137)	82	(322)	82
Party identification[a]								
Republican	(79)	44	(228)	42	(74)	46	(189)	48
Democrat	(54)	30	(156)	29	(43)	27	(96)	25
Independent	(38)	21	(126)	23	(38)	24	(92)	24
No preference	(8)	5	(36)	6	(5)	3	(12)	3
Political orientations[a]								
Far left	(1)	1	(6)	1	(0)	0	(2)	1
Very liberal	(15)	8	(37)	7	(9)	6	(30)	8
Somewhat liberal	(35)	19	(97)	18	(25)	16	(66)	17
Moderate	(54)	30	(167)	31	(50)	32	(111)	29
Somewhat conservative	(58)	32	(175)	33	(53)	34	(131)	34
Very conservative	(18)	10	(50)	9	(19)	12	(45)	11
Far right	(0)	0	(2)	1	(0)	0	(0)	0
Education[b]								
College degree or less	(33)	18	(139)	26	(21)	13	(116)	30
Master's degree	(51)	28	(149)	28	(49)	31	(93)	24
MBA	(25)	14	(64)	12	(21)	13	(52)	14
PhD	(56)	31	(140)	26	(53)	33	(85)	22
JD or LLM	(11)	6	(21)	4	(11)	7	(18)	5
MD	(6)	3	(22)	4	(5)	3	(18)	5
Profession[a]								
Business	(137)	73	(367)	66	(113)	69	(264)	66
Nonbusiness	(50)	27	(187)	34	(54)	32	(134)	34
Age[a]								
Born before 1945	(75)	40	(195)	35	(63)	37	(148)	37
Born 1945 to 1955	(38)	20	(129)	23	(50)	30	(93)	23
Born after 1955	(74)	40	(230)	41	(54)	32	(157)	40
Income[c]								
Less than $100,000	(29)	16	(159)	30	(24)	15	(120)	31
$100,000 to $999,999	(142)	77	(358)	67	(125)	77	(255)	65
More than $1,000,000	(13)	7	(17)	3	(14)	9	(14)	4

[a] This comparison was not significant in either 1999 or 2003.
[b] This comparison was not significant in 1999 but was significant at the .001 level in 2003.
[c] This comparison was significant at the .001 level in both 1999 and 2003.

Table 4.2 Did Either or Both of Your Parents ... (Check All That Apply)

	Check		No check	
	(n)	*%*	*(n)*	*%*
...come from a country other than the United States?				
1999 Cutting-Edgers (*n* = 187)[b]	(50)	27	(137)	73
1999 Other Leaders (*n* = 549)	(96)	17	(453)	83
2003 Cutting-Edgers (*n* = 167)[c]	(55)	33	(112)	67
2003 Other Leaders (*n* = 398)	(52)	13	(346)	87
...speak other languages in addition to English?				
1999 Cutting-Edgers (*n* = 187)[c]	(88)	47	(99)	53
1999 Other Leaders (*n* = 549)	(173)	32	(376)	68
2003 Cutting-Edgers (*n* = 167)[c]	(72)	43	(85)	57
2003 Other Leaders (*n* = 398)	(106)	27	(292)	73
...travel extensively?				
1999 Cutting-Edgers (*n* = 187)[c]	(73)	39	(114)	61
1999 Other Leaders (*n* = 549)	(136)	25	(413)	75
2003 Cutting-Edgers (*n* = 167)[c]	(70)	42	(97)	58
2003 Other Leaders (*n* = 398)	(83)	21	(315)	79
...take you on their travels when you were young?				
1999 Cutting-Edgers (*n* = 187)[a]	(84)	45	(103)	55
1999 Other Leaders (*n* = 549)	(195)	36	(354)	64
2003 Cutting-Edgers (*n* = 167)[a]	(81)	49	(86)	52
2003 Other Leaders (*n* = 398)	(147)	37	(251)	63

Note: Figures may not add to 100 owing to rounding.
[a] This comparison was significant at the .05 level.
[b] This comparison was significant at the .01 level.
[c] This comparison was significant at the .001 level.

comparisons of the two groups. One noteworthy pattern in table 4.1 stands out: for all the sizable differences between the two groups on the items that form the Involvement Index (see table 3.4) and that subsequent chapters also delineate, both the 1999 and the 2003 survey indicate that in some respects the two groups have similar backgrounds and characteristics even as they differ in ways that can be traced to the Cutting-Edgers' greater involvement in globalization.

Other interesting features of the data include the finding that, with one exception, less than one-fifth of the leaders in both years are women. Even smaller proportions (10 percent of the respondents in 1999 and 12 percent in 2003) reported being millionaires. Nevertheless, the income differential between the Cutting-Edgers and the Other Leaders is the only one that is significant in both years, with the former reporting greater wealth than

Table 4.3   With Respect to Your Country of Citizenship and Residence...

	Yes		No	
	(n)	*%*	*(n)*	*%*
...have you been a citizen of more than one country?				
1999 Cutting-Edgers (*n* = 186)[b]	(20)	11	(166)	89
1999 Other Leaders (*n* = 552)	(19)	3	(533)	97
2003 Cutting-Edgers (*n* = 166)[b]	(27)	16	(139)	84
2003 Other Leaders (*n* = 396)	(11)	3	(385)	97
...are you still a citizen of the country where you were born?				
1999 Cutting-Edgers (*n* = 187)[b]	(167)	90	(18)	10
1999 Other Leaders (*n* = 549)	(527)	97	(18)	3
2003 Cutting-Edgers (*n* = 165)[a]	(150)	91	(15)	9
2003 Other Leaders (*n* = 395)	(382)	97	(13)	3

...how many years have you lived in the country of which you
are now a resident?

	Average number
1999 Cutting-Edgers (*n* = 187)[b]	47.54
1999 Other Leaders (*n* = 549)	52.86
2003 Cutting-Edgers (*n* = 167)[b]	50.90
2003 Other Leaders (*n* = 398)	57.08

[a] This comparison was significant at the .01 level.
[b] This comparison was significant at the .001 level.

Table 4.4   Minority Statuses

	Yes		No	
	(n)	*%*	*(n)*	*%*
Have you ever thought of yourself as an expatriate?[*]				
Cutting-Edgers (*n* = 186)[b]	(71)	38	(115)	62
Other Leaders (*n* = 544)	(59)	11	(485)	89
Are you a member of an ethnic, racial, or religious minority in the country where you live?				
1999 Cutting-Edgers (*n* = 183)[a]	(48)	26	(135)	74
1999 Other Leaders (*n* = 533)	(183)	16	(447)	84
2003 Cutting-Edgers (*n* = 165)[a]	(43)	26	(120)	74
2003 Other Leaders (*n* = 395)	(64)	16	(331)	84

[*] 1999 survey only.
[a] This comparison was significant at the .01 level.
[b] This comparison was significant at the .001 level.

that of the latter. Similarly, small proportions of both groups were less than fifty years old. Another notable feature of the findings is the considerable education acquired by both Cutting-Edgers and Other Leaders. The two groups differed in 2003 in this regard, but the data nonetheless indicate, not surprisingly, that people do not normally occupy leadership positions without having earned advanced degrees. For both groups in both years, more than two-thirds reported having earned degrees after graduating from college, a finding comparable to another study of elites, one that found that "virtually all of those . . . interviewed, regardless of profession or organization, possessed advanced degrees in fields such as communications (i.e., journalism, public relations) the social sciences (e.g., economics psychology, anthropology), the health sciences, business, and law."[1] Nor is it particularly startling that both groups of leaders in the present era tend toward political conservatism. More than 40 percent of both groups in both surveys described their orientations as being "somewhat" or "very" conservative.

Still another conspicuous finding set forth in table 4.1 concerns the "profession" category. Recall that before we mailed the questionnaire to respondents, we identified them in two broad categories: those whose brief biographies indicated that they were business executives and those who lacked any indication that their professional accomplishments derived from success in the business world. This distinction allowed us to test one of the most common hypotheses in the globalization literature: that businessmen and businesswomen are central to the diverse processes of globalization. However, the test failed: in neither the 1999 nor the 2003 sample did the proportions of business and nonbusiness Cutting-Edgers differ significantly from the comparable proportions of Other Leaders.[2] From this we concluded that the Involvement Index performed well in identifying each respondent's participation in the diverse processes of globalization irrespective of his or her profession. It is a more valid and reliable measure of an individual's involvement in globalization than of simple attributes such as profession or income.

Hardly less noteworthy are the data in tables 4.2 and 4.3 that indicate that the Cutting-Edgers had significantly more extensive contacts with foreign cultures in their early years than those of their counterparts among the Other Leaders. By conspicuous margins in both surveys, the former reported having parents who came from a country other than the United States, who spoke more than one language, who traveled extensively, and who took their children with them when they traveled. Indeed, in 2003, when compared to Other Leaders, at least twice as many Cutting-Edgers reported having parents whose origins were external to the United States and who traveled extensively (see table 4.2). Moreover, in both surveys, at least three times as many Cutting-Edgers indicated that they had been a citizen of more than one country (table 4.3). A possible interpretation of these consistent findings on the early residence and experience of the Cutting-Edgers is that they reflect the growing hybridization of the United States, a process that in all likelihood began at the level of the society's most mobile leadership, or what one observer refers to as a "Mongrel leadership."[3]

Given the more extensive contacts with foreign cultures experienced by Cutting-Edgers in their early years, it is hardly surprising that in the one survey in which the question was posed (1999) more than three times as many of them recorded a greater willingness to view themselves as expatriates (table 4.4). On the other hand, why more of them than Other Leaders reported being members of an ethnic, racial, or religious minority is less clear-cut. Conceivably, and ironically, one's minority status may be an advantage in life on the cutting edge of globalization. The data hint at another possibility, however. Just as individuals worldwide seek shelter in immediate, local identities in the face of globalizing forces, it is plausible that Cutting-Edgers may also seek psychological comfort in identities that are rooted in concepts of place or locality. Rather than having asked the respondents, "Are you a member of an ethnic, racial or religious minority?" perhaps we should have asked, "Have you ever thought of yourself as, or do you consider yourself, a member of an ethnic, racial or religious minority?" In short, it may be that we have uncovered Cutting-Edgers' self-perceptions that result directly from their participation in the processes of globalization. They may undertake a psychological "localization" to counteract their participation in the processes of globalization.

HOW DO YOU KNOW A CUTTING-EDGER WHEN YOU ENCOUNTER ONE?

The answer to the question posed by the title of the chapter is far from self-evident in the personal attributes of leaders. The data on socioeconomic characteristics offer a mixed picture that defies a general conclusion. Unless one was to inquire into Cutting-Edgers' experiences abroad or patterns of foreign travel, Cutting-Edgers in the leadership ranks of the United States are in many ways too similar to Other Leaders to provide reliable bases for identifying the former through their personal attributes alone. Certainly the Involvement Index is a much more reliable basis in this regard, as are some of the variables analyzed in subsequent chapters.

* * *

Once the movie ends and the cabin lights come on, the two traveling companions are momentarily quiet, preferring to stare at each other, as if to ascertain whether the several differences between them are as pronounced as the data suggest. The Other Leader breaks the silence: "You may have more education than I do, and your income may be higher than mine, but I also travel a lot, and I know two languages. Indeed, that's why I am going abroad on this plane!"

"But I sense you are a Republican and conservative in your political orientations, whereas I tend in a liberal direction and vote for Democrats," the Cutting-Edger says.

"You have no way of knowing that," the Other Leader quickly replies, a note of annoyance in his voice.

"Wait a minute," the researcher interjects, eager to prevent the conversation from escalating into an argument. "Our friend is quite right. The data in table 4.1 reveal that both groups had virtually identical political affiliations and orientations in both 1999 and 2003. So there is no basis for asserting that one is more liberal or that one tends to vote for Democrats."

"It's just an intuition," the Cutting Edger responds.

"Intuitions can be widely off the mark," the researcher responds quickly, hoping to avert further squabbling. "If you play the statistics game, there is simply no room for intuition. Furthermore, remember, these are aggregate data. They do not necessarily say anything about a particular person. So let's move on to the ways in which each of you connect to the world."

Intent on maintaining a newfound camaraderie, the traveling companions agree to shift to a new subject, with the Cutting-Edger quelling an impulse to reiterate what he believes to be intuitively accurate.

NOTES

1. James Davison Hunter and Joshua Yates, "In the Vanguard of Globalization: The World of American Globalizers," in *Many Globalizations: Cultural Diversity in the Contemporary World*, ed. Peter L. Berger and Samuel P. Huntington (New York: Oxford University Press, 2002), 334.

2. For comparisons of the business and nonbusiness respondents along a variety of dimensions, see chapter 10.

3. This is title of chapter 8 in G. Pascal Zachary, *The Global Me: New Cosmopolitans and the Competitive Edge—Picking Globalism's Winners and Losers* (New York: PublicAffairs, 2000).

5

Connectivity on the Cutting Edge

When the movie, a James Bond film highlighting the power of corporations, comes to an end, the three travelers quickly agree that it is relevant to globalization. "How could Ian Fleming have so accurately anticipated the way the world has changed?" the Other Leader wonders.

"He must have intuited it," the Cutting-Edger responds playfully.

"Whether or not it was his intuition," the researcher intervenes, "the same theme recurs throughout his movies. Two of my colleagues published an analysis of his films, and they all, in one way or the other, posit a changing world and a changing balance between nongovernmental actors and the state."[1] He pauses and undertakes to redirect the discussion to the patterns whereby leaders maintain contact with the world.

"Why do you ask so many questions?" the Other Leader exclaims when different kinds of contact are posed.

The researcher, intent upon reinforcing the newfound camaraderie, deems it appropriate to offer a straightforward explanation: "I told you: we have to if we're to tell an accurate story. There's still a host of questions I'd like to explore, if you don't mind." Although sensitive to the likelihood they are about to be subjected to a long monologue, the traveling companions nod in agreement, then ask for another beer. The researcher draws the questions from the questionnaire, and the three-way conversation lapses into an exposition and analysis of the data.

CONNECTIVITY WITH THE WORLD

Throughout the globalization literature, it is often suggested that an individual's connectivity to the world transforms his or her attitudes toward

48

local, state, and international authorities.[2] Given their high scores on the Involvement Index (see table 3.4), Cutting-Edgers are also presumably more
cosmopolitan and less parochial, as well as more oriented toward international than national or local affairs, than are those who are not immersed
in global processes. Such a presumption does not mean, however, that
cosmopolitans are, so to speak, rootless. On the contrary, many may be
oriented toward and involved in world affairs even as they feel a sense
of connection to their local or national community. Persons with these
wide-ranging links have aptly been labeled "rooted cosmopolitans"—that
is, rooted in the sense of continuing to feel tied to their residences and
local communities but cosmopolitan in the sense of being inclined to follow or participate in processes unfolding abroad.[3] In the words of one
analyst, "what is 'rooted' in the concept of rooted cosmopolitanism is
that, as cosmopolitans move outside their spatial origins both cognitively
and physically, they continue to be linked to place; to the social networks
that inhabit that space, and to the resources, experiences and opportunities that place provides them with."[4] Another observer conceptualizes
the rooted cosmopolitan as a person who is "attached to a home of his
or her own, with its own cultural particularities, but taking pleasure from
the presence of other, different places that are home to other, different
people."[5]

We explored the notion of Cutting-Edgers' having cosmopolitan perspectives and experiences even as they maintain a sense of connection
with their local roots, by asking the respondents a number of questions
about their links to the world beyond the United States and their sense
of where "home" is located. The findings suggest that the Cutting-Edgers
shared with Other Leaders a tendency to feel close to their immediate
locales even as they were involved in globalizing processes. In effect, the
Cutting-Edgers exhibited the traits of rooted cosmopolitans.

One indication of this trait is their response to a simple yes/no question:
"Do you regard one country as 'home'?" As can be seen in table 5.1, while
the Cutting-Edgers answered "no" significantly more than did the Other
Leaders in 1999, they did not do so in 2003. More important, in both surveys
preponderant proportions of both groups indicated that they regard only
one country as "home." At the same time, the increased "yes" response on
the part of the Cutting-Edgers in 2003 and the absence of a significant difference between them and the Other Leaders may be the first of several indicators of the effects of the September 11 terrorist attacks, which occurred
between administration of the two surveys. Indeed, the difference between
the two Cutting-Edger groups was not significant, perhaps reflecting the
increase in sensitivity to home on the part of the Cutting-Edgers in 2003.

Additional indications of a correspondence between our respondents
and the characteristics of rooted cosmopolitanism is evident in the

Table 5.1   Do You Regard One Country as "Home"?

	Yes		No	
	(n)	%	(n)	%
1999 Cutting-Edgers (n = 185)[a]	(169)	91	(16)	9
1999 Other Leaders (n = 554)	(548)	99	(6)	1
2003 Cutting-Edgers (n = 164)[b]	(157)	96	(7)	4
2003 Other Leaders (n = 393)	(387)	98	(6)	2

[a] This comparison was significant at the .001 level.
[b] This comparison was not significant.

responses to two questions that sought to differentiate among the respondents' links to various aspects of their lives. One offered eight possible close-at-hand locales (table 5.2), and the other specified four possible ways in which the respondents' might regard more encompassing locales as their home (table 5.3). As can be seen in table 5.2, not only was no significant difference between the Cutting-Edgers and the Other Leaders recorded with respect to seven of the close-at-hand alternatives in 1999, but only small proportions of both groups indicated that they "did not regard any particular 'geographic' place as 'home.'" At the same time, at least two-thirds of both groups recorded the highest proportions with respect to the locale that is the least fixed in time and space and that is the most susceptible to change—"where my immediate family or partner lives"—thus suggesting that they carried their sense of rootedness whenever they moved to new locales. In the case of the "professional colleagues" query, on the other hand, the 2003 responses deviated from the 1999 distribution and differed significantly, with a higher proportion of Cutting-Edgers selecting this alternative than did the Other Leaders, a finding that is consistent with others noted later in the chapter, in which the Cutting-Edgers indicated a greater sensitivity to colleagues in the workplace and more extensive patterns of foreign travel and interaction with colleagues abroad than that indicated by the Other Leaders.

Viewed in this context, it is hardly surprising that the undifferentiated reactions of the two groups to the close-at-hand items did not persist when the respondents were asked about worlds more remote than their home (table 5.3). Given a choice of any or all of four conceptions along this line, the Cutting-Edgers differed significantly and substantially from the Other Leaders on two specific positive and behavioral alternatives that asked about movement around the world; however, the differences on two general alternatives and one negative alternative that inquired into orientations toward the world were not significant, presumably because they tapped dimensions of leadership irrespective of one's proximity to the cutting edge. The first sets of two rows in table 5.3 display the wide

Table 5.2   What Locale Do You Consider to Be Your "Home"? (Check All That Apply)

	Check		No check	
	(n)	%	*(n)*	%
Where I was raised[*]				
1999 Cutting-Edgers (*n* = 187)[a]	(84)	45	(103)	55
1999 Other Leaders (*n* = 554)	(227)	41	(327)	59
Where I am a citizen[*]				
1999 Cutting-Edgers (*n* = 187)[a]	(111)	59	(76)	41
1999 Other Leaders (*n* = 554)	(340)	61	(214)	39
Where my immediate family or partner lives[*]				
1999 Cutting-Edgers (*n* = 187)[a]	(125)	67	(62)	33
1999 Other Leaders (*n* = 554)	(390)	70	(164)	30
Where I feel a sense of ethnic, racial, or religious community				
1999 Cutting-Edgers (*n* = 187)[a]	(38)	21	(147)	79
1999 Other Leaders (*n* = 554)	(132)	24	(422)	76
2003 Cutting-Edgers (*n* = 167)[a]	(66)	40	(101)	60
2003 Other Leaders (*n* = 398)	(150)	38	(248)	62
Where I am employed				
1999 Cutting-Edgers (*n* = 187)[a]	(54)	29	(133)	71
1999 Other Leaders (*n* = 554)	(176)	32	(378)	68
2003 Cutting-Edgers (*n* = 167)[a]	(70)	42	(97)	58
2003 Other Leaders (*n* = 398)	(181)	45	(217)	55
Where I plan to retire				
1999 Cutting-Edgers (*n* = 187)[a]	(31)	17	(156)	83
1999 Other Leaders (*n* = 554)	(86)	16	(468)	84
2003 Cutting-Edgers (*n* = 167)[a]	(46)	28	(121)	72
2003 Other Leaders (*n* = 398)	(114)	29	(284)	71
Wherever my professional colleagues may be				
1999 Cutting-Edgers (*n* = 187)[a]	(14)	7	(173)	93
1999 Other Leaders (*n* = 554)	(45)	8	(509)	92
2003 Cutting-Edgers (*n* = 167)[b]	(30)	18	(137)	82
2003 Other Leaders (*n* = 398)	(30)	8	(368)	92
I do not regard any particular "geographic" place as "home"				
1999 Cutting-Edgers (*n* = 187)[a]	(15)	8	(172)	92
1999 Other Leaders (*n* = 554)	(31)	6	(523)	94
2003 Cutting-Edgers (*n* = 167)[a]	(23)	14	(144)	86
2003 Other Leaders (*n* = 398)	(41)	10	(357)	90

[*] Not included in the 2003 survey.
[a] This comparison was not statistically significant.
[b] This comparison was significant at the .001 level.

Table 5.3 In What Sense, If Any, Is the "World" Your Home? (Check All That Apply)

	Check		No check	
	(n)	%	(n)	%
In the sense that I have traveled widely				
1999 Cutting-Edgers (n = 187)[b]	(155)	83	(32)	17
1999 Other Leaders (n = 554)	(290)	52	(264)	48
2003 Cutting-Edgers (n = 167)[b]	(127)	76	(40)	24
2003 Other Leaders (n = 398)	(187)	47	(211)	53
In the sense that I earn my living in many parts of it				
1999 Cutting-Edgers (n = 187)[b]	(95)	51	(92)	49
1999 Other Leaders (n = 554)	(122)	22	(432)	78
2003 Cutting-Edgers (n = 167)[b]	(63)	38	(104)	62
2003 Other Leaders (n = 398)	(63)	16	(335)	84
In the sense that I feel a connection with humanity everywhere				
1999 Cutting-Edgers (n = 187)[a]	(116)	62	(71)	38
1999 Other Leaders (n = 554)	(336)	61	(218)	39
2003 Cutting-Edgers (n = 167)[a]	(107)	64	(60)	36
2003 Other Leaders (n = 398)	(232)	58	(166)	42
In the sense that I am keenly aware of the large extent to which the world is interdependent				
1999 Cutting-Edgers (n = 187)[a]	(157)	84	(30)	16
1999 Other Leaders (n = 554)	(451)	81	(103)	19
2003 Cutting-Edgers (n = 167)[a]	(136)	81	(31)	19
2003 Other Leaders (n = 398)	(310)	78	(88)	22
No, the "world" has no special meaning for me				
1999 Cutting-Edgers (n = 187)[a]	(5)	3	(182)	97
1999 Other Leaders (n = 554)	(14)	3	(540)	97
2003 Cutting-Edgers (n = 167)[a]	(5)	3	(162)	97
2003 Other Leaders (n = 398)	(19)	5	(379)	95

[a] This comparison was not statistically significant.
[b] This comparison was significant at the .001 level.

differences between the two groups on the specific behavioral alternatives (by 29 percent in three cases and 22 percent in the fourth instance) even as the last three sets of rows highlight the absence of statistical differences insofar as the general and attitudinal alternatives are concerned. In addition, the prevalence of a rooted cosmopolitanism is conspicuously evident in the small percentage of Cutting-Edgers who reported that "the 'world' had no special meaning" for them, despite indicating they traveled widely and were "keenly aware" of global interdependence.

Table 5.4 What Are the Bases for Your Contacts Abroad? (Check All That Apply)

	Check		No check	
	(n)	*%*	*(n)*	*%*
Your company's or organization's assignments				
1999 Cutting-Edgers[b] (*n* = 187)	(117)	63	(70)	37
1999 Other Leaders (*n* = 554)	(257)	46	(297)	54
2003 Cutting-Edgers[b] (*n* = 167)	(109)	65	(58)	35
2003 Other Leaders (*n* = 398)	(157)	39	(241)	61
Your freelance work involves foreign contacts				
1999 Cutting Edgers[b] (*n* = 187)	(71)	38	(116)	62
1999 Other Leaders (*n* = 554)	(91)	16	(463)	84
2003 Cutting-Edgers[b] (*n* = 167)	(55)	33	(112)	67
2003 Other Leaders (*n* = 398)	(61)	15	(337)	85
Your curiosity leads you to distant places				
1999 Cutting-Edgers[b] (*n* = 187)	(121)	65	(66)	35
1999 Other Leaders (*n* = 554)	(275)	50	(279)	50
2003 Cutting-Edgers[a] (*n* = 167)	(109)	65	(58)	35
2003 Other Leaders (*n* = 398)	(219)	55	(179)	45
The continuing globalization of world affairs				
1999 Cutting-Edgers[b] (*n* = 187)	(73)	39	(114)	61
1999 Other Leaders (*n* = 554)	(115)	21	(439)	79
2003 Cutting-Edgers[b] (*n* = 167)	(59)	35	(108)	65
2003 Other Leaders (*n* = 398)	(69)	17	(329)	83

[a] This comparison was significant at the .01 level.
[b] This comparison was significant at the .001 level.

While we assumed that the Cutting-Edgers would see themselves as having a professional expertise in demand abroad (row 1 of the Involvement Index presented in table 3.4), this was not the only basis of their foreign contacts. As can be seen in table 5.4, in both 1999 and 2003 Cutting-Edgers reported significantly greater connectivity to the world than did the Other Leaders along four dimensions. These distributions suggest that the sensitivity and proximity of Cutting-Edgers to globalizing dynamics is more broad-gauged than those of Other Leaders and that a multiplicity of reasons can underlie their movement to and on the cutting edge of globalization.

Perhaps even more compelling indicators of the large extent to which Cutting-Edgers are connected to the world outside the United States are evident in the findings generated by a list of twelve entities with which the Cutting-Edgers "feel a sense of identity." On ten of the alternatives—family

Table 5.5   To What Extent Do You Feel a Sense of Identity with Professional Associates at Home?

	Closely identified		Somewhat identified		Mildly identified		None	
	(n)	%	(n)	%	(n)	%	(n)	%
1999 Cutting-Edgers (n = 187)[a]	(102)	55	(73)	39	(12)	6	(0)	0
1999 Other Leaders (n = 552)	(204)	37	(256)	46	(82)	15	(10)	2
2003 Cutting-Edgers (n = 165)[a]	(94)	57	(61)	37	(10)	6	(0)	0
2003 Other Leaders (n = 391)	(170)	43	(163)	42	(51)	13	(7)	2

Note: Because both comparisons involve cells with fewer than five cases, the "none" category was collapsed into the "mildly identified" category when the significance level was calculated.
[a] This comparison was significant at the .001 level.

and friends, neighbors, community of residence, supervisors and/or supervisees, ethnic/racial group, political party or philosophy, country of birth, a region, fellow citizens, and humanity at large—the Cutting-Edgers and the Other Leaders did not differ significantly. It is hardly surprising that the Cutting-Edgers would report that they "closely" or "somewhat" identified with professional associates abroad (row 2 of the Involvement Index in table 3.4); however, what is equally indicative of the responsibilities that attach to their leadership roles is that, in both 1999 and 2003, they reported a significantly greater degree of identification with counterparts in their professions at home than did the Other Leaders. As can be seen in table 5.5, in both years more than half of the Cutting-Edgers "closely identified" with professional colleagues at home, and 94 percent reported feeling "closely" or "somewhat" identified with their counterparts in the United States. These findings suggest the degree to which networking dynamics are part and parcel of leadership in a globalizing world.

Connectivity through Travel

It is a virtual truism to assert that life on the cutting edge requires moving widely around the world. To be sure, on occasion top leaders may be inclined to have their subordinates travel on their behalf, but it is doubtful whether they can fully exercise their leadership by staying at home and using electronic avenues to establish and maintain their connectivity. More accurately, we reasoned that both face-to-face and electronic connections are prerequisites to the occupancy of global roles and thus included items in the questionnaire that sought to determine the extent to which Cutting-Edgers travel or otherwise interact with counterparts elsewhere in the world. Table 5.6 presents the 1999 and 2003 findings on the extent of Cutting-Edgers' business travels abroad in comparison to that of the

Table 5.6   Approximately How Many Times Have You Traveled Abroad on Business in the Past Two Years?

	Average number of trips
1999 Cutting Edgers (*n* = 186)[a]	2.17
1999 Other Leaders (*n* = 554)	0.88
2003 Cutting-Edgers (*n* = 153)[a]	2.59
2003 Other Leaders (*n* = 331)	1.02

[a] This comparison was significant at the .001 level.

Other Leaders. If the terrorist attacks in 2001 curbed the foreign travel of many Americans, such certainly was not the case for our 2003 sample of Cutting-Edgers: they reported averaging nearly three foreign trips in the prior two years.

As for the foreign destinations of their travels, this question was dropped in 2003 to free up space for items about the September 11 attacks. While we included in the Involvement Index the finding that Cutting-Edgers vacation abroad more often than do Other Leaders (row 4 of table 3.4), the 1999 data depict a large gap between the two groups in other kinds of travel, with the Cutting-Edgers making more than twice as many trips abroad for business purposes than those of the Other Leaders (table 5.6) and at least three times as many trips to each of five different regions of the world (table 5.7).[6]

On the other hand, while the Cutting-Edgers report more travel to a greater variety of places abroad, they travel domestically on business roughly as frequently as do Other Leaders. Table 5.8 indicates that domestically, for vacation or other personal matters, in both 1999 and 2003 the Cutting-Edgers traveled somewhat (though not significantly) less frequently than did Other Leaders: whereas the latter report taking an average of about eight trips within the United States each year, the Cutting-Edgers averaged five to six domestic trips. We can only speculate the reasons for

Table 5.7   Approximately How Many Times Have You Traveled in the Last Decade to Countries in . . .

1999 only	Average number of trips	
	Cutting-Edgers (*n* = 187)	Other Leaders (*n* = 554)
Africa?[a]	1.50	0.35
Asia?[a]	8.53	1.69
Europe?[a]	18.40	6.37
Middle East?[a]	2.61	0.45
South America?[a]	4.11	0.93

[a] This comparison was significant at the .001 level.

Table 5.8   Approximately How Many Times a Year Do You
Travel within Your Country But Outside Your City of Residence?

	Average no. of trips	(n)
On business		
1999 Cutting-Edgers[a]	16.96	(185)
1999 Other Leaders	15.61	(549)
2003 Cutting-Edgers[a]	15.87	(159)
2003 Other Leaders	12.34	(373)
For a vacation or other personal matters		
1999 Cutting-Edgers[a]	5.03	(187)
1999 Other Leaders	7.19	(550)
2003 Cutting-Edgers[a]	6.20	(163)
2003 Other Leaders	7.54	(391)

[a] This comparison was not statistically significant.

this difference. Not being statistically significant, it may not stem from systematic sources. Alternatively, the extensive international travel of Cutting-Edgers may conceivably deprive them of enough time to travel as much domestically.

Connectivity through Electronics

Not only do Cutting-Edgers travel abroad more than Other Leaders do, but they are also electronically connected to the world more extensively than the latter group. The findings relative to the electronic connectivity of the two leadership groups to the larger world affirm the more extensive contacts of the Cutting-Edgers. Table 5.9 highlights this significant difference for six technologies in 1999 and 2003. All these differences are substantial, even surprising and stunning: in response to both surveys, the Cutting-Edgers reported using all six technologies "very often" at least twice as frequently as did the Other Leaders, and in several instances the percentages of such responses were three or four times greater. It seems clear that, relatively speaking, rather than electronic communications substituting for the face-to-face interactions inherent in travel (or vice versa), a synergistic relationship between the two forms of interaction marks life on the cutting edge of globalization.

The synergism of travel and electronic connectivity is further reinforced and facilitated by the Cutting-Edgers' extensive use of laptop computers. As indicated in table 5.10, in both surveys they reported a much greater tendency to move around the world with a laptop than did the Other Leaders.

Table 5.9 How Often Do You Employ the Following Methods to Carry Forward Your Interactions with Counterparts Abroad? (Check Only One in Each Row)

	Very often		Occasionally		Seldom		Rarely		Never*	
	(n)	%	(n)	%	(n)	%	(n)	%	(n)	%
E-mail or other online services										
1999 Cutting-Edgers (n = 182)[a]	(131)	72	(39)	21	(5)	3	(4)	2	(3)	2
1999 Other Leaders (n = 535)	(189)	35	(191)	36	(42)	8	(41)	8	(72)	13
2003 Cutting-Edgers (n = 167)[a]	(116)	70	(40)	24	(4)	2	(5)	3	(2)	1
2003 Other Leaders (n = 385)	(137)	36	(139)	36	(25)	6	(32)	8	(52)	14
Cellular phone										
1999 Cutting-Edgers (n = 177)[a]	(25)	14	(39)	22	(34)	19	(26)	15	(53)	30
1999 Other Leaders (n = 500)	(26)	5	(67)	14	(55)	11	(76)	15	(276)	55
2003 Cutting-Edgers (n = 158)[a]	(23)	15	(50)	32	(24)	15	(25)	16	(36)	23
2003 Other Leaders (n = 370)	(16)	4	(59)	16	(52)	14	(65)	18	(178)	48
Regular telephone										
1999 Cutting-Edgers (n = 185)[a]	(106)	57	(62)	33	(11)	6	(5)	3	(1)	1
1999 Other Leaders (n = 533)	(118)	22	(214)	40	(62)	12	(72)	14	(67)	13
2003 Cutting-Edgers (n = 165)[a]	(62)	38	(71)	43	(14)	8	(11)	7	(7)	4
2003 Other Leaders (n = 380)	(48)	13	(133)	35	(52)	14	(69)	18	(78)	21
Teleconferencing										
1999 Cutting-Edgers (n = 174)[a]	(19)	11	(54)	31	(38)	22	(22)	13	(41)	24
1999 Other Leaders (n = 500)	(15)	3	(91)	18	(73)	15	(84)	17	(237)	47
2003 Cutting-Edgers (n = 158)[a]	(16)	10	(54)	34	(32)	20	(25)	16	(31)	20
2003 Other Leaders (n = 362)	(8)	2	(48)	13	(52)	14	(63)	18	(191)	53
Airmail										
1999 Cutting-Edgers (n = 182)[a]	(75)	41	(76)	42	(18)	10	(10)	5	(3)	2
1999 Other Leaders (520)	(106)	20	(215)	41	(63)	12	(65)	13	(71)	14
2003 Cutting-Edgers (n = 158)[a]	(43)	26	(63)	39	(34)	21	(16)	10	(6)	4
2003 Other Leaders (n = 370)	(29)	8	(136)	37	(59)	16	(67)	18	(79)	21
Fax										
1999 Cutting-Edgers (n − 184)[a]	(116)	63	(47)	25	(11)	6	(5)	3	(5)	3
1999 Other Leaders (n = 530)	(146)	28	(208)	39	(32)	6	(49)	9	(95)	18
2003 Cutting-Edgers (n = 164)[a]	(53)	32	(75)	46	(12)	7	(18)	11	(6)	4
2003 Other Leaders (n = 375)	(38)	10	(129)	35	(46)	12	(64)	17	(98)	26

* When the comparison involved cells with fewer than five cases, the "never" category was collapsed into the "rarely" category when the significance level was calculated.

[a] This comparison was significant at the .001 level.

Table 5.10   Do You Travel with a Laptop Computer?

	Yes		No	
	(n)	%	(n)	%
1999 Cutting-Edgers (n = 183)	(109)	60	(74)	40
1999 Other Leaders (n = 546)	(234)	43	(312)	57
2003 Cutting-Edgers (n = 165)	(100)	61	(65)	39
2003 Other Leaders (n = 396)	(160)	40	(236)	60

Although the use of computer and communications technologies indicate that Cutting-Edgers are highly connected, it does not necessarily suggest that they are a networked elite. Are they coordinated, as some theorists imply,[7] or are their actions on the cutting edge essentially independent of one another? Although our survey lacks a means of answering this question directly, hints of some networking can be seen in the finding that in both 1999 and 2003 they reported adding significantly more names to their address books, Rolodexes, or computer databases each month than did Other Leaders (table 5.11). While there is no way of knowing whether these added acquaintances are also global elites, the significant differences suggest that at a minimum Cutting-Edgers are more highly linked to other professionals than are Other Leaders.

CONCLUSION

Of the forty-nine comparisons of the Cutting-Edgers and Other Leaders analyzed in this chapter, thirty-five are marked by significant differences. In themselves, the differences are not surprising. Each of them involves the Cutting-Edgers being more connected to the processes of globalization, electronically and through travel, than the Other Leaders. Only the size of

Table 5.11   Approximately How Many Names Do You Add to Your Address Book, Rolodex, or Computer Each Month?

	26 or more		11–25		6–10		1–5		None	
	(n)	%	(n)	%	(n)	%	(n)	%	(n)	%
1999 Cutting-Edgers (n = 187)[a]	(19)	10	(36)	19	(67)	36	(65)	35	(0)	0
1999 Other Leaders (n = 551)	(22)	4	(70)	13	(136)	24	(297)	54	(26)	5
2003 Cutting-Edgers (n = 165)[b]	(14)	9	(22)	13	(55)	33	(73)	44	(1)	1
2003 Other Leaders (n = 391)	(19)	5	(41)	10	(100)	26	(217)	56	(14)	4

Note: Because these comparisons involve cells with fewer than five cases, the "none" category was collapsed into the "1–5" category when the significance level was calculated.
[a] This comparison was significant at the .001 level.
[b] This comparison was significant at the .01 level.

some of the differences is surprising. In some instances, the proportion of Cutting-Edgers who reported a high degree of connectivity is more than double—and even triple—that of the Other Leaders who responded to the same question. At the same time, with one possible exception (noted in interpreting table 5.1), there is no basis for concluding that the differences can be traced to the September 11 terrorist attacks or any other developments that occurred between the two surveys. It is only as the analysis turns in the next two chapters to probing the orientations and loyalties of the two groups toward globalization that traces of intervening events become manifest.

* * *

The Other Leader leans forward to look admiringly at the Cutting-Edger. "I had no idea you moved around the world so much more than I do," he says. "Don't you get tired?"

"Yes," comes the reply. "It is exhausting at times, but also very worthwhile. I figure it is my world, and I have to check up on it now and then! More seriously, all my trips abroad have a specific purpose. I have to take them to sustain my work. Isn't that also the case for you?"

"Of course, but the need for me to travel so extensively is not nearly as great as is the case for you. I guess I just don't live on the cutting edge of globalization as much as I might want to."

The researcher cannot resist: "Well, you both fulfilled our conception of how you might differ in your connectivity to the world. We're grateful for that!"

NOTES

1. David C. Earnest and James N. Rosenau, "The Spy Who Loved Globalization," *Foreign Policy* (September/October 2000): 88–90.

2. See, for example, Ulf Hannerz, "Cosmopolitans and Locals in World Culture," in *Global Culture: Nationalism, Globalization, and Modernity*, ed. Mike Featherstone (London: Sage, 1990), 237–52.

3. For a cogent formulation of the concept of rooted cosmopolitans, see Sidney Tarrow, *The New Transnational Contention* (Cambridge: Cambridge University Press, 2005).

4. Tarrow, *New Transnational Contention*.

5. Kwame Anthony Appiah, "Cosmopolitan Patriots," in *For Love of Country: Debating the Limits of Patriotism*, ed. Joshua Cohen (Boston: Beacon Press, 1996), 22.

6. These figures on foreign travel for both groups closely parallel comparable data for members of the U.S. Congress. See Eric Schmitt and Elizabeth Becker, "Insular Congress Appears to Be Myth," *New York Times*, November 4, 2000, A9.

7. See, for example, Peter L. Berger, "Four Faces of Global Culture," *National Interest*, no. 49 (Fall 1997): 23–29.

6

Leadership, Affiliations, and Loyalties

Both traveling companions seem puzzled. The Other Leader is the first to express doubt. "I'm impressed that Cutting-Edgers are much more connected to the world than my fellow Other Leaders," he says. "But do they have any sense of the advantages this may afford them? Assuming they are oblivious to that complex model of leadership you set forth earlier, are they nonetheless sensitive to being in a position to exercise the discretion your model says is available to them?"

The puzzlement of the Cutting-Edger goes even further: "Yes, I'm aware that my connectivity to the world provides certain opportunities others don't have," he says, adding, "after all, that's why I'm on this flight. Still, I have a gut feeling that many individuals are not as susceptible to revising their priorities and loyalties as I have been as a result of being on the cutting edge of globalization. Did your inquiry allow for the possibility that Cutting-Edgers have altered their affiliations and loyalties in response to their extensive connections and responsibilities around the world? Are they any different than Other Leaders in this respect?"

The Other Leader chimes in. "It seems to me that the priorities leaders attach to themselves, their organizations, and their country may well have been affected by the September 11 terrorist attacks. Did your 2003 survey probe that question?"

Acknowledging that any conception of leadership in an era of globalization cannot ignore whether the loyalties and patriotism of leaders undergo transformation when they participate more extensively in globalizing processes, the researcher then offers an extended presentation of how the two surveys shed light on such matters. "But," he adds, "while an effort to probe the conflicts of loyalty that may have been stoked by

Table 6.1   Do You Think of Yourself as . . .

	Among the top leaders of your organization or profession		Close to the top		In the middle range		Toward the bottom[*]	
	(n)	*%*	*(n)*	*%*	*(n)*	*%*	*(n)*	*%*
1999 Cutting-Edgers (*n* = 184)[a]	(99)	54	(59)	32	(25)	14	(1)	1
1999 Other Leaders (*n* = 536)	(205)	38	(193)	36	(116)	22	(22)	4
2003 Cutting-Edgers (*n* = 163)[b]	(71)	44	(65)	40	(25)	15	(2)	1
2003 Other Leaders (*n* = 385)	(136)	35	(136)	35	(104)	27	(9)	2

Note: Figures may not add to 100 owing to rounding.
[*] Because this comparison involves cells with fewer than five cases, the "toward the bottom" category was collapsed into the "in the middle range" category when the significance level was calculated.
[a] This comparison was significant at the .001 level.
[b] This comparison was significant at the .05 level.

the September 11 attacks and other recent developments was included in the 2003 survey, the potential consequences of how leaders manage to balance the priorities they attach to themselves, their organizations, and their country as a result of the several explosive issues that intervened between the two surveys are so important that we'll explore them separately."[1]

SELF-PERCEPTIONS

Although our construction of the Involvement Index and the procedure of treating those who scored in its top quartile as Cutting-Edgers meant that, by definition, we were bound to identify persons with leadership capacities more extensive than those of the others we surveyed, a key question remains to be addressed: Do Cutting-Edgers perceive themselves as occupants of leadership roles? As can be seen in table 6.1, the answer is clear-cut. In both 1999 and 2003, nearly nine-tenths of the Cutting-Edgers reported being at or near the top of their professions. Furthermore, as is also evident in table 6.1, these perceptions were significantly greater in 1999 (and marginally greater in 2003) than those of the Other Leaders, distributions that provide solid support for our use of the Involvement Index as a basis for distinguishing between the two groups; that is, both our objective measurement of Cutting-Edgers and their subjective self-evaluations were quite similar. At the same time, less than 5 percent of each group's members saw themselves as being located toward the bottom of the leadership ladder, thus validating our premise that we surveyed people drawn from the country's leadership ranks. Indeed, more than two-thirds of the Other Leaders in both surveys perceived themselves as being at or

Table 6.2   In General, Do You Feel You That You Control Change, or Does Change Control You?

	I control change		Change controls me		Not sure	
	(n)	%	(n)	%	(n)	%
1999 Cutting-Edgers (n = 148)[a]	(69)	46	(41)	28	(38)	26
1999 Other Leaders (n = 476)	(188)	40	(162)	34	(126)	26
2003 Cutting-Edgers (n = 140)[a]	(68)	49	(40)	28	(32)	23
2003 Other Leaders (n = 335)	(141)	42	(116)	35	(78)	23

[a] This comparison was not statistically significant.

close to the top of their organizations or professions, even if they did not match the Cutting-Edgers in this regard.[2]

But to perceive oneself as a top leader is not necessarily to believe one is free of constraining expectations and can thus exercise effective leadership. Perhaps high leadership positions conduce occupants to recognize the diverse limits on leadership posited by our perspective outlined in chapter 2. Or at least this would seem to be a reasonable interpretation of why, in sharp contrast to the reaction of protesters set forth in table 3.1, only a minority of both the Cutting-Edgers and the Other Leaders had self-perceptions in which they saw themselves as exercising control over change (table 6.2), with well over one-fourth of both groups indicating uncertainty on the issue either by answering the question directly or by not answering it at all.[3] This explanation also accounts for why the two groups did not record significantly different responses to the change question in both the 1999 and the 2003 survey. Whether a leader is on the cutting edge of globalization or not, he or she is likely to be sensitive to the limits within which change can be induced. Furthermore, the absence of a significant difference in attitudes toward change would seem to undermine the argument that Cutting-Edgers somehow feel more empowered in general than do Other Leaders.

Having assumed and found that the Cutting-Edgers perceive themselves to be in top leadership roles, we hypothesized that they would be more inclined than Other Leaders to overcome their doubts about controlling change and see themselves as being committed to using their positions on behalf of affecting global conditions. In other words, because Cutting-Edgers are more caught up in global processes than are Other Leaders, it seemed only logical that Cutting-Edgers would express a significantly greater sense of responsibility for the course of events in world affairs, an inclination both to worry about them more and to try to affect them more, and a sense of being less ineffective in influencing the course of events than Other Leaders. As can be seen in table 6.3, all four of these expectations

Table 6.3 With Respect to the Course of Events in World Affairs, Do You ...

	Often		Occasionally		Never	
	(n)	%	(n)	%	(n)	%
... have a sense of responsibility for them?						
1999 Cutting-Edgers (n = 185)[a]	(79)	43	(92)	50	(14)	8
1999 Other Leaders (n = 543)	(112)	·21	(344)	63	(87)	16
2003 Cutting-Edgers (n = 162)[a]	(76)	47	(70)	43	(16)	10
2003 Other Leaders (n = 388)	(115)	30	(202)	52	(71)	18
... worry about them?						
1999 Cutting-Edgers (n = 179)[b]	(89)	50	(79)	44	(11)	6
1999 Other Leaders (n = 536)	(186)	35	(316)	59	(34)	6
2003 Cutting-Edgers (n = 162)[c]	(99)	61	(59)	36	(4)	2
2003 Other Leaders (n = 394)	(212)	54	(166)	42	(16)	4
... try to affect them?						
1999 Cutting-Edgers (n = 180)[a]	(61)	34	(103)	57	(16)	9
1999 Other Leaders (n = 536)	(83)	15	(337)	63	(116)	22
2003 Cutting-Edgers (n = 161)[a]	(54)	34	(99)	61	(8)	5
2003 Other Leaders (n = 390)	(53)	14	(257)	66	(80)	20
... feel ineffective with respect to them?						
1999 Cutting-Edgers (n = 167)[b]	(41)	25	(88)	53	(38)	23
1999 Other Leaders (n = 529)	(228)	43	(208)	39	(93)	18
2003 Cutting-Edgers (n = 156)[c]	(42)	27	(85)	54	(29)	19
2003 Other Leaders (n = 391)	(156)	40	(168)	43	(67)	17

[a] This comparison was significant at the .001 level.
[b] This comparison was significant at the .01 level.
[c] This comparison was not statistically significant.

were upheld by the responses in both 1999 and 2003. Some traces of the effects of the events that intervened between 1999 and 2003 are also evident in the extent to which both groups in the later survey reported a greater sense of responsibility for the course of events and more worry about them. While these increases for the Cutting-Edgers were not significant, the Other Leaders recorded significant differences in both respects (see also table 9.4). Whether these increases were due to particular intervening events, such as the September 11 terrorist attacks or the surge in the antiglobalization protests, is a question addressed in chapter 9.

Another self-perception query involved the ways in which the respondents saw themselves as acting on behalf of their assessments of globalizing processes. As can be seen in table 6.4, in both years the Cutting-Edgers were significantly more likely to seek to advance globalization and less inclined

Table 6.4   To the Extent Your Work Is Relevant to the Processes of Globalization, Do You Usually . . . (Check Only One)

	Seek to advance the processes?		Seek to resist the processes?		Seek to redirect the processes?		Not think about its larger consequences?		My work has no relevance for globalization?[*]	
	(n)	%	(n)	%	(n)	%	(n)	%	(n)	%
1999 Cutting-Edgers (n = 177)[a]	(141)	80	(1)	1	(27)	15	(5)	3	(3)	2
1999 Other Leaders (n = 524)	(340)	65	(8)	2	(58)	11	(75)	14	(43)	8
2003 Cutting-Edgers (n = 159)[a]	(120)	75	(3)	2	(24)	15	(8)	5	(4)	3
2003 Other Leaders (n = 377)	(194)	51	(7)	2	(59)	16	(59)	16	(58)	15

Note: Figures may not add to 100 owing to rounding.
[*] Because the "no relevance" category had fewer than five entries in both years, it was excluded when the significance level was calculated. In addition, for the same reason, the "seek to resist the processes" and "not think about its larger consequences" categories were merged when the significance level was calculated.
[a] This comparison was significant at the .001 level.

to avoid thinking about its larger consequences than were Other Leaders. In these respects both sets of responses paint a picture of Cutting-Edgers feeling more empowered and ready to promote more actively the processes of globalization than the Other Leaders. Unlike that of the Cutting-Edgers, moreover, the readiness of the Other Leaders to advance globalizing process dropped off significantly in the 2003 survey (see also table 9.5).

A final set of self-perceptions probed the salience that both groups attached to certain aspects of globalization regarded as potential threats. The questionnaire included a nine-part item that sought to uncover how leaders personally experience—that is, feel threatened by—various dimensions of the current global scene. These are listed in table 6.5, in which it can be seen that only two of the nine possible threats resulted in statistically significant differences between the Cutting-Edgers and the Other Leaders in 1999, with the former more likely to see nationalism as a moderate or substantial threat and somewhat less likely to see globalization as threatening. Conversely—and not surprisingly—in 1999, only 4 percent of the Cutting-Edgers judged globalization to be a moderate or substantial threat, compared to 13 percent of the Other Leaders, figures that more than tripled for the former in 2003 and doubled for the latter, presumably in response

Table 6.5 To What Extent Do You Consider the Following a Threat to Your Well-Being?

	Not a threat at all		Mild threat		Moderate threat		Substantial threat		Not sure	
	(n)	%	(n)	%	(n)	%	(n)	%	(n)	%
Social movements										
1999 Cutting-Edgers (n = 179)[c]	(79)	44	(53)	30	(24)	13	(16)	9	(7)	4
1999 Other Leaders (n = 531)	(212)	40	(150)	28	(115)	22	(45)	8	(9)	2
2003 Cutting-Edgers (n = 166)[c]	(75)	45	(44)	27	(30)	18	(13)	8	(4)	2
2003 Other Leaders (n = 391)	(143)	37	(122)	31	(89)	23	(27)	7	(10)	3
Professional competitors										
1999 Cutting-Edgers (n = 182)[c]	(76)	42	(56)	31	(35)	19	(13)	7	(2)	1
1999 Other Leaders (n = 538)	(244)	45	(143)	27	(120)	22	(28)	5	(3)	1
2003 Cutting-Edgers (n = 166)[c]	(67)	40	(63)	38	(27)	16	(7)	4	(2)	1
2003 Other Leaders (n = 392)	(162)	41	(141)	36	(73)	19	(16)	4	(0)	0
Religious fundamentalism**										
2003 Cutting-Edgers (n = 166)[c]	(15)	9	(27)	16	(39)	23	(84)	51	(1)	—*
2003 Other Leaders (n = 396)	(62)	16	(59)	15	(87)	22	(183)	46	(5)	1
Multinational corporations										
1999 Cutting-Edgers (n = 182)[c]	(101)	55	(43)	24	(27)	15	(9)	5	(2)	1
1999 Other Leaders (n = 539)	(259)	48	(143)	26	(84)	16	(48)	9	(5)	1
2003 Cutting-Edgers (n = 165)[c]	(82)	50	(33)	20	(30)	18	(16)	10	(4)	2
2003 Other Leaders (n = 394)	(167)	42	(100)	25	(78)	20	(45)	12	(4)	1

Table 6.5 (continued)

	Not a threat at all		Mild threat		Moderate threat		Substantial threat		Not sure	
	(n)	%	(n)	%	(n)	%	(n)	%	(n)	%
Gap between rich and poor										
1999 Cutting-Edgers (n = 183)[c]	(36)	20	(56)	31	(45)	25	(42)	23	(4)	2
1999 Other Leaders (n = 543)	(121)	22	(143)	26	(133)	24	(139)	26	(7)	1
2003 Cutting-Edgers (n = 166)[c]	(28)	17	(52)	31	(42)	25	(38)	23	(6)	4
2003 Other Leaders (n = 396)	(81)	20	(103)	26	(106)	27	(102)	26	(4)	1
Certain individuals										
1999 Cutting-Edgers (n = 178)[c]	(44)	25	(56)	31	(40)	23	(29)	16	(9)	5
1999 Other Leaders (n = 531)	(148)	28	(181)	34	(97)	18	(79)	15	(26)	5
2003 Cutting-Edgers (n = 160)[b]	(23)	14	(44)	27	(35)	22	(49)	31	(9)	6
2003 Other Leaders (n = 393)	(97)	25	(107)	27	(87)	22	(85)	22	(17)	4
Certain countries										
1999 Cutting-Edgers (n = 182)[c]	(29)	16	(55)	30	(58)	32	(38)	21	(2)	1
1999 Other Leaders (n = 536)	(89)	17	(164)	31	(164)	31	(101)	19	(18)	3
2003 Cutting-Edgers (n = 164)[c]	(8)	5	(31)	19	(50)	30	(73)	45	(2)	1
2003 Other Leaders (n = 394)	(28)	7	(76)	19	(124)	32	(162)	41	(4)	1
Terrorist groups										
1999 Cutting-Edgers (n = 185)[c]	(4)	2	(45)	25	(56)	30	(80)	43	(0)	0
1999 Other Leaders (n = 543)	(25)	5	(127)	23	(177)	33	(212)	39	(2)	0
2003 Cutting-Edgers (n = 166)[c]	(0)	0	(21)	13	(30)	18	(115)	69	(0)	0
2003 Other Leaders (n = 397)	(6)	2	(40)	10	(89)	22	(260)	66	(2)	1

Table 6.5 (continued)

	Not a threat at all		Mild threat		Moderate threat		Substantial threat		Not sure	
	(n)	%	(n)	%	(n)	%	(n)	%	(n)	%
Nationalism										
1999 Cutting-Edgers (n = 182)[a]	(40)	22	(50)	27	(64)	35	(24)	13	(4)	2
1999 Other Leaders (n = 536)	(169)	32	(186)	35	(118)	22	(50)	9	(13)	2
2003 Cutting-Edgers (n = 166)[c]	(37)	22	(54)	33	(45)	27	(25)	15	(5)	3
2003 Other Leaders (n = 394)	(116)	29	(103)	26	(125)	32	(38)	10	(12)	3
Globalization										
1999 Cutting-Edgers (n = 182)[b]	(137)	75	(34)	19	(1)	1	(6)	3	(4)	2
1999 Other Leaders (n = 537)	(357)	67	(99)	18	(46)	9	(24)	4	(11)	2
2003 Cutting-Edgers (n = 166)[a]	(112)	67	(21)	13	(19)	11	(6)	4	(8)	5
2003 Other Leaders (n = 389)	(211)	54	(82)	21	(63)	16	(22)	6	(11)	3
Environmental degradation*										
2003 Cutting-Edgers (n = 167)[c]	(15)	9	(48)	29	(44)	26	(58)	35	(2)	1
2003 Other Leaders (n = 394)	(35)	9	(106)	27	(119)	30	(131)	33	(3)	1

Note: Figures may not add to 100 owing to rounding. Because the "not sure" category had fewer than five entries in most of the subparts of the question, that category was excluded when the significance level was calculated. In the case of the "terrorist groups" and "globalization" subparts, however, there were at least two categories with fewer than five entries, thus leading to the merger of the "substantial" and "moderate" categories when significance levels were calculated. None of these changes altered the significance level of the comparisons.
[a] This comparison was significant at the .01 level.
[b] This comparison was significant at the .05 level.
[c] This comparison was not significant.
* Not included in the 1999 survey.

to the greater uncertainty that prevailed globally in that year. For both groups, however, the percentages on globalization as a moderate or substantial threat are noticeably lower than is the case for the other eight types of threats. Indeed, more than 70 percent of both the Cutting-Edgers and the Other Leaders assessed "terrorists groups" as moderate or substantial threats in 1999, and after the September 11 terrorist attacks on the World

Trade Center towers and the Pentagon these figures rose to 87 percent for both groups. Although not quite as large, noticeable increases for both groups marked their judgments about "certain countries," perhaps reflecting the war against the Taliban in Afghanistan and the buildup to similar action in Iraq that intervened between the two surveys. In short, while an upbeat quality marks some of the data presented previously, the findings presented in table 6.5 indicate that a more pessimistic set of concerns were also operative.

Priorities and Loyalties

Presumably the attachments of Cutting-Edgers to their country, professions, organizations, and careers require establishing a complex balance among the demands on their loyalties. After all, to be on the cutting edge of globalization is to enter a role with a new set of informal expectations and, as table 6.3 indicates, to evolve responsibilities and worries that are global in scope or at least much more extensive than is the case for leadership in national or local contexts. Traces that such reasoning is well grounded have already been uncovered in our findings: not only do Cutting-Edgers report engaging in significantly more extensive travel and not only do they earn their living in significantly more extensive parts of the world than do the Other Leaders (table 5.2), but they are also significantly less likely to view one country as home (table 5.1). These hints and the fact that such reasoning pervades the literature on cosmopolitanism highlight several questionnaire items that probed how Cutting-Edgers and Other Leaders prioritize their various attachments.[4]

Yet, despite earlier intimations that Cutting-Edgers may have different conceptions of patriotism than do Other Leaders as well as different priorities if their professional or organizational goals and obligations conflict with their civic duties, such reasoning was not upheld in response to the data on conceptions of patriotism and potential conflicts among various loyalties. Three questions focused on potential conflicts among responsibilities, and three multiple-part queries probed issues of patriotism. The distributions in response to the former are presented in the three parts of table 6.6. Here it can be seen that, confronted with hypothetical conflicts among their professional, organizational, national, and civic obligations, the two groups of respondents in both 1999 and 2003 did not differ significantly in their responses to any of the conflicts. Interestingly, while both the Cutting-Edgers and the Other Leaders were substantially more likely in 1999 and 2003 to attach a higher priority to the interests of their countries than to those of their companies or organizations, they did so to a greater degree in response to the latter survey, a pattern that was not significant in either case but that could be interpreted as a trace of the consequences

Table 6.6 Potential Conflicts among Role Requirements

Table 6.6a If a vital choice involving your company or organization could not be avoided, would you put its interests ahead of those of your country?

	Yes		No		I avoid such choices		Not sure	
	(n)	%	(n)	%	(n)	%	(n)	%
1999 Cutting-Edgers (n = 186)[a]	(22)	12	(119)	64	(10)	5	(35)	19
1999 Other Leaders (n = 546)	(39)	7	(337)	62	(34)	6	(135)	25
2003 Cutting-Edgers (n = 162)[a]	(10)	6	(124)	77	(7)	4	(21)	13
2003 Other Leaders (n = 394)	(19)	5	(271)	69	(18)	4	(86)	22

Table 6.6b If a vital choice involving your career could not be avoided, would you put your professional needs ahead of those of your company or organization?

1999 Cutting-Edgers (n = 182)[a]	(100)	55	(45)	25	(7)	4	(30)	16
1999 Other Leaders (n = 545)	(314)	58	(108)	20	(17)	3	(105)	19
2003 Cutting-Edgers (n = 164)[a]	(91)	55	(41)	25	(6)	4	(26)	16
2003 Other Leaders (n = 394)	(223)	57	(86)	22	(13)	3	(72)	18

Table 6.6c If your professional responsibilities and your civic obligations come into conflict, which are likely to prevail most of the time?

	Professional obligations		Civic obligations		I avoid such conflicts		Not sure	
	(n)	%	(n)	%	(n)	%	(n)	%
1999 Cutting-Edgers (n = 183)[a]	(82)	45	(60)	33	(14)	8	(27)	15
1999 Other Leaders (n = 545)	(269)	49	(131)	24	(41)	8	(104)	19
2003 Cutting-Edgers (n = 161)[a]	(70)	43	(53)	33	(16)	10	(22)	14
2003 Other Leaders (n = 393)	(173)	44	(109)	28	(32)	8	(79)	20

[a] This comparison was not statistically significant.

fostered by the September 11 attacks. Most notably, it suggests a resurgence of rooted cosmopolitanism in response to the terrorism. At the same time, it is noteworthy that between a fourth and a third of both groups in both years did not accord the highest priority to their countries (the first, third, and fourth columns in table 6.6a) and that unusually large proportions of both groups selected the "not sure" alternative, suggesting that loyalty issues are problematic and the source of more than a little ambivalence. These findings also indicate the likelihood that patriotism has different meanings for different people.[5]

No less telling, an indicator of ambivalence over their concern for their political communities is evident in the finding that both groups in both surveys valued their professional needs over their civic obligations. The aforementioned notion that leadership on the cutting edge tends to foster cosmopolitan attitudes favoring civil society is called into question by the finding that both groups attached considerably higher priority to their professional obligations than to their civic obligations. If it is assumed that civic obligations draw on the same wellsprings from which patriotism gathers strength, it would appear that the patriotism of no more than a third of the leaders accorded the highest priority to the state of worlds beyond their professions and careers.

Perhaps the most salient pattern in table 6.6 is the recurrent commitment to the world of work, to the professional requirements of the respondents' positions, or (as stated in terms of our leadership model set forth in chapter 2) to the informal and formal expectations of the leadership roles they occupied. Put differently, signs of self-centeredness can be discerned among both the Cutting-Edgers and the Other Leaders: more than half of both groups in both surveys indicated that, given an unavoidable choice, they would place the professional needs of their careers ahead of the companies or organizations with which they were affiliated. Unfortunately, we did not pursue the self-centered theme by inquiring directly into the relative priority of the loyalties they attached to their countries and careers, but the fact that less than two-thirds put the interests of their countries ahead of those of their companies or organizations in 1999 suggests that a country–career comparison might yield more than a few leaders who accord a lower priority to their countries.

In sum, the fact that table 6.6 depicts the absence of significant differences between the Cutting-Edgers and the Other Leaders tends to disconfirm the various assertions in the impressionistic literature about the loyalties of leaders on the cutting edge of globalization.[6] Rather, the distribution of responses suggests that the priorities of all elites—not just those on the cutting edge—are inconsistent with traditional notions of identity and loyalty, that national loyalties are problematic for more than a few leaders, that more than half of both groups value their own well-being ahead of their organizational ties, and that no more than a third of both groups attach unqualified priority to their civic obligations relative to their professional obligations. Accordingly, while these findings say more about leaders in general than about those on the cutting edge of globalization, it can be argued that the absence of differences between the two groups hint at two theoretically interesting possibilities: that our samples contain some self-centered leaders from the baby boomer generation whose members have difficulty committing to values not encompassed by their narrow self-interests (though the mean age of our respondents, fifty-five years old in 1999 and fifty-eight in 2003, may refute this interpretation) or that the processes of globalization may have consequences for all leaders, irrespective of whether they are active on the cutting edge. While the survey lacks a

Table 6.7   Would You Say Patriotism Is . . . (Check All That Apply)

. . . an increasingly obsolete sentiment?

	Check		No check	
1999 survey only	*(n)*	*%*	*(n)*	*%*
Cutting-Edgers (*n* = 187)[a]	(28)	15	(159)	85
Other Leaders (*n* = 553)	(94)	17	(459)	83

. . . of continuing major importance?

Cutting-Edgers (*n* = 187)[a]	(118)	63	(69)	37
Other Leaders (*n* = 553)	(370)	67	(183)	33

. . . of largely symbolic or psychological significance?

Cutting-Edgers (*n* = 187)[a]	(73)	39	(114)	61
Other Leaders (*n* = 553)	(197)	36	(356)	64

. . . no longer relevant to the course of events?

Cutting-Edgers (*n* = 187)[a]	(5)	3	(182)	97
Other Leaders (*n* = 553)	(17)	3	(536)	97

[a] This comparison was not statistically significant.

means to distinguish between these possibilities, the responses to the three questions do suggest the presence of self-centered priorities.

Patriotism

Several multipart questions directly addressed the question of national loyalties. One of the 1999 questions (table 6.7) was posed more elaborately in 2003. Both items offered the same characterizations of patriotism, but in 2003 we expanded the characterizations to determine whether the assessments varied under three conditions (table 6.8). In 2003 we also added an item that called for a judgment as to whether the September 11 terrorist attacks had consequences for the patriotism of the respondents personally, for the United States, and for most of the world (table 6.9).

In none of these questions was a significant difference uncovered between the responses of the Cutting-Edgers and those of the Other Leaders. As far as patriotism is concerned, it apparently does not matter whether a leader is on the cutting edge of globalization or not. At the same time, a widespread consensus can be discerned in the substantial proportions of both groups in both surveys who either avoided treating patriotism as "an increasingly obsolete sentiment" or rejected the proposition that patriotism is "no longer relevant to the course of events." Indeed, another indication

Table 6.8 Would You Say Patriotism Is ...(Check All That Apply)

2003 survey only	For you personally				For the United States				For the most of the world			
	Check		No check		Check		No check		Check		No check	
	(n)	%	(n)	%	(n)	%	(n)	%	(n)	%	(n)	%
...an increasingly obsolete sentiment?												
Cutting-Edgers (n = 167)[a]	(11)	8	(154)	92	(10)	6	(157)	94	(16)	10	(151)	90
Other Leaders (n = 398)	(25)	6	(373)	94	(16)	4	(382)	96	(38)	10	(360)	90
...of continuing major importance?												
Cutting-Edgers (n = 167)[a]	(116)	69	(51)	31	(123)	74	(44)	26	(91)	54	(76)	46
Other Leaders (n = 398)	(278)	70	(120)	30	(306)	77	(92)	23	(215)	54	(183)	46
...of largely symbolic or psychological significance?												
Cutting-Edgers (n = 167)[a]	(40)	24	(127)	76	(38)	23	(129)	77	(54)	32	(113)	68
Other Leaders (n = 398)	(96)	24	(302)	76	(79)	20	(319)	80	(125)	31	(273)	69
...no longer relevant to the course of events?												
Cutting-Edgers (n = 167)[a]	(3)	2	(164)	98	(3)	2	(164)	98	(5)	3	(162)	97
Other Leaders (n = 398)	(5)	1	(393)	99	(5)	1	(393)	99	(13)	3	(385)	97

[a] This comparison was not statistically significant.

Table 6.9   Would You Say Patriotism Has ... (Check Only One in Each Row)

	Temporarily increased since September 11		Permanently increased since September 11		Remained unchanged since September 11	
2003 survey only	*(n)*	*%*	*(n)*	*%*	*(n)*	*%*
... for you personally?						
Cutting-Edgers (*n* = 167)[a]	(25)	15	(56)	35	(82)	50
Other Leaders (*n* = 398)	(60)	15	(153)	39	(181)	46
... for the United States?						
Cutting-Edgers (*n* = 165)[a]	(85)	51	(67)	41	(13)	8
Other Leaders (*n* = 395)	(207)	53	(167)	42	(21)	5
... for most of the world?						
Cutting-Edgers (*n* = 154)[a]	(48)	31	(22)	14	(84)	55
Other Leaders (*n* = 380)	(124)	33	(44)	11	(212)	56

[a] This comparison was not statistically significant.

of a resurgent rooted cosmopolitanism can be discerned in the finding that some two-thirds of both groups perceived patriotism as being "of continuing major importance"[7] for them personally and for the United States, even as only slightly more than half of both groups in 2003 believed that it was of major importance for most of the world. Given an opportunity to explain the continuing importance of patriotism by describing it as being "of largely symbolic or psychological significance," nearly two-fifths of both groups opted for this explanation in 1999, but that figure dropped to less than one-fourth for them personally and for the United States in 2003 and to less than one-third when asked about its significance "for most of the world."

Nor did the Cutting-Edgers and the Other Leaders record significantly different reactions to the impact that the September 11 terrorist attacks had on patriotism. Members of both groups perceived the attacks as being highly consequential for their own patriotism and for the that of the United States while perceiving less of an impact on patriotism throughout the world. As can be seen in table 6.9, more than half the respondents in both groups responded that their own patriotism either temporarily or permanently increased as a consequence of the September 11 attacks. The figures for their perception of the impact on the United States are even more indicative of the powerful consequences of the attacks: perhaps influenced by the plethora of flags that subsequently marked the American scene, more than nine-tenths of both groups responded that patriotism increased temporarily or permanently after the September 11 attacks. Probably this assessment of the U.S. reaction accounts for the finding that fewer respondents in both groups perceived that patriotism in the rest of the world was altered by the attacks.

CONCLUSION

The findings of this chapter present a mixed picture insofar as the differences between the Cutting-Edgers and the Other Leaders are concerned. On the one hand, all the comparisons of their self-perceptions involved significant differences in both 1999 and 2003, but the opposite was the case for all the comparisons of the assessment of patriotism and the priorities the respondents attach to their key affiliations. However, this mix is not as contradictory as it might seem at first glance. It speaks to the scope of a person's leadership, to the breadth of the stage on which leaders exercise their responsibilities. Our data clearly indicate that the concern of leaders for the course of world affairs is heightened the more their positions involve them in the processes of globalization. Indeed, not only is it remarkable, even stunning, that at least nine-tenths of the Cutting-Edgers often or occasionally experience a sense of responsibility for the course of world affairs and that similar proportions worry about and try to affect them, but such findings also suggest that the dynamics of globalization have led to the emergence of leaders whose concerns are not confined within national boundaries.

Such an interpretation, however, is not contradicted by the absence of differences between the two groups in their affiliative priorities and notions of patriotism. This finding suggests the common elements of leadership that operate irrespective of whether globalizing processes are involved. As far as careers, jobs, organizations, and civic obligations are concerned, it matters little whether a leader is on the cutting edge of globalization or not. The patriotism of both Cutting-Edgers and Other Leaders, moreover, affirms the notion that their cosmopolitanism does not involve a commitment to world citizenship so much as it is expressive of rooted cosmopolitanism, a perspective that has been voiced by a number of nonpolitical leaders in the United States.[8]

* * *

Both travelers express considerable agitation. "I can't believe that more than half of both your 1999 and your 2003 samples gave greater weight to their professional needs than to those of their companies," the Cutting-Edger exclaims. "That's certainly not true of me!"

"And I resist the idea that my patriotism was not altered by the September 11 attacks," the Other Leader adds. "My patriotism has never been more intense."

Aware that the findings had touched sensitive issues, the researcher reminds his companions that the aggregate data do not necessarily apply to any single individual. "You've forgotten the point of this kind of inquiry," he says reassuringly. "Our findings describe overall patterns that may or may not be relevant to you in particular."

The Other Leader responds, "Still, it amazes me that no more than half of your elites reported that their patriotism remained unchanged after September 11. I thought those terrorist attacks were supposed to have profoundly altered everyone's perspective. Everyone I know seems more devoted to the United States now than before the attacks."

Raising his voice, the Cutting-Edger asserts, "My patriotism remained unchanged, and, in fact, I don't feel very patriotic, either now or prior to September 11!"

Sensing that a needless argument is brewing, the researcher repeats that one cannot personalize quantified findings. "Look, fellows," he repeats firmly, "I've been talking about central tendencies that may or may not describe you. Besides, we're going to look more closely later at the differences between the 1999 and 2003 patterns. The whole of chapter 9 is devoted to the subject. So be patient and let me first recount for you what we found with respect to orientations toward globalization and world affairs."

NOTES

1. See chapter 9.

2. Although the distributions for both the Cutting-Edgers and the Other Leaders indicate that their perceptions of themselves as being at the top of their organizations or professions dropped from 1999 to 2003, neither comparison of the responses of each group to the two surveys resulted in a significant difference.

3. The number of respondents to this question is conspicuously lower than that for a preponderance of other items. Indeed, offered a chance to specify in writing an alternative response, seventy-two respondents in 1999 and sixty-nine in 2003 indicated (either in writing or by checking both alternatives) that they controlled change *and* were controlled by it.

4. See, for example, several essays in Joshua Cohen, ed., *For Love of Country: Debating the Limits of Patriotism* (Boston: Beacon Press, 1996).

5. For a cogent analysis of the variability that can attach to the concept of patriotism, see Janny Scott, "The Changing Face of Patriotism," *New York Times*, July 6, 2003, sec. 4., 1.

6. See, for example, Rosabeth Moss Kanter, *World Class: Thriving Locally in the Global Economy* (New York: Simon & Schuster, 1995), chap. 1; and Robert B. Reich, *The Future of Success* (New York: Knopf, 2000), chap. 4.

7. For a journalistic interpretation along these lines, see William Safire, "The New Patriotism," *New York Times*, July 2, 2001, A19.

8. See Cohen, *For Love of Country*.

7

Orientations toward Globalization

The Other Leader seems exasperated. "You've answered queries about connectivity and affiliations, but that doesn't tell me very much. I don't carry a laptop, and my loyalties have become more intense, but what does that say about my attitudes toward globalization?"

The Cutting-Edger nods in agreement. "For all you know, the two of us have similar reactions to the implications of globalization. There must be more to your story than what you've told us thus far. Surely you asked both your 1999 and your 2003 samples questions about globalizing processes."

After the researcher assures the two travelers that, indeed, such questions were asked and that they generated complex findings, the three-way conversation yields to another monologue as the questions and their complex responses are elaborated.

GENERAL ATTITUDES TOWARD GLOBALIZATION

To be located on the cutting edge of globalization is not necessarily to be unqualifiedly in favor of the processes that promote and sustain it. Recall from the previous chapter that in both 1999 and 2003 large proportions of the Cutting-Edgers perceived themselves as seeking to advance these processes and that they did so significantly more than did the Other Leaders (table 6.4). When our questions moved from self-perceptions in general to attitudes toward globalization in particular, however, traces of ambivalence toward globalization's processes became manifest. Not only were few significant differences between the two groups recorded, but in a number of instances both groups indicated less-than-wholehearted support for what were then perceived as the dynamics of globalization.

Illustrating first the positive side of the ambivalence, table 7.1 reveals at least four-fifths of both groups in both surveys who assessed globalization as enhancing human rights, economic integration, and capitalism, as well as three-fourths of both groups in both years who regarded the enhancement of political democracy as being among the consequences of globalizing processes. Substantial majorities also perceived the creation of jobs, cultural diversity, and ecological sensitivities as having been enhanced by globalization. On the other hand, less than half of both groups in both surveys, perhaps reflecting the continuing tensions in the Middle East, regarded globalization as having undermined ethnic identities and religion as much as it enhanced them. Perhaps equally indicative, traces of mounting ambivalence can be discerned in the finding that virtually every actor or issue included in table 7.1 was perceived by both the Cutting-Edgers and the Other Leaders as being less enhanced and more undermined by globalization in 2003 than in 1999.[1]

Another way to interpret the data in table 7.1 is to view them as reflecting consensus among leaders irrespective of their proximities to the cutting edge of globalization. With one possible exception, the two groups recorded similar reactions to the actors, issues, or institutions listed in the table. Their differences with respect to the "creation of jobs" alternative might be explained in terms of the large extent to which the period between the two surveys was marked by growing unemployment; however, it is not easy to account for why this alternative was the only consequence that differentiated the two groups in both surveys, inasmuch as their similar reactions in both surveys to eight of the alternatives and in one survey to two of the alternatives depict a degree of agreement that can readily be called a consensus. Although they responded to different degrees, with exceptions being that of ethnic identities and religion, the two groups viewed globalization as enhancing rather than undermining nine actors, issues, or institutions: in eight instances, the respondents recorded at least a three-to-one margin in favor of enhancement; in five of these cases, the margin is seven to one or better. In sum, while table 7.1 does not point to an unqualified consensus in support of globalizing processes, it does reflect a consensus nevertheless.

Another measure of mixed assessments of the virtues of globalizing processes is evident in the responses to direct questions about whether its processes are good or bad and whether they can or should be facilitated. We probed these assessments in slightly different ways in the two surveys, but in both cases positive responses—"mostly good" or "good"—were recorded by only about half the leaders (table 7.2 and the first subpart of

Table 7.1 On Balance, How Would You Assess the Impact of the Diverse Processes of Globalization on ...

	Undermining		Enhancing		Having no effect	
	(n)	%	(n)	%	(n)	%
...local communities?						
1999 Cutting-Edgers (n = 182)[a]	(43)	24	(97)	53	(42)	23
1999 Other Leaders (n = 529)	(136)	26	(255)	48	(138)	26
2003 Cutting-Edgers (n = 161)[a]	(46)	28	(72)	45	(43)	27
2003 Other Leaders (n = 384)	(132)	34	(144)	38	(108)	28
...individual altruism?						
1999 Cutting-Edgers (n = 181)[a]	(30)	17	(91)	50	(60)	33
1999 Other Leaders (n = 520)	(92)	18	(214)	41	(214)	41
2003Cutting-Edgers (n = 155)[c]	(19)	12	(70)	45	(66)	43
2003 Other Leaders (n = 384)	(87)	23	(143)	37	(154)	40
...human rights?						
1999 Cutting-Edgers (n = 187)[a]	(14)	7	(160)	86	(13)	7
1999 Other Leaders (n = 535)	(42)	8	(464)	87	(29)	5
1999 Cutting-Edgers (n = 163)[a]	(14)	8	(138)	85	(11)	7
2003 Other Leaders (n = 389)	(53)	14	(313)	80	(23)	6
...political democracy?						
1999 Cutting-Edgers (n = 182)[b]	(14)	8	(159)	87	(9)	5
1999 Other Leaders (n = 530)	(48)	9	(442)	83	(40)	8
2003 Cutting-Edgers (n = 161)[a]	(22)	14	(120)	74	(19)	12
2003 Other Leaders (n = 385)	(64)	17	(291)	75	(30)	8
...economic integration?[**]						
1999 Cutting-Edgers (n = 184)[a]	(8)	4	(173)	94	(3)	2
1999 Other Leaders (n = 536)	(29)	5	(488)	91	(19)	4
2003 Cutting-Edgers (n = 162)[a]	(8)	5	(150)	93	(4)	2
2003 Other Leaders (n = 381)	(36)	9	(336)	88	(9)	2
...creation of jobs[**]						
1999 Cutting-Edgers (n = 181)[d]	(10)	6	(167)	92	(4)	2
1999 Other Leaders (n = 529)	(59)	11	(437)	83	(33)	6
2003 Cutting-Edgers (n = 159)[b]	(22)	14	(127)	80	(10)	6
2003 Other Leaders (n = 384)	(88)	23	(261)	68	(35)	9
...cultural diversity?						
1999 Cutting-Edgers (n = 186)[a]	(44)	24	(129)	71	(9)	5
1999 Other Leaders (n = 552)	(91)	17	(410)	77	(32)	6
2003 Cutting-Edgers (n = 165)[a]	(39)	24	(117)	71	(9)	5
2003 Other Leaders (n = 383)	(85)	22	(283)	74	(15)	4

Table 7.1 (continued)

	Undermining		Enhancing		Having no effect	
	(n)	%	(n)	%	(n)	%
...ecological sensitivities?						
1999 Cutting-Edgers (n = 180)[a]	(37)	21	(122)	68	(21)	12
1999 Other Leaders (n = 531)	(88)	17	(361)	68	(82)	15
2003 Cutting-Edgers (n = 160)[a]	(37)	23	(99)	62	(24)	15
2003 Other Leaders (n = 381)	(120)	32	(222)	58	(39)	10
...ethnic identities?						
1999 Cutting-Edgers (n = 178)[a]	(77)	43	(78)	44	(23)	13
1999 Other Leaders (n = 526)	(222)	42	(212)	40	(92)	17
2003 Cutting-Edgers (n = 162)[a]	(72)	45	(59)	36	(31)	19
2003 Other Leaders (n = 377)	(165)	44	(154)	41	(58)	15
...capitalism?						
1999 Cutting-Edgers (n = 182)[a]	(11)	6	(160)	88	(11)	6
1999 Other Leaders (n = 529)	(32)	6	(455)	86	(42)	8
2003 Cutting-Edgers (n = 161)[a]	(10)	6	(142)	88	(9)	6
2003 Other Leaders (n = 389)	(38)	10	(335)	86	(16)	4
...religion?[*]						
2003 Cutting-Edgers (n = 160)[a]	(40)	25	(50)	31	(70)	44
2003 Other Leaders (n = 379)	(117)	31	(100)	26	(162)	43

[*] In the 2003 survey only.
[**] Because the "having no effect" category had fewer than five entries in this subpart of the question, the category was excluded when the significance level was calculated.
[a] This comparison was not statistically significant.
[b] This comparison was significant at the .05 level.
[c] This comparison was significant at the .01 level.
[d] This comparison was significant at the .001 level.

Table 7.2 On Balance, What Have Been the Consequences of Globalization for the United States?

	Mostly good		Both good and bad		Mostly bad		Neither good nor bad[*]	
2003 survey only	(n)	%	(n)	%	(n)	%	(n)	%
Cutting-Edgers (n = 167)[a]	(80)	48	(78)	47	(7)	4	(2)	1
Other Leaders (n = 391)	(141)	36	(218)	55	(22)	6	(10)	3

[*] Because the "neither good nor bad" category had fewer than five entries in this subpart of the question, that category was excluded when the significance level was calculated.
[a] This comparison was significant at the .05 level.

table 7.3). To be sure, small proportions of both groups judged the consequences to be "mostly bad" or "bad" (table 7.2 and the second subpart of
table 7.3), but enough opted for the middle, "both good and bad" option
(table 7.2 and the third subpart of table 7.3) to restrict a consensus forming
around the positive alternatives. Put differently, only with respect to the
negative alternatives did both groups register a widespread and clear-cut
consensus.[2]

The question about the desirability of globalizing processes probed
whether the processes can or should be facilitated and whether they can
or should be altered, hindered, or retarded. As can be seen in the last four
parts of table 7.3, these additional queries did not result in significant differences between the evaluations of the Cutting-Edgers and those of the
Other Leaders, but the differences did yield some interesting findings. One
is that only one respondent, a Cutting-Edger, perceived globalization as a
"bad set of processes," thus suggesting that at least the 1999 leaders shared
a near-unanimous and positive approach to the dynamics of globalization.
Second, a quick glance down the two columns of table 7.3 suggests a computer or transcription error was made in calculating the 2003 responses
to the "a set of processes that can be facilitated" subpart of the question.
After carefully checking the original questionnaires, however, we deter-
mined that no error had been made: the 2003 responses to that subpart
are indeed contrary to the 1999 responses and to the other subparts of the
question. Further investigation and reflection then led to a logical explanation. While these responses can be interpreted as those stemming from a
methodological bias,[3] they can be interpreted more persuasively as those
stemming from substantive dynamics precipitated by the battle of Seattle
and similar protests that intervened between the two surveys. This interpretation is analyzed at length in chapter 9, where diachronic comparisons
are employed to analyze the data (table 9.12).

It might also be argued that these mixed findings were the result of
Cutting-Edgers being more optimistic or feeling more empowered in
general—not just toward the consequences of globalization—than is the
case for Other Leaders. However, this reasoning does not hold up in the
light of responses to the aforementioned question that probed their self-
perceptions on controlling change (see table 6.2). The absence of a significant difference between the two groups in their attitudes toward change
undermines the argument that Cutting-Edgers feel more empowered in
general than do Other Leaders.

Another general question that probed for indicators of optimism or pes-
simism focused on expectations for the future, and it too did not result in a
statistically significant difference between the two groups. Table 7.4 reveals
that both the Cutting-Edgers and the Other Leaders leaned in an optimistic
direction, even though their responses were essentially undifferentiated.

Table 7.3 On Balance Do You Believe Globalization Is ... (Check All That Apply)

	Check		No check	
	(n)	*%*	*(n)*	*%*
...a "good" set of processes?[*]				
1999 Cutting-Edgers (*n* = 186)[b]	(103)	55	(83)	45
1999 Other Leaders (*n* = 547)	(249)	46	(298)	54
...a "bad" set of processes?[*]				
1999 Cutting-Edgers (*n* = 186)[a]	(1)	1	(185)	100
1999 Other Leaders (*n* = 554)	(16)	3	(531)	97
...a "good" set of processes for some and a "bad" set for others?[*]				
1999 Cutting-Edgers (*n* = 186)[a]	(87)	47	(99)	53
1999 Other Leaders (*n* = 547)	(281)	51	(266)	49
...a set of processes that can be facilitated?				
1999 Cutting-Edgers (*n* = 186)[a]	(82)	44	(104)	56
1999 Other Leaders (*n* = 547)	(228)	42	(319)	58
2003 Cutting-Edgers (*n* = 167)[c]	(115)	69	(52)	31
2003 Other Leaders (*n* = 398)	(238)	60	(160)	40
...a set of processes that should be facilitated?				
1999 Cutting-Edgers (*n* = 186)[d]	(109)	59	(77)	41
1999 Other Leaders (*n* = 547)	(261)	48	(286)	52
2003 Cutting-Edgers (*n* = 167)[c]	(102)	61	(65)	39
2003 Other Leaders (*n* = 398)	(190)	48	(208)	52
...a set of processes that can be altered, hindered, or retarded?				
1999 Cutting-Edgers (*n* = 186)[a]	(58)	31	(128)	69
1999 Other Leaders (*n* = 547)	(174)	32	(373)	68
2003 Cutting-Edgers (*n* = 167)[a]	(67)	40	(100)	60
2003 Other Leaders (*n* = 398)	(192)	48	(206)	52
...a set of processes that should be altered, hindered, or retarded?				
1999 Cutting-Edgers (*n* = 186)[a]	(18)	10	(168)	90
1999 Other Leaders (*n* = 547)	(65)	12	(482)	88
2003 Cutting-Edgers (*n* = 167)[a]	(19)	11	(148)	89
2003 Other Leaders (*n* = 398)	(61)	15	(337)	85

Note: Figures may not add to 100 owing to rounding.
[*] Not included in the 2003 survey.
[a] This comparison was not statistically significant.
[b] This comparison was significant at the .05 level in the bivariate test. It was not significant in the multivariate test, which revealed that the bivariate difference was due to the business–nonbusiness distinction rather than the Cutting-Edger–Other Leader distinction.
[c] This comparison was significant at the .05 level in the bivariate test. It was not significant in the multivariate test, which revealed that the only significant factor was the gender of the respondents.
[d] This comparison was significant at the .01 level.

Table 7.4   How Would You Characterize Your Expectations for the Next Generation When Its Members Reach Your Age?

	Much better		Better		Same		Worse		Much worse[*]	
	(n)	%	(n)	%	(n)	%	(n)	%	(n)	%
1999 Cutting-Edgers (n = 176)[a]	(28)	16	(94)	53	(26)	15	(23)	13	(5)	3
1999 Other Leaders (n = 537)	(56)	10	(261)	49	(111)	21	(96)	18	(13)	2
2003 Cutting-Edgers (n = 158)[b]	(23)	15	(63)	40	(25)	16	(45)	28	(2)	1
2003 Other Leaders (n = 391)	(22)	6	(147)	38	(85)	22	(123)	31	(14)	3

[*] Because the "much worse" category had fewer than five entries in this subpart of the question, that category was excluded when the significance level was calculated.
[a] This comparison was not statistically significant.
[b] This comparison was significant at the .01 level.

This finding is similar to, but pales in comparison with, the central pattern of a study of 1,020 chief executive officers, who were found to be "almost uniformly upbeat about growth prospects for their companies over the coming three years. No fewer than 91 percent are 'extremely' or at very least 'somewhat' optimistic about those prospects."[4]

However, the interpretation that the respondents leaned in an optimistic direction requires qualification. Table 7.4 reveals a significantly higher proportion of respondents in both groups that answered "worse" in 2003 than in 1999, a shift that can be traced to the impact of the September 11 attacks, the war on terrorism, the downturn of the global economy, and the antiglobalization protests, all of which rose to the top of the global agenda between the two surveys.[5] These traces are explored further in chapter 9.

Orientations toward the Consequences of Globalization

The surprising absence of differences in general attitudes toward globalization carries over to the leaders' orientations toward the consequences of globalization. Indeed, with one less-than-startling exception, the similarity of the responses of the two groups is striking even as they also reflect an upbeat set of orientations toward the impact of globalizing forces. Confronted with a series of positive and negative alternatives about the consequences of the "diverse processes of globalization," Cutting-Edgers and Other Leaders differed substantially on only one alternative (more so in 2003 than in 1999): that globalization "sharpens the skills of individuals" (table 7.5). A conjecture explaining why this is the sole significant difference might be that Cutting-Edgers exceed Other Leaders in this respect because of a greater sensitivity to the role that workers, entrepreneurs, computer specialists, and other highly skilled professions play in the processes of globalization. Whatever the reason, however, it is not as if the

Table 7.5 On Balance, Do You Regard the Diverse Processes of Globalization as ... (Check All That Apply)

	Check		No check	
	(n)	*%*	*(n)*	*%*
...making people more selfish?				
1999 Cutting-Edgers (*n* = 186)[a]	(24)	13	(162)	87
1999 Other Leaders (*n* = 551)	(61)	11	(490)	89
2003 Cutting-Edgers (*n* = 167)[a]	(25)	15	(142)	85
2003 Other Leaders (*n* = 398)	(71)	18	(327)	82
...sharpening the skills of individuals?				
1999 Cutting-Edgers (*n* = 186)[b]	(147)	79	(39)	21
1999 Other Leaders (*n* = 552)	(378)	68	(174)	32
2003 Cutting-Edgers (*n* = 167)[c]	(134)	80	(33)	20
2003 Other Leaders (*n* = 398)	(236)	59	(162)	41
...fostering political apathy?				
1999 Cutting-Edgers (*n* = 186)[a]	(25)	13	(161)	87
1999 Other Leaders (*n* = 552)	(60)	11	(492)	89
2003 Cutting-Edgers (*n* = 167)[a]	(25)	15	(142)	85
2003 Other Leaders (*n* = 398)	(59)	15	(339)	85
...promoting the power of corporations?				
1999 Cutting-Edgers (*n* = 186)[a]	(106)	57	(80)	43
1999 Other Leaders (*n* = 552)	(310)	56	(242)	44
2003 Cutting-Edgers (*n* = 186)[a]	(98)	59	(69)	41
2003 Other Leaders (*n* = 398)	(245)	62	(153)	38
...sensitizing people to other cultures?				
1999 Cutting-Edgers (*n* = 186)[a]	(155)	83	(31)	17
1999 Other Leaders (*n* = 552)	(442)	80	(110)	20
2003 Cutting-Edgers (*n* = 167)[b]	(138)	83	(29)	17
2003 Other Leaders (*n* = 398)	(283)	71	(115)	29
...widening the gap between rich and poor nations?				
1999 Cutting-Edgers (*n* = 186)[a]	(59)	32	(127)	68
1999 Other Leaders (*n* = 552)	(148)	27	(404)	73
2003 Cutting-Edgers (*n* = 186)[a]	(47)	28	(120)	72
2003 Other Leaders (*n* = 398)	(124)	31	(274)	69
...widening the gap between rich and poor individuals?				
1999 Cutting-Edgers (*n* = 186)[a]	(67)	36	(119)	64
1999 Other Leaders (*n* = 552)	(160)	29	(392)	71
2003 Cutting-Edgers (*n* = 167)[a]	(53)	32	(114)	68
2003 Other Leaders (*n* = 398)	(132)	33	(266)	67

Table 7.5   (continued)

	Check		No check	
	(n)	*%*	*(n)*	*%*
. . . creating too much homogeneity?				
1999 Cutting-Edgers (*n* = 186)[a]	(23)	12	(163)	88
1999 Other Leaders (*n* = 552)	(68)	12	(484)	88
2003 Cutting-Edgers (*n* = 398)[a]	(26)	16	(141)	84
2003 Other Leaders (*n* = 167)	(64)	16	(334)	84

[a] This comparison was not statistically significant.
[b] This comparison was significant at the .01 level.
[c] This comparison was significant at the .001 level.

Other Leaders dismissed the impact on individual skills: more than two-thirds of them also checked this alternative, a proportion exceeded only by their assessment of how globalization tends to sensitize people to other cultures. This proportion stands in sharp contrast to the small proportion that checked the three other consequences involving individuals, their self-ishness, their political apathy, and their tendency toward homogeneity. Equally noteworthy is the apparent lack of concern among both Cutting-Edgers and Other Leaders for the rich–poor gaps separating people and nations. Contrary to much of the literature on the subject, two-thirds of both groups did not perceive globalization as a source of the rich–poor gaps even as a majority of both subsamples also perceived globalization as promoting the power of corporations—a finding that is consistent with a proglobalization orientation.[6]

Indeed, the responses to the one globalization crisis that did occur prior to the mailing of the 1999 survey—the Asian financial crisis precipitated in 1997 by the collapse of Thailand's currency—suggest upbeat attitudes toward globalization. As can be seen in table 7.6, when confronted with four reactions to the financial crisis, substantially less than a third of both the Cutting-Edgers and the Other Leaders indicated that it gave them pause as to the virtues of globalization. Only a small minority in both groups responded that it affirmed their negative orientations toward globalization. Interestingly, when compared to that of the Other Leaders, a significantly greater proportion of the Cutting-Edgers reported that the crisis actually reinforced their positive orientations, and even larger proportions of both groups indicated that the crisis had no impact on their views of global-ization. These findings suggest the durability and strength of favorable attitudes toward globalization held by elites in 1999: the orientations of more than two-thirds of both groups were either reinforced or not under-mined ("had no impact") in the face of a so-called crisis of globalization.

Table 7.6 Did the Advent of the Financial Crisis That Began in Thailand in 1997 and then Spread Around the World ... (Check All That Apply)

	Check		No check	
1999 survey only	*(n)*	*%*	*(n)*	*%*
... give you pause as to the virtues of globalization?				
Cutting-Edgers (n = 186)[a]	(51)	27	(135)	73
Other Leaders (n = 547)	(130)	24	(417)	76
... affirm your negative orientations toward globalization?				
Cutting-Edgers (n = 186)[a]	(8)	4	(178)	96
Other Leaders (n = 547)	(35)	6	(512)	94
... reinforce your positive orientations toward globalization?				
Cutting-Edgers (n = 186)[b]	(57)	31	(129)	69
Other Leaders (n = 547)	(104)	19	(443)	81
... had no impact on your views of globalization?				
Cutting-Edgers (n = 186)[b]	(72)	39	(114)	61
Other Leaders (n = 547)	(289)	53	(258)	47

[a] This comparison was not statistically significant.
[b] This comparison was significant at the .01 level.

In 2003, however, we employed a slightly different format to explore attitudes toward the vulnerability of globalization to financial (and other) international crises (table 7.7) and turned up traces of slippage in the positive orientations of both groups. More than a third of the Cutting-Edgers and the Other Leaders were led during the years between the surveys to experience pause over the Asian financial crisis, and in the case of the Other Leaders the difference between their responses to the two surveys was significant at the .001 level. Put in substantive terms, these findings point to differences driven by the Other Leaders, since it was they and not the Cutting-Edgers who were significantly more inclined to be given pause by the financial crisis. A clear-cut interpretation follows: by 2003, leaders who were not on the cutting edge of globalization became more suspect of globalizing processes than the Cutting-Edgers, who were no more skeptical than they were in 1999. It seems that involvement in global processes makes one more supportive of globalization, or at least less skeptical.[7]

Table 7.7 also suggests that two other major intervening events—the acceleration of the protests against globalization and the September 11 terrorist attacks—were a source of proglobalization slippage. More than two-fifths of both groups had their negative attitudes affirmed or were given pause by the terrorist attacks. The proportions for the globalization

Table 7.7 How Would You Characterize Your Reactions to the Following Recent Events? (Check One Item in Each Row)

	Gave you pause as to the virtues of globalization		Affirmed your negative attitude toward globalization		Reinforced your positive orientations toward globalization		Had no impact on your views of globalization	
2003 survey only	(n)	%	(n)	%	(n)	%	(n)	%
Asian financial crisis (1997–1999)								
Cutting-Edgers (n = 166)ᶜ	(60)	36	(9)	6	(37)	22	(60)	36
Other Leaders (n = 394)	(142)	36	(27)	7	(51)	13	(174)	44
Protests against international economic institutions								
Cutting-Edgers (n = 165)ᵃ	(42)	25	(9)	5	(43)	26	(71)	43
Other Leaders (n = 393)	(117)	30	(40)	10	(81)	21	(155)	39
Terrorist attacks of September 11, 2001								
Cutting-Edgers (n = 167)ᵇ	(57)	34	(14)	8	(42)	25	(54)	32
Other Leaders (n = 397)	(119)	30	(56)	14	(82)	21	(140)	35
Contested presidential election of 2000*								
Cutting-Edgers (n = 166)ᵃ	(10)	6	(4)	3	(17)	10	(135)	81
Other Leaders (n = 394)	(28)	7	(16)	4	(26)	7	(324)	82
Israel–Palestine conflict								
Cutting-Edgers (n = 166)ᵈ	(37)	22	(10)	6	(53)	32	(66)	40
Other Leaders (n = 393)	(89)	23	(54)	14	(72)	18	(178)	45
Enron scandal (2001)								
Cutting-Edgers (n = 167)ᵇ	(29)	17	(15)	9	(15)	9	(108)	65
Other Leaders (n = 394)	(56)	14	(50)	13	(13)	3	(275)	70

* Because the "negative attitude" category had fewer than five entries in this subpart of the question, it was collapsed into the "no impact" category when the significance level was calculated.
ᵃ This comparison was not statistically significant.
ᵇ This comparison was significant at the .05 level.
ᶜ This comparison was significant at the .01 level.
ᵈ This comparison was significant at the .001 level.

protests were somewhat smaller but nevertheless substantial. These findings are further validated by the response to a crisis, the contested 2000 presidential election, which was purposely included because of its essential irrelevance to globalizing processes: more than four-fifths of both groups responded that the election "had no impact" on their orientations toward globalization.[8] The same six issues were also posed as possible causes or consequences of globalization (table 7.8), and it is noteworthy that all these

Table 7.8   Which of the Following Recent Events Do You Consider a Cause or Consequence of Globalization? (Check One Item in Each Row)

2003 survey only	A cause of globalization (n)	%	A consequence of globalization (n)	%	Both a cause and a consequence (n)	%	Neither a cause nor a consequence (n)	%	Not sure (n)	%
Asian financial crisis (1997–1999)										
Cutting-Edgers (n = 165)[b]	(2)	1	(61)	37	(45)	27	(50)	30	(7)	4
Other Leaders (n = 392)	(9)	2	(122)	31	(120)	31	(95)	24	(46)	12
Protests against international economic institutions										
Cutting-Edgers (n = 166)[a]	(2)	1	(112)	67	(26)	16	(18)	11	(8)	5
Other Leaders (n = 393)	(6)	2	(262)	67	(68)	17	(42)	11	(15)	4
Terrorist attacks of September 11, 2001										
Cutting-Edgers (n = 165)[a]	(3)	2	(51)	31	(32)	19	(76)	46	(3)	2
Other Leaders (n = 394)	(18)	5	(118)	30	(70)	18	(174)	44	(14)	4
Contested presidential election of 2000										
Cutting-Edgers (n = 166)[a]	(0)	0	(4)	2	(2)	1	(156)	94	(4)	2
Other Leaders (n = 392)	(1)	—*	(7)	2	(16)	4	(351)	90	(17)	4
Israel–Palestine conflict										
Cutting-Edgers (n = 165)[b]	(4)	2	(9)	5	(31)	19	(118)	72	(3)	2
Other Leaders (n = 393)	(13)	3	(43)	11	(80)	20	(243)	62	(14)	4
Enron scandal (2001)										
Cutting-Edgers (n = 166)[b]	(0)	0	(11)	7	(23)	14	(123)	74	(9)	5
Other Leaders (n = 393)	(6)	2	(60)	15	(39)	10	(267)	68	(21)	5

Note: Even though the "cause of globalization" and "not sure" categories had cells with fewer than five cases, these were not collapsed into an adjoining category, because it would not have made substantive sense to do so and because in no case would the comparisons have been statistically significant at the .001 level. Likewise, since the election item was not significant despite the few entries in four of the five cells, no adjustments were made in this case.
* Less than one-half of 1 percent.
[a] This comparison was not statistically significant.
[b] This comparison was significant at the .05 level.

issues were perceived by only a few respondents in both groups as being exclusively a source of globalizing processes. And, again, both groups evidenced sensitivity to the impact of the Asian financial crisis, the antiglobalization protests, and the September 11 terrorist attacks: roughly a third of both groups regarded these issues as consequences of globalization, and, indeed, two-thirds of the Cutting-Edgers and the Other Leaders cited the protests as having been fostered by globalizing dynamics. If those who viewed the protests as both a cause and a consequence of globalization are taken into account, this figure rises to almost seven-eighths of both groups. Once again, large majorities of both groups rejected both the Enron scandal and the 2000 election as being either causal or consequential with respect to globalizing processes. As for the differences between the two groups, table 7.7 reveals that only the Israel–Palestine conflict separated them to any significant extent, albeit possible reasons for this difference are not easily discerned.

These data highlight again a surprising lack of differences in opinion between the Cutting-Edgers and the Other Leaders, as well as a minimum of negative orientations toward the consequences of globalization. In general, both groups express positive attitudes toward globalizing processes and their consequences, even in the face of dire circumstances, such as the 1997 Asian financial crisis and the September 11 terrorist attacks. These strong positive orientations suggest a consensus in favor of globalization among the elites that we surveyed, not simply those whom we have categorized as Cutting-Edgers.

All told, of the sixty comparisons between the two groups presented in this chapter, only three involved significant differences at the .001 level, and fifty-seven did not. At the same time, some of the data revealed hints that during the period between 1999 and 2003 several events reduced commitments to globalization or at least planted doubts about some of its dynamics. The impact of intervening events is examined more closely in chapter 9.

* * *

A trace of doubt comes over the face of the Cutting-Edger. "I'm not sure your interpretation is correct. Isn't it possible that the absence of significant differences between the two groups of leaders reflects a consensus that the world is experiencing 'Americanization' rather than undergoing globalization? Perhaps we American elites perceive what you call 'globalization' not as a worldwide phenomenon that originates in various and diverse countries but rather as the result of forces at work in this country."

The researcher replies, "It's not clear to me how that follows. Even though the Other Leaders expressed similar orientations toward globalization, the fact remains that in other respects we have already discussed, Other Leaders differ from those of you who are on the cutting edge."

NOTES

1. Four of the differences between the 1999 and 2003 responses of each group were significant at the .001 level, and these can be found in table 9.14.

2. Conceivably, the finding that 99 percent of the Cutting-Edgers and 97 percent of the Other Leaders did not opt for the "bad" judgment was partially influenced by the fact that our sample consisted entirely of Americans. Thus, since globalization benefits some countries more than others, these percentages may at least partly be a reflection of sample bias.

3. It is conceivable, though unlikely, that the addition of three subparts at the outset of the seven-part question somehow altered the context in which responses to the last four subparts were answered and thus intruded a methodological bias into the distributions. What this bias might be, however, defies the imagination and can thus be discounted.

4. PricewaterhouseCoopers, *Inside the Mind of the CEO*, 5 (see chap. 3, note 2).

5. The comparison of the responses of the Cutting-Edgers in 1999 and 2003 was significant at the .01 level. For the Other Leaders, the difference was significant at the .001 level.

6. Works that focus on various dimensions of the rich–poor gap include J. Brecher and T. Costello, *Global Village or Global Pillage: Economic Reconstruction from the Bottom Up* (Boston: South End Press, 1994); David C. Korten, *When Corporations Rule the World* (West Hartford, Conn.: Kumarian Press, 1995); and Saskia Sassen, *Globalization and Its Discontents: Essays on the New Mobility of People and Money* (New York: New Press, 1998).

7. It should be noted, moreover, that these differences were recorded despite the fact that in 1999 the respondents were instructed to "select as many as you like" among the given alternatives, whereas in 2003 they were asked to "check only one alternative." From a strictly methodologically perspective, therefore, fewer respondents could have been expected to select the "gave you pause" alternative in 2003. That an increase in the selection of this alternative occurred suggests that the different responses to the two surveys are even more robust than the tests of significance indicate.

8. The Enron scandal was also included as a "dummy" item to validate the reactions to the September 11 attacks and the antiglobalization protests, but in this case a somewhat lesser proportion of both groups, perhaps because of the relevance of corporate behavior, indicated that the scandal "had no impact" on their orientations.

8

Attitudes toward World Affairs

"We may have different interpretations, but I certainly was right when I said we weren't far apart on questions of globalization," the Cutting-Edger says, as if to gloat over having outsmarted the researcher.

The Other Leader also presses hard: "Furthermore, there's more to world affairs than globalization. You haven't said a thing about the United States and its policies, as if your research team presumed that everyone in the samples is a cosmopolitan who doesn't attach any importance to what this country and international agencies do. I can't believe you were so oblivious to the real world that you ignored current issues and institutions!"

Aware that his traveling companions are prone to resist the research methods and findings outlined, the researcher is quick to respond. "You misread us. Of course, we investigated these matters with a view to determining whether involvement in globalizing processes correlated with the issues that are currently high on the global agenda and the institutions that sustain them. Let me elaborate."

Here we go again, the Other Leader thinks to himself.

ATTITUDES TOWARD ISSUES AND INSTRUMENTS OF GLOBALIZATION

Although both Cutting-Edgers and Other Leaders gave voice to positive orientations toward globalization and its consequences, the survey probed their attitudes further by asking, in 1999, for their assessments of nine current issues high on the global agenda and, in 2003, for an additional four issues, resulting in twenty-one comparisons between the two groups.

Table 8.1 indicates that in none of these comparisons did the responses of the two groups differ at the most stringent level of significance. However, it is perhaps a noteworthy pattern that the proportion of Cutting-Edgers exceeded or tied that of the Other Leaders in seventeen of the comparisons. These differences may not have been statistically significant, but their common direction can readily be interpreted as forming a pattern.

Interestingly, perhaps with the Balkans or Afghanistan in mind, both groups identified the issue of ethnic conflict as being essential by a larger proportion than all but one of the other issues: terrorism. Unsurprisingly, in the light of the September 11 attacks and the subsequent stress on the war to prevent future attacks, the issue of terrorism far exceeded all the other issues in the number of respondents who perceived it as being essential in response to the one survey (2003) when it was included among the listed issues. Equally noteworthy, and in sharp contrast to the attention that the burgeoning academic literature pays to problems of global governance,[1] this issue evoked markedly smaller proportions of concern on the part of both groups than any other issue.

Another issue—trade—was singled out as a separate question because of its presumed immediacy to the work of those Cutting-Edgers in the business community. Table 8.2 presents the responses to the issue, and the expectation of its relevance is readily apparent. In both surveys, the Cutting-Edgers registered pro–free trade sentiments significantly more than did the Other Leaders, while only one-quarter of the former registered a "selectively protectionist" or "protectionist" preference.

A more qualified support for other kinds of economic issues was recorded in response to a question about the way in which faltering economies of other countries should be handled. As can be seen in table 8.3a, only two-fifths of the Cutting-Edgers and roughly one-third of the Other Leaders perceived it to be "necessary" to ameliorate the economic problems of Russia and Brazil. Nonetheless, the two groups did not register statistically significant different reactions to the question in 1999. The perceptions along this line did not change significantly when Brazil was omitted from the question in the 2003 survey (table 8.3b).

With regard to the instruments of globalization, the respondents were asked to assess twelve international actors and the role they play in world affairs. Table 8.4 presents the reactions, and once again the absence of differences between the two groups of leaders stands out. Only four of the twenty comparisons exceeded the .001 level of significance. There are two features of table 8.4, however, that are conspicuous and lend themselves to a logical interpretation. One is the substantial differences between the importance attached to the eight international governmental organizations listed as instruments and the two international nongovernmental organizations (INGOs). With one exception—the Association of Southeast Asian

Table 8.1 Which of the Following Do You Regard as Essential Global Issues That Need to Be Addressed in the Next Decade? (Check All That Apply)

	Check		No check	
	(n)	%	*(n)*	%
Strengthening the United Nations*				
2003 Cutting-Edgers (*n* = 167)[a]	(81)	49	(86)	52
2003 Other Leaders (*n* = 398)	(185)	46	(213)	54
Stability of the world economy				
1999 Cutting-Edgers (*n* = 186)[a]	(132)	71	(54)	29
1999 Other Leaders (*n* = 553)	(396)	72	(157)	28
2003 Cutting-Edgers (*n* = 167)[a]	(108)	65	(59)	35
2003 Other Leaders (*n* = 398)	(254)	64	(144)	36
Climate change				
1999 Cutting-Edgers (*n* = 186)[a]	(106)	57	(80)	43
1999 Other Leaders (*n* = 553)	(302)	55	(251)	45
2003 Cutting-Edgers (*n* = 167)[a]	(88)	53	(79)	47
2003 Other Leaders (*n* = 398)	(199)	50	(199)	50
Worldwide arms control				
1999 Cutting-Edgers (*n* = 186)[a]	(108)	58	(78)	42
1999 Other Leaders (*n* = 553)	(270)	49	(283)	51
2003 Cutting-Edgers (*n* = 167)[a]	(116)	69	(51)	31
2003 Other Leaders (*n* = 398)	(264)	66	(134)	34
Ethnic conflicts				
1999 Cutting-Edgers (*n* = 186)[c]	(154)	83	(32)	17
1999 Other Leaders (*n* = 553)	(411)	74	(142)	26
2003 Cutting-Edgers (*n* = 167)[a]	(121)	72	(46)	28
2003 Other Leaders (*n* = 398)	(265)	67	(133)	33
Transnational organized crime				
1999 Cutting-Edgers (*n* = 186)[a]	(121)	65	(65)	35
1999 Other Leaders (*n* = 553)	(338)	61	(215)	39
2003 Cutting-Edgers (*n* = 167)[a]	(103)	62	(64)	38
2003 Other Leaders (*n* = 398)	(210)	53	(188)	47
Promoting democracy*				
2003 Cutting-Edgers (*n* = 167)[a]	(98)	59	(69)	41
2003 Other Leaders (*n* = 398)	(202)	51	(196)	49
Global governance				
1999 Cutting-Edgers (*n* = 186)[c]	(70)	38	(116)	62
1999 Other Leaders (*n* = 553)	(140)	25	(413)	75
2003 Cutting-Edgers (*n* = 167)[a]	(43)	26	(124)	74
2003 Other Leaders (*n* = 398)	(84)	21	(314)	79

Table 8.1 (continued)

	Check		No check	
	(n)	*%*	*(n)*	*%*
Terrorism*				
2003 Cutting-Edgers (*n* = 167)[a]	(148)	89	(19)	11
2003 Other Leaders (*n* = 398)	(363)	91	(35)	9
Corruption*				
2003 Cutting-Edgers (*n* = 167)[b]	(98)	59	(69)	41
2003 Other Leaders (*n* = 398)	(200)	50	(198)	50
Disposition of nuclear materials				
1999 Cutting-Edgers (*n* = 186)[a]	(131)	70	(55)	30
1999 Other Leaders (*n* = 547)	(402)	73	(151)	27
2003 Cutting-Edgers (*n* = 167)[b]	(133)	80	(34)	20
2003 Other Leaders (*n* = 398)	(290)	73	(108)	27
Epidemics				
1999 Cutting-Edgers (*n* = 186)[a]	(111)	60	(75)	40
1999 Other Leaders (*n* = 547)	(342)	62	(211)	38
2003 Cutting-Edgers (*n* = 167)[a]	(95)	57	(72)	43
2003 Other Leaders (*n* = 398)	(216)	54	(182)	46
International drug trafficking*				
2003 Cutting-Edgers (*n* = 167)[a]	(116)	69	(51)	31
2003 Other Leaders (*n* = 398)	(274)	69	(124)	31

Note: Figures may not add to 100 owing to rounding.
* Not included in the 1999 survey.
[a] This comparison was not significant.
[b] This comparison was significant at the .05 level.
[c] This comparison was significant at the .01 level.

Table 8.2 How Would You Describe Your Views on Trade Issues?

	Pro–free trade		Selectively protectionist		Protectionist		Not sure	
	(n)	*%*	*(n)*	*%*	*(n)*	*%*	*(n)*	*%*
1999 Cutting-Edgers (*n* = 184)[a]	(141)	77	(37)	20	(1)	1	(5)	3
1999 Other Leaders (*n* = 537)	(338)	63	(166)	31	(11)	2	(22)	4
2003 Cutting-Edgers (*n* = 164)[b]	(119)	73	(40)	24	(1)	—*	(4)	2
2003 Other Leaders (*n* = 385)	(216)	56	(150)	39	(12)	3	(7)	2

Note: Figures may not add to 100 owing to rounding.
* Because the "protectionist" and "not sure" categories had fewer than five entries in one or both years, the "protectionist" and "selectively protectionist" categories were merged and the "not sure" category was dropped when the significance level was calculated.
[a] This comparison was significant at the .01 level.
[b] This comparison was significant at the .001 level.

Table 8.3 Faltering Economies of Other Countries

Table 8.3a Do you regard efforts to bail out countries in economic trouble, like Russia and Brazil, as . . . (check only one)[*]

1999 survey	Necessary		Worthwhile		Questionable		Futile		Unsure	
	(n)	%	(n)	%	(n)	%	(n)	%	(n)	%
Cutting-Edgers (n = 168)[b]	(67)	40	(45)	27	(46)	27	(7)	4	(3)	2
Other Leaders (n = 523)	(169)	32	(127)	24	(166)	32	(39)	7	(22)	4

Table 8.3b Do you regard efforts to bail out countries in economic trouble, like Russia, as . . . (check only one)

2003 survey	Necessary		Worthwhile		Questionable		Futile		Unsure	
	(n)	%	(n)	%	(n)	%	(n)	%	(n)	%
Cutting Edgers (n = 166)[a]	(57)	34	(48)	29	(46)	28	(8)	5	(7)	4
Other Leaders (n = 379)	(122)	32	(125)	33	(96)	25	(24)	7	(12)	3

[*] Because one of the "unsure" category had fewer than five entries, the entries in this category were dropped when the significance level was calculated.
[a] This comparison was not significant.
[b] This comparison was significant at the .01 level.

Nations (ASEAN)—all of the former were perceived by at least three-fourths of both groups in both surveys as either "very" or "somewhat" important, whereas the comparable figure for the two INGOs (Amnesty International and Greenpeace) was no more than three-fifths in one case and less than two-fifths in the other. In short, given that only the INGOs evoked substantial proportions of both groups' ranking them as being not very important or unimportant, it seems clear that both the Cutting-Edgers and the Other Leaders tended to put considerable stock in the role of international organizations and institutions and were not convinced of the efficacy of global civil society. Second, especially noteworthy is the huge consensus on the importance of the United States: as might be expected of any single-country survey, virtually every respondent of both groups ranked the United States as being very or somewhat important, a ranking that also suggests a perception held by American leaders of their country's hegemonic role in world affairs.

The consensus around the global role of the United States is mirrored in the responses to an eight-part question that was included in only the 1999 survey and sought to trace degrees of agreement with propositions about the lessons that the United States should have learned from past experiences. As can be seen in table 8.5, the Cutting-Edgers and Other Leaders did not record a statistically significant difference on any of the eight parts. Moreover, perhaps because the propositions listed in table 8.5 were included to facilitate comparison with the results of earlier surveys

Table 8.4   How Would You Rank the Role the Following Can Play in World Affairs?

	Very important		Somewhat important		Not very important		Un-important		Not sure	
	(n)	*%*	*(n)*	*%*	*(n)*	*%*	*(n)*	*%*	*(n)*	*%*
United Nations										
1999 Cutting-Edgers (*n* = 185)[a]	(93)	50	(68)	37	(17)	9	(7)	4	(0)	0
1999 Other Leaders (*n* = 546)	(282)	52	(189)	35	(60)	11	(12)	2	(3)	1
2003 Cutting-Edgers (*n* = 165)[a]	(92)	56	(52)	32	(14)	8	(6)	4	(1)	1
2003 Other Leaders (*n* = 396)	(223)	56	(120)	30	(37)	9	(13)	3	(3)	1
World Bank										
1999 Cutting-Edgers (*n* = 186)[a]	(126)	68	(47)	25	(10)	5	(2)	1	(1)	1
1999 Other Leaders (*n* = 542)	(333)	62	(173)	32	(22)	4	(7)	1	(7)	1
2003 Cutting-Edgers (*n* = 165)[a]	(72)	44	(74)	45	(17)	10	(2)	1	(0)	0
2003 Other Leaders (*n* = 395)	(210)	53	(158)	40	(21)	5	(3)	1	(3)	1
World Trade Organization										
1999 Cutting-Edgers (*n* = 184)[a]	(108)	59	(65)	35	(9)	5	(0)	0	(2)	1
1999 Other Leaders (*n* = 538)	(281)	52	(209)	39	(29)	5	(8)	1	(11)	2
2003 Cutting-Edgers (*n* = 165)[a]	(85)	52	(68)	41	(10)	6	(2)	1	(0)	0
2003 Other Leaders (*n* = 395)	(180)	46	(174)	44	(32)	8	(2)	1	(7)	2
Amnesty International										
1999 Cutting-Edgers (*n* = 182)[a]	(40)	22	(70)	38	(45)	25	(21)	12	(6)	3
1999 Other Leaders (*n* = 539)	(95)	18	(216)	40	(146)	27	(49)	9	(33)	6
2003 Cutting-Edgers (*n* = 164)[a]	(41)	25	(47)	28	(52)	32	(21)	13	(3)	2
2003 Other Leaders (*n* = 392)	(79)	20	(133)	34	(126)	32	(40)	10	(14)	4

Table 8.4   (continued)

	Very important		Somewhat important		Not very important		Un-important		Not sure	
	(n)	%	(n)	%	(n)	%	(n)	%	(n)	%
International Monetary Fund										
1999 Cutting-Edgers (n = 184)[d]	(97)	53	(74)	40	(7)	4	(2)	1	(4)	2
1999 Other Leaders (n = 522)	(218)	42	(193)	37	(42)	8	(9)	2	(60)	11
2003 Cutting-Edgers (n = 163)[a]	(70)	43	(71)	44	(17)	10	(2)	1	(3)	2
2003 Other Leaders (n = 384)	(136)	35	(174)	45	(38)	10	(7)	2	(29)	8
G7**										
1999 Cutting-Edgers (n = 182)[d]	(89)	49	(67)	37	(16)	9	(3)	2	(7)	4
1999 Other Leaders (n = 519)	(173)	33	(217)	42	(40)	8	(12)	2	(77)	15
NATO										
1999 Cutting-Edgers (n = 183)[b]	(95)	52	(69)	38	(19)	10	(0)	0	(0)	0
1999 Other Leaders (n = 539)	(235)	44	(242)	45	(46)	9	(11)	2	(5)	1
2003 Cutting-Edgers (n = 165)[b]	(80)	48	(67)	41	(16)	10	(1)	1	(1)	1
2003 Other Leaders (n = 392)	(157)	40	(180)	46	(43)	11	(5)	1	(7)	2
NAFTA**										
1999 Cutting-Edgers (n = 183)[b]	(67)	37	(89)	49	(27)	15	(0)	0	(0)	0
1999 Other Leaders (n = 528)	(126)	24	(286)	54	(85)	16	(11)	2	(20)	4
European Union										
1999 Cutting-Edgers (n = 185)[d]	(126)	68	(52)	28	(6)	3	(1)	1	(0)	0
1999 Other Leaders (n = 539)	(262)	49	(222)	41	(29)	5	(5)	1	(21)	4
2003 Cutting-Edgers (n = 165)[a]	(89)	54	(65)	39	(9)	5	(2)	1	(0)	—*
2003 Other Leaders (n = 189)	(196)	50	(154)	40	(31)	8	(3)	1	(5)	1

Table 8.4 (continued)

	Very important		Somewhat important		Not very important		Un-important		Not sure	
	(n)	%	(n)	%	(n)	%	(n)	%	(n)	%
United States										
1999 Cutting-Edgers (n = 186)[a]	(160)	86	(26)	14	(0)	0	(0)	0	(0)	0
1999 Other Leaders (n = 547)	(444)	81	(96)	18	(3)	1	(1)	—*	(3)	1
2003 Cutting-Edgers (n = 165)[a]	(146)	88	(19)	12	(0)	0	(0)	0	(0)	0
2003 Other Leaders (n = 397)	(352)	89	(41)	10	(4)	1	(0)	0	(0)	0
ASEAN**										
1999 Cutting-Edgers (n = 180)[d]	(47)	26	(87)	48	(32)	18	(1)	—*	(13)	7
1999 Other Leaders (n = 510)	(73)	14	(216)	42	(86)	17	(12)	2	(123)	24
Greenpeace**										
1999 Cutting-Edgers (n = 185)[a]	(17)	9	(49)	26	(78)	42	(37)	20	(4)	2
1999 Other Leaders (n = 532)	(40)	8	(132)	25	(206)	39	(127)	24	(27)	5

Note: Because the "unimportant" and "not sure" categories had fewer than five entries in one or both years, the "unimportant" and "not very important" categories were merged and the "not sure" category was dropped when the significance level was calculated. NATO = North Atlantic Treaty Organization; NAFTA = North American Free Trade Agreement; G7 = France, United States, Britain, Germany, Japan, Canada, and Italy; ASEAN = Association of Southeast Asian Nations. Figures may not add to 100 owing to rounding.
* Less than one-half of 1 percent.
** Not included in the 2003 survey.
[a] This comparison was not significant.
[b] This comparison was significant at the .05 level.
[c] This comparison was significant at the .01 level.
[d] This comparison was significant at the .001 level.

conducted during the Cold War, it is noteworthy that neither group indicated much enthusiasm for any of the eight lessons that might have been learned.[2] Except for the item on the United Nations, none of the other questions evoked as much as a quarter of the respondents registering strong agreement.

Quite a different picture emerges from the pattern of responses to the fifteen subparts of a question that probed assessments of issues that have persisted since the end of the Cold War. With two exceptions, table 8.6 reveals substantial majorities—from about two-thirds to nearly all in two

Table 8.5   This Question Asks You to Indicate Your Position on Certain Propositions That Are Sometimes Described as Lessons That the United States Should Have Learned from Past Experiences Abroad. (Please Indicate How Strongly You Agree or Disagree with Each Statement.)

1999 survey only	Agree strongly		Agree somewhat		Disagree somewhat		Disagree strongly		No opinion[*]	
	(n)	%	(n)	%	(n)	%	(n)	%	(n)	%
There is considerable validity in the "domino theory" that when one nation falls to aggressor nations, others nearby will soon follow a similar path.										
Cutting-Edgers (n = 186)[a]	(20)	11	(84)	45	(61)	33	(20)	11	(1)	1
Other Leaders (n = 548)	(65)	12	(253)	46	(148)	27	(73)	13	(9)	2
Any communist victory is a defeat for America's national interest.										
Cutting-Edgers (n = 186)[a]	(31)	17	(59)	32	(60)	32	(32)	17	(4)	2
Other Leaders (n = 542)	(92)	17	(183)	33	(162)	30	(98)	18	(12)	2
It is vital to enlist the cooperation of the UN in settling international disputes.										
Cutting-Edgers (n = 186)[a]	(64)	34	(82)	44	(25)	13	(13)	7	(2)	1
Other Leaders (n = 552)	(195)	35	(233)	42	(84)	15	(32)	6	(8)	1
Russia is generally expansionist rather than defensive in its foreign policy goals.										
Cutting-Edgers (n = 185)[a]	(15)	8	(55)	30	(81)	44	(25)	14	(9)	5
Other Leaders (n = 547)	(28)	5	(168)	31	(255)	47	(61)	11	(35)	6
There is nothing wrong with using the CIA to try to undermine hostile governments.										
Cutting-Edgers (n = 185)[a]	(29)	16	(51)	28	(58)	31	(44)	24	(3)	2
Other Leaders (n = 546)	(76)	14	(195)	36	(145)	27	(117)	21	(13)	2
The U.S. should give economic aid to poorer countries even if it means high prices at home.										
Cutting-Edgers (n = 186)[a]	(25)	13	(80)	43	(54)	29	(23)	12	(4)	2
Other Leaders (n = 551)	(45)	8	(229)	42	(176)	32	(94)	17	(7)	1
The U.S. should take all steps including the use of force to prevent aggression by any expansionist power.										
Cutting-Edgers (n = 186)[a]	(32)	17	(91)	49	(50)	27	(11)	6	(2)	1
Other Leaders (n = 546)	(119)	22	(226)	41	(147)	27	(46)	8	(8)	1
Rather than simply countering our opponents thrusts, it is necessary to strike at the heart of the opponent's power.										
Cutting-Edgers (n = 183)[a]	(31)	17	(75)	41	(46)	25	(18)	10	(13)	7
Other Leaders (n = 543)	(126)	23	(188)	35	(135)	25	(73)	13	(21)	4

Note: Figures may not add to 100 owing to rounding.
[*] Because the "no opinion" category had fewer than five entries on all but two issues, it was dropped when the significance level was calculated.
[a] This comparison was not significant.

Table 8.6 Turning to More General Considerations, Here Is a List of Possible Foreign Policy Goals That the United States Might Have. Indicate How Much Importance You Think Should Be Attached to Each Goal.

	Very important		Moderately important		Slightly important		Not at all important		Not sure	
	(n)	%	(n)	%	(n)	%	(n)	%	(n)	%
Containing communism[**]										
1999 Cutting-Edgers (n = 185)[a]	(40)	22	(48)	26	(58)	31	(39)	21	(0)	0
1999 Other Leaders (n = 548)	(118)	22	(174)	32	(143)	26	(112)	20	(1)	0
Preventing the spread of nuclear weapons[***]										
2003 Cutting-Edgers (n = 165)[a]	(149)	90	(11)	7	(3)	2	(2)	1	(0)	0
2003 Other Leaders (n = 397)	(355)	89	(31)	8	(12)	3	(0)	0	(0)	0
Combating international terrorism[***]										
2003 Cutting-Edgers (n = 164)[b]	(144)	87	(15)	9	(4)	2	(1)	—[*]	(1)	—[*]
2003 Other Leaders (n = 396)	(363)	91	(29)	7	(3)	1	(1)	—[*]	(1)	—[*]
Helping to improve the standard of living in less developed countries										
1999 Cutting-Edgers (n = 186)[c]	(100)	54	(64)	34	(18)	10	(4)	2	(0)	0
1999 Other Leaders (n = 552)	(222)	40	(221)	40	(96)	17	(13)	2	(0)	0
2003 Cutting-Edgers (n = 163)[b]	(70)	43	(49)	30	(39)	24	(5)	3	(0)	0
2003 Other Leaders (n = 394)	(123)	31	(150)	38	(103)	26	(17)	5	(1)	—[*]
Worldwide arms control[**]										
1999 Cutting-Edgers (n = 186)[a]	(124)	67	(50)	27	(7)	4	(4)	2	(0)	0
1999 Other Leaders (n = 552)	(352)	64	(147)	27	(39)	7	(8)	1	(4)	1
Combating world hunger										
1999 Cutting-Edgers (n = 185)[a]	(114)	62	(48)	26	(20)	11	(3)	2	(0)	0
1999 Other Leaders (n = 550)	(312)	57	(149)	27	(75)	14	(14)	3	(0)	0
2003 Cutting-Edgers (n = 164)[a]	(90)	55	(48)	29	(22)	13	(4)	2	(0)	0
2003 Other Leaders (n = 395)	(206)	52	(130)	33	(50)	13	(9)	2	(0)	0
Improving the global environment[***]										
2003 Cutting-Edgers (n = 165)[a]	(81)	49	(54)	33	(23)	14	(6)	4	(1)	—[*]
2003 Other Leaders (n = 395)	(182)	46	(139)	35	(64)	16	(8)	2	(2)	1
Strengthening the United Nations										
1999 Cutting-Edgers (n = 185)[a]	(50)	27	(86)	47	(28)	15	(21)	11	(0)	0
1999 Other Leaders (n = 550)	(164)	30	(204)	37	(116)	21	(62)	11	(4)	1
2003 Cutting-Edgers (n = 162)[a]	(59)	36	(43)	27	(34)	21	(25)	15	(1)	—[*]
2003 Other Leaders (n = 393)	(112)	29	(134)	34	(84)	21	(56)	14	(7)	2

Table 8.6   (continued)

	Very important		Moderately important		Slightly important		Not at all important		Not sure	
	(n)	%	(n)	%	(n)	%	(n)	%	(n)	%
Invading Iraq to overthrow Saddam Hussein***										
2003 Cutting-Edgers (n = 155)[a]	(39)	23	(41)	25	(31)	19	(44)	27	(11)	7
2003 Other Leaders (n = 367)	(90)	23	(94)	24	(83)	21	(100)	25	(28)	7
Promoting and defending human rights in other countries***										
2003 Cutting-Edgers (n = 155)[c]	(71)	43	(62)	37	(30)	18	(3)	2	(0)	0
2003 Other Leaders (n = 367)	(123)	31	(175)	45	(77)	20	(18)	5	(0)	0
Protecting weaker nations against aggression***										
2003 Cutting-Edgers (n = 165)[d]	(73)	44	(67)	41	(24)	15	(1)	—[*]	(0)	0
2003 Other Leaders (n = 397)	(110)	28	(193)	49	(77)	19	(12)	3	(5)	1
Helping to bring a democratic form of government to other nations***										
2003 Cutting-Edgers (n = 155)[b]	(50)	30	(61)	37	(40)	24	(13)	8	(1)	1
2003 Other Leaders (n = 367)	(80)	20	(153)	39	(120)	30	(37)	9	(6)	2
Controlling and reducing illegal immigration***										
2003 Cutting-Edgers (n = 166)[a]	(56)	34	(48)	29	(48)	29	(13)	8	(1)	—[*]
2003 Other Leaders (n = 396)	(150)	38	(115)	29	(99)	25	(29)	7	(3)	1
Stopping the flow of illegal drugs***										
2003 Cutting-Edgers (n = 165)[a]	(97)	59	(37)	22	(21)	13	(5)	3	(5)	3
2003 Other Leaders (n = 396)	(227)	57	(98)	25	(50)	13	(18)	5	(3)	1
Fostering international cooperation to solve common problems, such as food, inflation and energy**										
1999 Cutting-Edgers (n = 186)[a]	(136)	73	(37)	20	(12)	6	(1)	1	(0)	0
1999 Other Leaders (n = 552)	(401)	73	(115)	21	(30)	5	(5)	1	(1)	—[*]

Note: Because the "not at all important" and "not sure" categories had fewer than five entries in one or both years, the "not at all important" and "slightly important" categories were merged and the "not sure" category was dropped when the significance level was calculated.
[*] Less than one-half of 1 percent.
[**] Not included in the 2003 survey.
[***] Not included in the 1999 survey.
[a] This comparison was not significant.
[b] This comparison was significant at the .05 level.
[c] This comparison was significant at the .01 level.
[d] This comparison was significant at the .001 level.

cases—of both groups perceiving the issues that have continued to persist since the Cold War as being very or moderately important. One of the two exceptions ("containing communism") can be readily explained as pertaining more to the Cold War than to the post–Cold War period, but the other exception is interesting in the sense that it anticipates the ambivalence of American society over the policy of preemption that led to the invasion of Iraq two months after the questionnaire was mailed. Fewer than half of both the Cutting-Edgers and the Other Leaders perceived such an invasion as being "very" or "moderately important," and at least a quarter of both groups perceived it as being "not at all important," figures that are in sharp contrast with responses to the other thirteen issues. (Indeed, responding two months before the Iraq invasion, 29 percent of all the leaders, a proportion that includes the 234 individuals who were not classified as either Cutting-Edgers or Other Leaders, responded that the invasion was "not at all important.") Not only does table 8.6 depict large proportions of both groups' having assessed the other issues as being very or moderately important, but in most instances an infinitesimal number reported viewing these issues as being not at all important.

Another interesting dimension of table 8.6 is the common nature of the one issue on which the difference between the Cutting-Edgers and the Other Leaders was significant and the four issues on which their differences exceeded the .05 or .01 cutoff criteria. All of these issues posit the United States as being, so to speak, ranged on the side of underdogs abroad, while the other subparts are more oriented toward statecentric goals. More than that, in each of the five instances, the Cutting-Edgers attached more importance to the well-being of the underdogs than that of the Other Leaders. This finding suggests that those who live and travel on the cutting edge of globalization are more sensitized to the plight of peoples abroad than are Other Leaders, whose foreign travels and connections are less extensive.

The questionnaire contained three domestic policy items or, more accurately, philosophical questions that probed dimensions of cosmopolitanism, especially with respect to the role of government in the economy and diversity in the workplace. Since all the respondents occupied leadership positions in an era dominated by neoliberal economic policies, it is not surprising that the Cutting-Edgers and Other Leaders did not record statistically significant differences at the .001 level on these more philosophical items (see tables 8.7, 8.8, and 8.9). On the other hand, it is clear that both

Table 8.7 Do You Believe an Organization with a Workforce That Shares the Same Background Is More Productive than One that Has Diverse Backgrounds?

	Same background		Diverse backgrounds	
1999 survey only	(n)	%	(n)	%
Cutting-Edgers (n = 167)[a]	(40)	24	(127)	76
Other Leaders (n = 450)	(118)	26	(332)	74

[a] This comparison was not significant.

Table 8.8   How Would You Summarize Your Views on the Proper Role of Government in Economic Matters?

	Minimum regulation		Some regulation		Maximum regulation		Not sure	
	(n)	%	(n)	%	(n)	%	(n)	%
1999 Cutting-Edgers (n = 184)[a]	(68)	37	(111)	60	(4)	2	(1)	1
1999 Other Leaders (n = 545)	(162)	30	(364)	67	(14)	3	(5)	1
2003 Cutting-Edgers (n = 165)[a]	(37)	22	(124)	75	(3)	2	(1)	1
2003 Other Leaders (n = 390)	(86)	22	(281)	72	(17)	4	(6)	2

Note: Because the "maximum regulation" and "not sure" categories had fewer than five entries in one or both years, the "maximum regulation" and "some regulation" categories were merged and the "not sure" category was dropped when the significance level was calculated. Figures may not add to 100 owing to rounding.
[a] This comparison was not significant.

groups of leaders were committed to an open trading regime that provides some governmental regulation by way of performing service roles and protecting against unfair competition but that does not otherwise protect against foreign competition.

Of course, it is not enough merely to note the points at which the Cutting-Edgers and Other Leaders did and did not differ in their orientations toward public affairs. An important outstanding question is whether the behavior of the two groups reflects their different attitudes toward the issues and instruments of globalization. One query sought to shed light on this question by asking about patterns of charitable giving, and the responses suggest that Cutting-Edgers do indeed engage in significantly different behavior than do Other Leaders. The data in table 8.10 reveal that the Cutting-Edgers give significantly more each year to international charities and significantly less to local charities than do Other Leaders. Though popular rhetoric advocates thinking globally and acting locally, our data indicate that, compared to other leaders, elites on the cutting edge of globalization are much more inclined to think globally and—as far as putting their money where their values are—act globally as well.

* * *

Both traveling companions seem bewildered. The researcher asks, "Why are you making those faces?"

"You've given us so much," the Other Leader replies. "Do you really expect your readers to go over all those tables? They're so lengthy. And they seem too readily subject to diverse and contradictory interpretations. Should we simply accept your interpretation of what the significant differences mean or imply?"

Table 8.9 What Do You Regard as the Proper Roles of National Governments with Regard to Private Firms and the Global Economy? (Check All That Apply)

	Check		No check	
	(n)	%	*(n)*	%
A service role (providing infrastructure, police protection, health, and education, etc.)				
1999 Cutting-Edgers (*n* = 184)[b]	(171)	93	(13)	7
1999 Other Leaders (*n* = 549)	(467)	85	(82)	15
2003 Cutting-Edgers (*n* = 167)[a]	(148)	89	(19)	11
2003 Other Leaders (*n* = 398)	(338)	85	(60)	15
Prevent potential monopolies/cartels and ensure fair and honest competition				
1999 Cutting-Edgers (*n* = 184)[a]	(148)	80	(36)	20
1999 Other Leaders (*n* = 549)	(418)	76	(131)	24
2003 Cutting-Edgers (*n* = 167)[a]	(140)	84	(27)	16
2003 Other Leaders (*n* = 398)	(325)	82	(73)	18
Protect domestic firms and jobs from foreign competition				
1999 Cutting-Edgers (*n* = 184)[a]	(18)	10	(166)	90
1999 Other Leaders (*n* = 549)	(70)	13	(479)	87
2003 Cutting-Edgers (*n* = 167)[a]	(19)	11	(148)	89
2003 Other Leaders (*n* = 398)	(66)	17	(332)	83
Subsidize lagging economic sectors to aid their competitiveness in foreign markets				
1999 Cutting-Edgers (*n* = 184)[a]	(20)	11	(164)	89
1999 Other Leaders (*n* = 549)	(65)	12	(484)	88
2003 Cutting-Edgers (*n* = 167)[a]	(23)	14	(144)	86
2003 Other Leaders (*n* = 398)	(60)	15	(338)	85
Subsidize promising economic sectors to aid their competitiveness in foreign markets				
1999 Cutting-Edgers (*n* = 184)[a]	(57)	31	(127)	69
1999 Other Leaders (*n* = 549)	(152)	28	(397)	72
2003 Cutting-Edgers (*n* = 167)[a]	(50)	30	(117)	70
2003 Other Leaders (*n* = 398)	(117)	29	(281)	71

[a] This comparison was not significant.
[b] This comparison was significant at the .05 level.

The researcher responds, "No, by all means feel free to interpret them as seems right to you. We are the last to claim that there is only one correct interpretation or even that our interpretations are sufficient. And you're right, there are a lot of tables, and they contain huge amounts of data. We don't expect that everyone will ponder the tables at length. We simply felt obliged to present the data for those who may be interested in the details.

Table 8.10 Approximately What Proportion of Your Charitable Donations Each Year Goes to ...

	Cutting-Edgers		Other Leaders	
	Mean proportion	(n)	Mean proportion	(n)
1999 Local charities[c]	54.80	(174)	60.63	(501)
1999 National charities[a]	32.52	(174)	31.58	(501)
1999 International charities[d]	12.68	(174)	7.80	(501)
2003 Local charities[d]	54.53	(153)	65.38	(374)
2003 National charities[b]	33.20	(153)	28.72	(374)
2003 International charities[d]	12.26	(153)	5.89	(374)

[a] This comparison was not significant.
[b] This comparison was significant at the .05 level.
[c] This comparison was significant at the .01 level.
[d] This comparison was significant at the .001 level.

You could easily skim through them, even ignore them, if all you want is the big picture."

The Cutting-Edger still seems bewildered. "But what is the big picture?" he asks, a note of annoyance in his voice. "By my hasty calculations, all told you made a total of 285 comparisons between the Cutting-Edgers and the Other Leaders, but less than a quarter of these—66 to be exact, or 23 percent—were statistically significant at the .001 level of probability. That's not a very high percentage. Doesn't it undermine your premise that leaders on the cutting edge of globalization can be readily distinguished from other elites? What story do those differences tell about those of us active on the cutting edge of globalization?"

"No," the researcher says, "these figures don't undermine the premises of our inquiry. It would be more disconcerting if the proportion of significant findings at the .001 approached 100 percent. Then we would have no way of differentiating the meaningful patterns from those that are essentially mundane. As for the story that can be derived from our findings, it is premature to undertake to tell it."

Bewilderment returns to the faces of the travelers. "What does that mean? Why is it premature?" the Other Leader asks.

"Brace yourselves, my friends," the researcher responds. "There's still more to tell."

"What!" they both exclaim simultaneously, with the Other Leader adding, "I thought you gave us the results of your comparisons on all the queries posed by your two surveys. What more is there to say?"

"It's true that I have now confronted you with all the questions and the responses to them of the Cutting-Edgers and Other Leaders," the researcher replies.

"So why don't you quit while you're ahead!"

"Because there are still two sets of comparisons that need to be made. We need to compare the business executives in our samples with those whose biographies made no mention of business leadership, and, perhaps even more important, there is still the diachronic comparisons to make."

"The what?"

"The comparisons across time. We need to ascertain whether the events that intervened between 1999 and 2003 altered the perspectives of the respondents."

Resigned, the two travelers order still another round of beer and settle back to hear how the passage of more than three years and the respondents' occupations may have shaped the reactions of the leaders surveyed.

NOTES

1. Entries in this exploding literature include David Held, *Democracy and the Global Order* (Stanford, Calif.: Stanford University Press, 1995); Martin Hewson and Timothy J. Sinclair, eds., *Approaches to Global Governance Theory* (Albany: State University of New York Press, 1999); and Oran R. Young, ed., *Global Governance: Drawing Insights from the Environmental Experience* (Cambridge: MIT Press, 1997).

2. Six surveys were conducted every presidential year between 1974 and 1994. For the use of the comparable questions, see Ole R. Holsti and James N. Rosenau, *American Leadership in World Affairs: Vietnam and the Breakdown of Consensus* (Boston: George Allen & Unwin, 1984), appendix.

9

From 1999 to 2003: Did Intervening Events Make a Difference?

Having endured the lengthy monologues and puzzled over forty-eight tables of data, the two traveling companions sip their beers, suspend their skepticism, and yield to camaraderie. "Okay," the Cutting-Edger says. "I'm convinced that you have managed to shed some light on leadership in a globalizing world. But those two big questions still remain: In what ways, if any, did the events that intervened between your two surveys affect your findings? And what about the differences between the two of us, between those of us in the business world and those who toil in other vineyards?"

"Let me start with the first question," the researcher replies. "It was precisely because the September 11 terrorist attacks seemed likely to induce attitudinal and behavioral changes that we felt obliged to send out the second questionnaire in January 2003. Indeed, it can be argued that we should do it a third time in order to trace the affects of the United States' preemptive war on Iraq and its messy aftermath."

"You're asking for trouble," the Other Leader responds. "Life is a never-ending series of calamities so that you'll want to be doing a fourth iteration and then a fifth. It will be endless. You'll never be able to bring your project to a close."

"You've got a point. We'll have to see. In the meantime let me spell out the key differences between our two surveys."

* * *

Diachronic analysis is complicated and difficult, especially if it involves assessing data generated through survey research rather than through a controlled experiment. More specifically, since it is never unmistakably clear what events underlie any changes that are uncovered between two points in time, the analysis must proceed with caution and recognize that different responses to a questionnaire item at time 2 compared to those at time 1 may stem from a multiplicity of events. No less relevant is the methodological problem that stems from the fact that while we surveyed the same samples at two points in time, presumably those who responded in 2003 were not exactly the same people who answered in 1999 (see tables 3.2, 3.3, and 4.1). As we acknowledged earlier, our research does not amount to a panel study, thus adding to the difficulty of interpreting the changes revealed by comparing the two sets of survey results.[1]

Still, it makes little sense not to seek out the patterns and possible sources of change that may explain the temporal differences. As long as grand claims are avoided and as long as appropriate qualifications are made in interpreting the data depicting changes across time, differences between the two surveys can usefully be considered. Such is the purpose of this chapter: first, to determine whether significant differences mark those questionnaire items that seem especially subject to behavioral or attitudinal changes as a result of salient developments between 1999 and 2003; and, second, to discern whether the changes can be traced to the orientations and activities of the Cutting-Edgers.

A set of findings independent of orientations toward leadership and globalization highlights the potential of comparing the responses to the two surveys. Between 1999 and 2003, the cell phone became a conventional feature of American life and partially replaced landline phones as a central means of voice-to-voice communications. By 1999, moreover, e-mail and traveling with a laptop computer had become a standard and widely employed means of exchanging ideas and information electronically and, in so doing, diminished reliance on airmail, faxes, and the telephone as means of communications.[2]

Traces of these empirical transformations can be readily discerned in our data. As can be seen in table 9.1, the use of e-mail and laptops did not change between the two surveys: the overall comparison of the two surveys and the comparisons of both the Cutting-Edgers and the Other Leaders yielded differences that are not significant. On the other hand, the use of airmail, the fax machine, and regular telephones "very often" dropped substantially across the period between the two surveys. Consequently, the comparisons of the 1999 and 2003 responses on all three of these media for both the Cutting-Edgers and the Other Leaders, as well as for the whole samples, involved significant differences in which the "very often" responses were substantially lower in the later survey. Indeed, the use of faxes "very often" was more than halved by the overall samples and the Other Leaders and virtually halved by the Cutting-Edgers during the interval. Since the discrepancies in the communications patterns depicted

Chapter 9

Table 9.1   Comparisons between the 1999 and 2003 Surveys on Various Forms of Communication

Table 9.1a Do you travel with a laptop or handheld computer?

	Yes		No	
	(n)	*%*	*(n)*	*%*
All 1999 Respondents (*n* = 874)[a]	(391)	45	(483)	55
All 2003 Respondents (*n* = 821)	(391)	48	(434)	52
1999 Cutting Edgers (*n* = 183)[a]	(109)	60	(74)	40
2003 Cutting Edgers (*n* = 165)	(100)	61	(65)	39
1999 Other Leaders (*n* = 546)[a]	(234)	43	(312)	57
2003 Other Leaders (*n* = 396)	(160)	40	(236)	60

Table 9.1b How often do you employ the following methods to carry forward your interactions with counterparts abroad? (check only one in each row)

	Very often		Occasionally		Seldom		Rarely		Never	
	(n)	*%*	*(n)*	*%*	*(n)*	*%*	*(n)*	*%*	*(n)*	*%*
E-mail or other online services										
All 1999 Respondents (*n* = 849)[a]	(390)	46	(256)	30	(55)	7	(52)	6	(96)	11
All 2003 Respondents (*n* = 802)	(378)	47	(252)	32	(49)	6	(49)	6	(74)	9
1999 Cutting-Edgers (*n* = 182)[a]	(131)	72	(39)	21	(5)	3	(4)	2	(3)	2**
2003 Cutting-Edgers (*n* = 167)	(116)	70	(40)	24	(4)	2	(5)	3	(2)	1
1999 Other Leaders (*n* = 535)[a]	(189)	35	(191)	36	(42)	8	(41)	8	(72)	13
2003 Other Leaders (*n* = 385)	(137)	36	(139)	36	(25)	6	(32)	8	(52)	14
Cellular phone										
All 1999 Respondents (*n* = 792)[b]	(63)	8	(125)	16	(99)	12	(117)	15	(388)	49
All 2003 Respondents (*n* = 746)	(65)	9	(149)	20	(103)	14	(132)	18	(297)	39
1999 Cutting-Edgers (*n* = 177)[a]	(25)	14	(39)	22	(34)	19	(26)	15	(53)	30
2003 Cutting-Edgers (*n* = 158)	(23)	15	(50)	32	(24)	15	(25)	16	(36)	23
1999 Other Leaders (*n* = 500)[a]	(26)	5	(67)	13	(55)	11	(76)	15	(276)	55
2003 Other Leaders (*n* = 370)	(16)	4	(59)	16	(52)	14	(65)	18	(178)	48

Table 9.1 (continued)

Table 9.1b How often do you employ the following methods to carry forward your interactions with counterparts abroad? (check only one in each row)

	Very often		Occasionally		Seldom		Rarely		Never	
	(n)	%	(n)	%	(n)	%	(n)	%	(n)	%
Regular telephone										
All 1999 Respondents (n = 848)[b]	(277)	33	(313)	37	(82)	10	(88)	10	(88)	10
All 2003 Respondents (n = 781)	(167)	21	(293)	38	(96)	12	(111)	14	(114)	15
1999 Cutting-Edgers (n = 185)[b]	(106)	57	(62)	34	(11)	6	(5)	3	(1)	—*
2003 Cutting-Edgers (n = 165)	(62)	38	(71)	43	(14)	8	(11)	7	(7)	4
1999 Other Leaders (n = 533)[b]	(118)	22	(214)	40	(62)	12	(72)	13	(67)	13
2003 Other Leaders (n = 380)	(48)	13	(133)	35	(52)	14	(69)	18	(78)	20
Airmail										
All 1999 Respondents (n = 827)[b]	(222)	26	(336)	41	(93)	11	(87)	11	(89)	11
All 2003 Respondents (n = 765)	(116)	15	(294)	38	(126)	17	(115)	15	(114)	15
1999 Cutting-Edgers (n = 182)[b]	(75)	41	(76)	42	(18)	10	(10)	5	(3)	2
2003 Cutting-Edgers (n = 162)	(43)	26	(63)	39	(34)	21	(16)	10	(6)	4
1999 Other Leaders (520)[b]	(106)	20	(215)	41	(63)	12	(65)	13	(71)	14
2003 Other Leaders (n = 370)	(29)	8	(136)	37	(59)	16	(67)	18	(79)	21
Fax										
All 1999 Respondents (n = 839)[b]	(317)	38	(285)	34	(52)	6	(64)	8	(121)	14
All 2003 Respondents (n = 771)	(130)	17	(300)	39	(89)	12	(108)	14	(144)	18
1999 Cutting-Edgers (n = 184)[b]	(116)	63	(47)	25	(11)	6	(5)	3	(5)	3
2003 Cutting-Edgers (n = 164)	(53)	32	(75)	46	(12)	7	(18)	11	(6)	4
1999 Other Leaders (n = 530)[b]	(146)	28	(208)	39	(32)	6	(49)	9	(95)	18
2003 Other Leaders (n = 375)	(38)	10	(129)	35	(46)	12	(64)	17	(98)	26

* Less than one-half of 1 percent.
** Because the "seldom," "rarely," and "never" categories had fewer than five entries, these categories were combined when the significance levels were calculated.
a This comparison was not significant.
b This comparison was significant at the .001 level.

in tables 9.1a and 9.1b are independent of attitudinal and behavioral responses to globalization, we interpret them as supporting the validity of the substantive findings assessed in subsequent tables.

OVERALL DIACHRONIC PATTERNS

Three developments that unfolded between the two surveys seem especially likely to have induced significant alterations in the response patterns of the leaders. Perhaps the most salient of these were the September 11 terrorist attacks and the subsequent preoccupation with the war on terror, developments that are widely assumed to have made an indelible mark on the perspectives and behavior of Americans. Second, the 1999–2003 period witnessed the evolution, even the institutionalization, of the antiglobalization movement, thereby perhaps altering, if not transforming, the ways in which leaders assess the virtues and defects of globalizing processes. Third, and related, during this period the global economy sputtered both generally and more severely in many parts of the world, thus perhaps occasioning second thoughts about the virtues and defects of globalization on the part of both the Cutting-Edgers and the Other Leaders. Needless to say, reactions to each of these developments may have been reinforced by the other two so that clear-cut interpretations of the response patterns cannot be offered in many cases; nevertheless, several of the questions directly addressed one or another of the three situations and thus allow for more confident observations.

Generalizing beyond the three developments just cited, it can readily be argued that for the United States and its citizens, if not for people everywhere, the world was a much more threatening place in 2003 than in 1999. In addition to the preoccupation with terrorism as an ever-present threat, the lag in many national economies, and the commotion sustained by the antiglobalization protests, the tenor of world affairs was also agitated by the intensification and violence of Israeli–Palestinian tensions, the growing likelihood of military action against Saddam Hussein, the war on the Taliban and persistent problems in Afghanistan, the introduction of nuclear weapons into India–Pakistan tensions over Kashmir, the continuing spread of AIDS in Africa and elsewhere, the surfacing of corrupt business practices in the United States, talk of challenges posed by the "axis of evil"—to cite only some of the developments that may have cumulatively deepened insecurities during the interval between the two surveys. Accordingly, it is reasonable to anticipate that a comparison of the responses to the same items in the two questionnaires would yield numerous significant differences.

Table 9.2   Number of Comparisons between the 1999 and 2003 Surveys at Four Levels of Significance (*N* = 138)

Significance levels	p < .001	p < .01	p < .05	Not significant
All respondents	39	21	15	63
Cutting-Edgers	17	9	11	101
Other Leaders	28	12	21	77

All told, 138 questions were identically worded in the 1999 and 2003 surveys. Of these, comparisons of all the respondents to the two surveys yielded 63 that were not significant, while 39, 21, and 15 were, respectively, significant at the .001, .01, and .05 levels of probability. As noted, however, since the comparisons involved large numbers of respondents (889 in 1999 and 830 in 2003), the ensuing analysis again focuses on the comparisons that were significant at the most stringent level of probability and can reasonably be linked to developments that intervened between the surveys. The comparable figures for the Cutting-Edgers and the Other Leaders at each level of significance are presented in table 9.2. Here can be seen the interesting finding that neither group (the members of which are distinguished by their having responded to all the items forming the Involvement Index) registered more shifts between the two surveys than those for all the respondents in each survey. While 75 comparisons of the entire sample recorded significant differences in the responses to the two surveys, the Cutting-Edgers were found to have only 37 such differences and the Other Leaders registered 61 differences in this regard.

Perhaps the most interesting aspects of table 9.2 is the number of non-significant differences recorded by the Cutting-Edgers and the fact that they had the fewest significant comparisons at the other three levels. These findings suggest either that they are more consistent and less impervious to immediate happenings in their orientations toward world affairs or, less likely, that their perspectives on the course of events are more rigid than those of leaders not on the cutting edge of globalization. Of course, the data in table 9.2 are far from the whole diachronic story. They do not depict the direction of the findings, and it is also quite conceivable that some of the nonsignificant comparisons are of interest.

The most revealing overall indicator that the leaders in the 2003 sample perceived the world as being more threatening than that found by their counterparts in 1999 is provided by the responses to the aforementioned question about their expectations for the future (see table 7.4). Whatever the degree to which the September 11 attacks and a variety of other factors underlay their answers, the proportion selecting the two positive alternatives ("much better" and "better") in 2003 declined by 15 percentage points, just as those who favored the two negative alternatives ("worse" and "much worse") increased by the same amount (table 9.3a). These patterns were reinforced by both the Other Leaders and the Cutting-Edgers. Although the differences are not significant, similar generalized patterns of a less-promising future can be traced in the declines in the perceptions of all the respondents, the Cutting-Edgers, and the Other Leaders as being among the top leaders of their organizations or professions (table 9.3b).

Given the cumulative insecurities that had deepened by 2003, it is hardly surprising that a significantly greater number of all the leaders in that year reported worrying about the course of events than they did in 1999. Even more indicative was the difference they recorded in the degree of worry about the future direction of world affairs: 17 percent divided the respondents of the two samples on whether they worried "often" in this regard, a percentage that is one of the largest uncovered in the 138 diachronic comparisons (table 9.4). Interestingly, table 9.4 also reveals that the Other Leaders contributed more to this difference than did the Cutting-Edgers.

On the other hand, the greater worry did not give rise to greater motivations to do something about the circumstances that prevailed in 2003. Neither all the leaders nor the Cutting-Edgers, as if paralyzed by their worries, recorded a greater sense of responsibility for them. Only the Other Leaders registered a significant increase in their sense of responsibility for the course of events. Even more telling, table 9.4 discloses that none of the three groups reported an increased readiness to affect those aspects of world affairs that worried them.

Similarly, despite the foregoing finding that the 2003 leaders indicated greater worry about the course of world affairs than that of their 1999 counterparts, neither all the leaders nor the Cutting-Edgers nor the Other Leaders expressed a readiness to advance, redirect, or resist the processes of globalization. Rather, further suggesting some dismay over the state of world affairs, smaller proportions of respondents in all three comparisons replied in 2003 that they sought to advance the processes, and only in the case of the Cutting-Edgers was the decline not statistically significant (table 9.5).

Still another sign of sensitivity to a more threatening world in 2003 is discernible in responses that reflected rooted cosmopolitanism through greater attachments to the local and familiar dimensions of a leader's life, suggesting that these dimensions were viewed as being more meaningful in the post–September 11 era. In the case of the question that asked about their sense of identity with ten diverse groups to which they might be linked, for example, the three most local and familiar subgroups evoked significant differences in the same direction: significantly more respondents reported feeling "closely identified" with their neighbors, communities of residence, and fellow citizens in 2003 than was the case in 1999. In each of these cases,

Table 9.3   Expectations for the Future and Self-Perception

Table 9.3a How would you characterize your expectations for the next generation when its members reach your age?

	Much better		Better		Same		Worse		Much worse	
	(n)	%	*(n)*	%	*(n)*	%	*(n)*	%	*(n)*	%
All 1999 Respondents (n = 847)[b]	(101)	12	(419)	49	(166)	20	(141)	17	(20)	2
All 2003 Respondents (n = 804)	(69)	9	(296)	37	(165)	20	(245)	30	(29)	4
1999 Cutting-Edgers (n = 176)[a]	(28)	16	(94)	53	(26)	15	(23)	13	(5)	3
2003 Cutting-Edgers (n = 158)	(23)	15	(63)	40	(25)	16	(45)	28	(2)	1*
1999 Other Leaders (n = 537)[b]	(56)	10	(261)	49	(111)	21	(96)	18	(13)	2
2003 Other Leaders (n = 391)	(22)	6	(147)	38	(85)	22	(123)	31	(14)	3

Table 9.3b Do you think of yourself as . . .

	Among the top leaders of your organization or profession		Close to the top		In the middle range		Toward the bottom	
	(n)	%	*(n)*	%	*(n)*	%	*(n)*	%
All 1999 Respondents (n = 844)[d]	(364)	43	(290)	34	(163)	19	(27)	3
All 2003 Respondents (n = 786)	(294)	37	(293)	37	(186)	24	(13)	2
1999 Cutting-Edgers (n = 184)[c]	(99)	54	(59)	32	(25)	14	(1)	—**
2003 Cutting-Edgers (n = 163)	(71)	44	(65)	40	(25)	15	(2)	1
1999 Other Leaders (n = 536)[c]	(205)	38	(193)	36	(116)	22	(22)	4
2003 Other Leaders (n = 385)	(136)	35	(136)	35	(104)	27	(9)	2

* Because this comparison involved a cell with fewer than five cases, the "much worse" category was collapsed into the "worse" category when the significance levels were calculated.

** Less than one-half of 1 percent. Because the "toward the bottom" category had fewer than five entries in both years, that category was merged with the "in the middle range" category when the significance levels were calculated.

[a] This comparison was significant at the .05 level.

[b] This comparison was significant at the .001 level.

[c] This comparison was not significant.

[d] This comparison was significant at the .01 level in the bivariate test but not significant in the multivariate test, with profession, gender, and education explaining the observed significant difference in the bivariate test.

Table 9.4   With Respect to the Course of Events in World Affairs, Do You ...

	Often		Occasionally		Never	
	(n)	*%*	*(n)*	*%*	*(n)*	*%*
...worry about them?						
All 1999 respondents (*n* = 837)[c]	(325)	39	(450)	54	(62)	7
All 2003 respondents (*n* = 801)	(448)	56	(326)	41	(27)	3
1999 Cutting-Edgers (*n* = 179)[b]	(89)	50	(79)	44	(11)	6
2003 Cutting-Edgers (*n* = 162)	(99)	61	(59)	36	(4)	2*
1999 Other Leaders (*n* = 536)[c]	(186)	35	(316)	59	(34)	6
2003 Other Leaders (*n* = 394)	(212)	54	(166)	42	(16)	4
...have a sense of responsibility for them?						
All 1999 respondents (*n* = 856)[a]	(236)	27	(495)	58	(125)	15
All 2003 respondents (*n* = 791)	(266)	34	(390)	49	(135)	17
1999 Cutting-Edgers (*n* = 185)[a]	(79)	43	(92)	50	(14)	8
2003 Cutting-Edgers (*n* = 162)	(76)	47	(70)	43	(16)	10
1999 Other Leaders (*n* = 543)[c]	(112)	21	(344)	63	(87)	16
2003 Other Leaders (*n* = 388)	(115)	30	(202)	52	(71)	18
...try to affect them?						
All 1999 respondents (*n* = 842)[a]	(166)	20	(515)	61	(161)	19
All 2003 respondents (*n* = 793)	(155)	20	(506)	64	(132)	17
1999 Cutting-Edgers (*n* = 180)[a]	(61)	34	(103)	57	(16)	9
2003 Cutting-Edgers (*n* = 161)	(54)	34	(99)	61	(8)	5
1999 Other Leaders (*n* = 536)[a]	(83)	15	(337)	63	(116)	22
2003 Other Leaders (*n* = 390)	(53)	14	(257)	66	(80)	20

*   Because the "never" category had fewer than five entries, it was merged with the "occasionally" category when the significance levels were calculated.
[a]   This comparison was not significant.
[b]   This comparison was significant at the .05 level.
[c]   This comparison was significant at the .001.

the differences were no less than 9 percent for those who "closely identified" in 2003 (table 9.6). A fourth subgroup, "political party or philosophy," also evoked a significant difference, but its immediacy to a leader's life is more ambiguous, as is perhaps indicated by the smaller difference (7 percent) between those in the 1999 and 2003 surveys who selected the "closely identified" alternative.

Another noteworthy pattern in table 9.6 is the degree to which the differences along these dimensions were not reflective of comparable data for the Cutting-Edgers and the Other Leaders. Except for the Other Leaders' response to the community residence subpart of the question, neither group contributed substantially to the overall difference that marked the two surveys, a finding that can be interpreted as indicating greater local

Table 9.5   To the Extent Your Work Is Relevant to the Processes of Globalization, Do You Usually ... (Check Only One)

	Seek to advance the processes		Seek to resist the processes		Seek to redirect the processes		Not think about its larger processes		My work has no relevance for globalization	
	(n)	%	(n)	%	(n)	%	(n)	%	(n)	%
All 1999 Respondents (n = 828)[c]	(559)	68	(9)	1	(101)	12	(94)	11	(65)	8
All 2003 Respondents (n = 762)	(449)	59	(15)	2	(115)	15	(93)	12	(90)	12
1999 Cutting-Edgers (n = 177)[a]	(141)	80	(1)	1	(27)	15	(5)	3	(3)	2*
2003 Cutting-Edgers (n = 159)	(12C)	75	(3)	2	(24)	15	(8)	5	(4)	3
1999 Other Leaders (n = 524)[b]	(34C)	65	(8)	2	(58)	11	(75)	14	(43)	8
2003 Other Leaders (n = 377)	(194)	51	(7)	2	(59)	16	(59)	16	(58)	15

* Because the "no relevance" and "seek to resist" categories had fewer than five entries, they were excluded when the significance level was calculated.
[a] This comparison was not significant.
[b] This comparison was significant at the .01 level.
[c] This comparison was significant at the .001 level.

Table 9.6 To What Extent Do You Feel a Sense of Identity With...

	Closely identified		Somewhat identified		Mildly identified		None*	
	(n)	%	(n)	%	(n)	%	(n)	%
...neighbors?								
All 1999 respondents (n = 870)[d]	(196)	23	(411)	47	(239)	27	(24)	3
All 2003 respondents (n = 817)	(275)	34	(355)	43	(165)	20	(22)	3
1999 Cutting-Edgers (n = 187)[a]	(37)	20	(87)	46	(58)	31	(5)	3
2003 Cutting-Edgers (n = 165)	(44)	27	(80)	48	(36)	22	(5)	3
1999 Other Leaders (n = 551)[b]	(138)	25	(254)	46	(142)	26	(17)	3
2003 Other Leaders (n = 397)	(139)	35	(167)	42	(81)	20	(10)	3
...the community where you reside?								
All 1999 respondents (n = 872)[d]	(320)	37	(366)	42	(173)	20	(13)	1
All 2003 respondents (n = 819)	(413)	50	(309)	38	(90)	11	(7)	1
1999 Cutting-Edgers (n = 187)[c]	(61)	33	(83)	44	(42)	22	(1)	1
2003 Cutting-Edgers (n = 167)	(78)	47	(67)	40	(20)	12	(2)	1
1999 Other Leaders (n = 551)[d]	(211)	38	(228)	41	(102)	19	(10)	2
2003 Other Leaders (n = 396)	(212)	53	(143)	36	(38)	10	(3)	1
...fellow citizens?								
All 1999 respondents (n = 856)[d]	(234)	27	(404)	47	(198)	23	(20)	2
All 2003 respondents (n = 809)	(291)	36	(359)	44	(147)	18	(12)	1
1999 Cutting-Edgers (n = 184)[d]	(42)	23	(90)	49	(49)	27	(3)	1
2003 Cutting-Edgers (n = 163)	(67)	41	(65)	40	(30)	18	(1)	1
1999 Other Leaders (n = 543)[c]	(149)	27	(258)	48	(122)	22	(14)	3
2003 Other Leaders (n = 397)	(140)	35	(177)	45	(75)	19	(5)	1
...political party or philosophy?								
All 1999 respondents (n = 863)[d]	(181)	21	(290)	34	(279)	32	(113)	13
All 2003 respondents (n = 808)	(231)	28	(291)	36	(216)	27	(70)	9
1999 Cutting-Edgers (n = 187)[a]	(42)	22	(65)	35	(59)	32	(21)	11
2003 Cutting-Edgers (n = 165)	(49)	30	(57)	34	(43)	26	(16)	10
1999 Other Leaders (n = 545)[b]	(107)	20	(186)	34	(179)	33	(73)	13
2003 Other Leaders (n = 397)	(101)	26	(144)	36	(112)	28	(38)	10

* The "none" category was collapsed into the "mildly identified" category when the significance level was calculated.
[a] This comparison was not significant
[b] This comparison was significant at the .05 level.
[c] This comparison was not significant at the .01 level.
[d] This comparison was not significant at the .001 level.

concerns on the part of the respondents who did not record a score on the Involvement Index.

Further indications that the leaders responded to the events that intervened between 1999 and 2003 by attaching greater importance to the close and familiar aspects of their lives is provided by the absence of statistical differences in their responses to the five subparts of the question not included in table 9.6. These asked about the leaders' sense of identity with the less-local and more-remote dimensions of their lives—their sense of identity with respect to their "supervisors" (and/or those they supervise), their "professional associates abroad," their "professional associates at home," their "ethnic or racial group," and "humanity at large"—and none of the comparisons of their responses to these items met the .001 criterion of significance.[3]

The differences in the locales that the respondents considered to be "home" provide additional evidence suggesting that it is reasonable to interpret the several intervening developments between the surveys as having heightened the awareness of respondents to the fragility of the world scene and thus having increased rooted cosmopolitanism through a readiness to appreciate the close-at-hand and familiar aspects of their lives. As can be seen in table 9.7, all the respondents recorded substantial increases with respect to those locales that can reasonably be regarded as being familiar and close at hand. To a large extent, both the Cutting-Edgers and the Other Leaders reinforced these increases.

Finally, to further assess the extent to which greater uncertainties prevailed in 2003, we thought it instructive to determine which of the previously identified eight global issues regarded as "essential" (table 8.1) evoked different responses and greater concern in 2003. The responses to all eight issues are listed in table 9.8, and they tend to run counter to the proposition that the intervening years heightened the uncertainties felt by leaders. More accurately, our data suggest that the changes precipitated by the passage of time resulted less in specific concerns about developments abroad and more in the personal concerns delineated in tables 9.3 through 9.7. Such an inference is discernible in the fact that significant diachronic differences were recorded with respect to only three of the eight global issues, and two of these (ethnic conflict and transnational crime) involved a decline in the proportion of leaders who appraised them in 2003 as being essential. On only one of the eight issues, worldwide arms control, did the appraisal reflect a significant (and substantial) increase in its essentiality.[4]

The Impact of September 11

The greater unease in 2003 can also be linked more specifically to the September 11 terrorist attacks. Hints of these links have already been uncovered, once in the query as to what the respondents regarded as "essential" global issues and again in their assessments of threats to their well-being. In the former instance (table 8.1), both the Cutting Edgers and the Other Leaders selected "terrorism" by a huge margin over twelve other

Table 9.7   What Locale Do You Consider to Be Your "Home"? (Check All That Apply)

	Check		No check	
	(n)	%	(n)	%
Where I feel a sense of ethnic, racial, or religious community				
All 1999 respondents (*n* = 881)ᶜ	(203)	23	(678)	77
All 2003 respondents (*n* = 830)	(317)	38	(513)	62
1999 Cutting-Edgers (*n* = 185)ᶜ	(38)	21	(147)	79
2003 Cutting-Edgers (*n* = 167)	(66)	40	(101)	60
1999 Other Leaders (*n* = 554)ᶜ	(132)	24	(422)	76
2003 Other Leaders (*n* = 398)	(150)	38	(248)	62
Where I am employed				
All 1999 respondents (*n* = 884)ᶜ	(261)	30	(623)	70
All 2003 respondents (*n* = 830)	(349)	42	(481)	58
1999 Cutting-Edgers (*n* = 187)ᵃ	(54)	29	(133)	71
2003 Cutting-Edgers (*n* = 167)	(70)	42	(97)	58
1999 Other Leaders (*n* = 554)ᶜ	(176)	32	(378)	68
2003 Other Leaders (*n* = 398)	(181)	45	(217)	55
Where I plan to retire				
All 1999 respondents (*n* = 884)ᶜ	(136)	15	(748)	85
All 2003 respondents (*n* = 830)	(244)	29	(586)	71
1999 Cutting-Edgers (*n* = 187)ᵇ	(31)	17	(156)	83
2003 Cutting-Edgers (*n* = 167)	(46)	28	(121)	72
1999 Other Leaders (*n* = 554)ᶜ	(86)	16	(468)	84
2003 Other Leaders (*n* = 398)	(114)	29	(284)	71

ᵃ This comparison was significant at the .05 level.
ᵇ This comparison was significant at the .01 level.
ᶜ This comparison was significant at the .001 level.

issues listed as being essential. In the latter case (table 6.5), larger proportions of both groups in 2003 cited terrorist groups as "substantial" threats to a far greater extent than any of the other ten possible threats listed. Indeed, the 26 percent and 27 percent jumps on the part of all the leaders, the Cutting-Edgers, and the Other Leaders who perceived terrorist groups as a "substantial threat" were the largest of all the comparisons between the two surveys. Furthermore, as evident in table 9.9, in addition to terrorist groups being perceived as significantly more threatening in 2003, two of the three other subparts of the eleven-part question marked by differences at the .001 level of significance—"certain individuals" and "certain countries"—can reasonably be traced to the September 11 attacks. Likewise, the conspicuous decreases in the degree to which the individuals and countries were perceived as "mild" threats or "not at all a threat" may

Table 9.8 Which of the Following Do You Regard as Essential Global Issues That Need to Be Addressed in the Next Decade? (Check All That Apply)

	Check		No check	
	(n)	%	*(n)*	%
Stability of the world economy				
All 1999 respondents (*n* = 876)[c]	(626)	71	(250)	29
All 2003 respondents (*n* = 830)	(534)	64	(296)	36
1999 Cutting-Edgers (*n* = 186)[a]	(132)	71	(54)	29
2003 Cutting-Edgers (*n* = 167)	(108)	65	(59)	35
1999 Other Leaders (*n* = 553)[b]	(396)	72	(157)	28
2003 Other Leaders (*n* = 398)	(254)	64	(144)	36
Climate change				
All 1999 respondents (*n* = 876)[b]	(486)	55	(390)	45
All 2003 respondents (*n* = 830)	(418)	50	(412)	50
1999 Cutting-Edgers (*n* = 186)[a]	(106)	57	(80)	43
2003 Cutting-Edgers (*n* = 167)	(88)	53	(79)	47
1999 Other Leaders (*n* = 553)[a]	(302)	55	(251)	45
2003 Other Leaders (*n* = 398)	(199)	50	(199)	50
Worldwide arms control				
All 1999 respondents (*n* = 876)[d]	(447)	51	(429)	49
All 2003 respondents (*n* = 830)	(553)	67	(277)	33
1999 Cutting-Edgers (*n* = 186)[b]	(108)	58	(78)	42
2003 Cutting-Edgers (*n* = 167)	(116)	69	(51)	31
1999 Other Leaders (*n* = 553)[d]	(270)	49	(283)	51
2003 Other Leaders (*n* = 398)	(264)	66	(134)	34
Ethnic conflicts				
All 1999 respondents (*n* = 876)[d]	(664)	76	(212)	24
All 2003 respondents (*n* = 830)	(556)	67	(274)	33
1999 Cutting-Edgers (*n* = 186)[c]	(154)	83	(32)	17
2003 Cutting-Edgers (*n* = 167)	(121)	72	(46)	28
1999 Other Leaders (*n* = 553)[c]	(411)	74	(142)	26
2003 Other Leaders (*n* = 398)	(265)	67	(133)	33
Transnational organized crime				
All 1999 respondents (*n* = 876)[d]	(542)	62	(334)	38
All 2003 respondents (*n* = 830)	(435)	52	(395)	48
1999 Cutting-Edgers (*n* = 186)[a]	(121)	65	(65)	35
2003 Cutting-Edgers (*n* = 167)	(103)	62	(64)	38
1999 Other Leaders (*n* = 553)[c]	(338)	61	(215)	39
2003 Other Leaders (*n* = 398)	(210)	53	(188)	47

Table 9.8   (continued)

	Check		No check	
	(n)	*%*	*(n)*	*%*
Global governance				
All 1999 respondents (*n* = 876)[c]	(254)	29	(622)	71
All 2003 respondents (*n* = 830)	(188)	23	(642)	77
1999 Cutting-Edgers (*n* = 186)[a]	(70)	38	(116)	62
2003 Cutting-Edgers (*n* = 167)	(43)	26	(124)	74
1999 Other Leaders (*n* = 553)[a]	(140)	25	(413)	75
2003 Other Leaders (*n* = 398)	(84)	21	(314)	79
Disposition of nuclear materials				
All 1999 respondents (*n* = 876)[a]	(618)	71	(258)	29
All 2003 respondents (*n* = 830)	(618)	74	(212)	26
1999 Cutting-Edgers (*n* = 186)[b]	(131)	70	(55)	30
2003 Cutting-Edgers (*n* = 167)	(133)	80	(34)	20
1999 Other Leaders (*n* = 547)[a]	(402)	73	(151)	27
2003 Other Leaders (*n* = 398)	(290)	73	(108)	27
Epidemics				
All 1999 respondents (*n* = 876)[b]	(536)	61	(340)	39
All 2003 respondents (*n* = 830)	(450)	54	(380)	46
1999 Cutting-Edgers (*n* = 186)[a]	(111)	60	(75)	40
2003 Cutting-Edgers (*n* = 167)	(95)	57	(72)	43
1999 Other Leaders (*n* = 547)[a]	(342)	62	(211)	38
2003 Other Leaders (*n* = 398)	(216)	54	(182)	46

[a] This comparison was not significant.
[b] This comparison was significant at the .05 level.
[c] This comparison was significant at the .01 level.
[d] This comparison was significant at the .001 level.

well have reflected concern about Osama bin Laden, Saddam Hussein, and the "axis of evil," as well as the September 11 attacks.

Interestingly, as much as the terrorist attacks of September 11 may have affected those in the leadership samples, they were perceived as having a greater impact on the patriotism of the country at large than on themselves. As has already been seen in table 6.9 and is further demonstrated in table 9.10, higher proportions of the respondents in 2003 regarded patriotism as being both "temporarily" and "permanently" increased and less "unchanged" for the country than for them "personally" as well as for "most of the world." Indeed, probably because patriotism was so widely and vividly displayed in the United States after September 11, the 94 percent who judged patriotism to have subsequently been either "temporarily or "permanently" increased is impressively larger than the 53 percent or

Table 9.9 To What Extent Do You Consider the Following a Threat to Your Well-Being?

	Not a threat at all		Mild threat		Moderate threat		Substantial threat		Not sure**	
	(n)	%	(n)	%	(n)	%	(n)	%	(n)	%
Certain individuals										
All 1999 respondents (n = 832)[b]	(241)	29	(259)	31	(166)	20	(118)	14	(48)	6
All 2003 respondents (n = 783)	(164)	21	(201)	26	(176)	22	(196)	25	(46)	6
1999 Cutting Edgers (n = 178)[b]	(44)	25	(56)	31	(40)	22	(29)	16	(9)	5
2003 Cutting-Edgers (n = 160)	(23)	14	(44)	28	(35)	22	(49)	31	(9)	6
1999 Other Leaders (n = 531)[b]	(148)	28	(181)	34	(97)	18	.(79)	15	(26)	5
2003 Other Leaders (n = 393)	(97)	25	(107)	27	(87)	22	(85)	22	(17)	4
Certain countries										
All 1999 respondents (n = 845)[b]	(143)	17	(248)	29	(268)	32	(162)	19	(24)	3
All 2003 respondents (n = 790)	(57)	7	(143)	18	(253)	32	(321)	41	(16)	2
1999 Cutting Edgers (n = 182)[b]	(29)	16	(55)	30	(58)	32	(38)	21	(2)	1
2003 Cutting-Edgers (n = 164)	(8)	5	(31)	19	(50)	30	(73)	45	(2)	1
1999 Other Leaders (n = 536)[b]	(89)	17	(164)	31	(164)	31	(101)	19	(18)	3
2003 Other Leaders (n = 394)	(28)	7	(76)	19	(124)	31	(162)	41	(4)	1
Terrorist groups										
All 1999 respondents (n = 863)[b]	(37)	4	(201)	23	(267)	31	(356)	41	(2)	—*
All 2003 respondents (n = 808)	(13)	2	(81)	10	(165)	21	(546)	68	(3)	—*
1999 Cutting Edgers (n = 185)[b]	(4)	2	(45)	24	(56)	30	(80)	43	(0)	0
2003 Cutting-Edgers (n = 166)	(0)	0	(21)	13	(30)	18	(115)	69	(0)	0
1999 Other Leaders (n = 543)[b]	(25)	5	(127)	23	(177)	33	(212)	39	(2)	0
2003 Other Leaders (n = 397)	(6)	2	(40)	10	(89)	22	(260)	65	(2)	—*

Table 9.9   (continued)

	Not a threat at all		Mild threat		Moderate threat		Substantial threat		Not sure**	
	(n)	%	(n)	%	(n)	%	(n)	%	(n)	%
Globalization										
All 1999 respondents (n = 847)[b]	(578)	68	(158)	19	(52)	6	(36)	4	(23)	3
All 2003 respondents (n = 784)	(449)	57	(143)	18	(122)	16	(40)	5	(30)	4
1999 Cutting Edgers (n = 182)[b]	(137)	75	(34)	19	(1)	—*	(6)	3	(4)	2
2003 Cutting-Edgers (n = 166)	(112)	67	(21)	13	(19)	11	(6)	4	(8)	5
1999 Other Leaders (n = 537)[b]	(357)	66	(99)	18	(46)	9	(24)	4	(11)	2
2003 Other Leaders (n = 389)	(211)	54	(82)	21	(63)	16	(22)	6	(11)	3

* Less than one-half of 1 percent.
** Whenever the "not sure" category had fewer than five entries in a subpart of the question, that category was excluded when the significance level was calculated. In the case of the "terrorist groups," however, the "not a threat at all" category and "mild threat" also had fewer than five entries and thus were merged when the significance level was calculated. Likewise, a merger of the "moderate threat" and "substantial threat" categories was necessitated by too few entries in the case of "globalization."
[a] This comparison was significant at the .05 level.
[b] This comparison was significant at the .001 level.

Table 9.10   Would You Say Patriotism Has ... (Check Only One in Each Row)

2003 survey only	Temporarily increased since September 11		Permanently increased since September 11		Remained unchanged since September 11	
	(n)	%	(n)	%	(n)	%
...for you personally?						
All respondents (802)	(124)	15	(300)	37	(378)	47
...for the United States?						
All respondents (808)	(419)	52	(338)	42	(51)	6
...for most of the world?						
All respondents (766)	(244)	32	(101)	13	(481)	55

Table 9.11 How Would You Characterize Your Reactions to the Following Recent Events? (Check One Item in Each Row)

2003 survey only	Gave you pause as to the virtues of globalization		Affirmed your negative attitude toward globalization		Reinforced your positive orientations toward globalization		Had no impact on your views of globalization	
	(n)	*%*	*(n)*	*%*	*(n)*	*%*	*(n)*	*%*
Asian financial crisis (1997–1999)								
All respondents (802)	(289)	36	(55)	7	(109)	13	(357)	44
Protests against international economic institutions								
All respondents (806)	(231)	29	(70)	9	(177)	22	(328)	41
Terrorist attacks of September 11, 2001								
All respondents (818)	(257)	31	(104)	13	(183)	22	(274)	34
Contested presidential election of 2000								
All respondents (808)	(50)	6	(34)	4	(64)	8	(660)	82
Israel–Palestine conflict								
All respondents (808)	(189)	23	(87)	11	(177)	22	(355)	44
Enron scandal (2001)								
All respondents (808)	(128)	16	(85)	10	(43)	5	(557)	69

less who made the same judgments about both themselves and the world outside the United States.

While the nationwide links between September 11 and patriotism were assessed to be considerable by the responding leaders, the same cannot be said about the links they perceived between globalization and the terrorist attacks. As indicated in table 7.7 and further evident in tables 9.11 and 9.12, the September 11 attacks do not stand out among six "recent events" as having evoked notably different responses with respect to leaders' attitudes toward globalization (table 9.11) or their perception of whether the attacks were a cause or a consequence of globalization (table 9.12). To be sure, leaving aside the two domestic issues (the presidential election and the Enron scandal), a smaller proportion of respondents said that the attacks "had no impact" on their views of globalization than that for the other three international issues, but the distribution for the terrorism issue is not otherwise distinguishable from these three issues.

Table 9.12 Which of the Following Recent Events Do You Consider a Cause or Consequence of Globalization? (Check One Item in Each Row)

	A cause of globalization		A consequence of globalization		Both a cause and a consequence		Neither a cause nor a consequence		Not sure	
2003 survey only	(n)	%	(n)	%	(n)	%	(n)	%	(n)	%
Asian financial crisis (1997–1999)										
All respondents (797)	(18)	2	(261)	33	(225)	28	(207)	26	(86)	11
Protests against international economic institutions										
All respondents (801)	(17)	2	(527)	66	(126)	16	(90)	11	(41)	5
Terrorist attacks of September 11, 2001										
All respondents (802)	(35)	4	(251)	31	(142)	18	(342)	43	(32)	4
Contested presidential election of 2000										
All respondents (802)	(3)	0	(18)	2	(25)	3	(721)	90	(35)	4
Israel–Palestine conflict										
All respondents (798)	(24)	3	(71)	9	(153)	19	(513)	64	(37)	5
Enron scandal (2001)										
All respondents (797)	(11)	1	(95)	12	(93)	12	(550)	69	(48)	6

The Impact of Antiglobalization Protests

Whatever they may indicate with respect to the September 11 terrorist attacks, the findings presented in tables 9.9 and 9.10 highlight the relevance of other developments that marked the interval between the two surveys. Most notably, there are several indicators of sensitivity on the part of the respondents to the economic foundations of globalization and especially to the emergence of the antiglobalization movement. The collapse of Thailand's currency and the ensuing Asian financial crisis of 1997 to 1999, for example, evoked more than a little concern in 1999 (table 7.6), and in 2003 more of the respondents were given pause by this issue than for any of the other five issues (table 9.11). Likewise, nearly two-thirds of the 2003 respondents judged the Asian financial crisis to be "both a cause and a consequence" of globalizing dynamics (table 9.12). Along the same line, it is probably indicative of sensitivities to the economic dimensions of world affairs that globalization was one of the issues that evoked a significant difference at the .001 level on the question of "threats to your well-being" (table 9.9). The difference was a 10 percent decrease in respondents perceiving globalization as "not a threat at all" in 2003, even as this difference was offset by a comparable increase in those that viewed it as a "moderate threat."

And why should "globalization" have been the source of an increased level of threat? A reasonable answer lies in the response to the query on the protests against international economic institutions. Starting with the battle of Seattle in late 1999, protests accompanied virtually every subsequent meeting of the boards of the International Monetary Fund, the World Trade Organization, and the World Bank, as well as UN conferences on particular issues—a pattern that, by the mailing of the second survey in early 2003, came to be widely regarded as an antiglobalization movement.[5] That this pattern was highly salient for the respondents is plainly indicated in table 9.12 by the two-thirds who indicated that the protests were a consequence of globalization (a proportion that at least doubled the figure for any of the other five issues) and by 16 percent who perceived them as both a cause and a consequence. A sense of concern over the implications of the protests on the part of the respondents, most of whom were positively inclined toward globalizing processes, can also be readily inferred from the number of both Cutting-Edgers and Other Leaders who perceived each of nine issues (table 7.1) as being more enhancing than undermining of globalization. Indeed, in the case of five of the issues—human rights, political democracy, economic integration, job creation, and capitalism—large proportions recorded such perceptions, just as infinitesimally small proportions characterized the consequences of globalization as being "mostly bad" for the United States (tables 7.2 and 7.3).

Further indications of sensitivity to the antiglobalization protests can be inferred from the assessments of four international institutions charged with some responsibility for the processes of globalization. As can be seen in table 9.13, which indicates the importance ascribed to the roles played by the United Nations, the World Bank, the World Trade Organization, and the International Monetary Fund, only the first of these recorded an increase in the degree to which it was viewed as being "very important" in 2003, while a significant decrease marked the responses of all the leaders and the Cutting-Edgers to the World Bank's role, presumably because it was a prime target of the antiglobalization movement.

But the protest movement was not without consequences for the leadership samples. Although they regarded globalization as having enhanced a variety of aspects of the world scene, a nuanced analysis points to some evidence that such positive evaluations were not invulnerable to the protest movement. As can be seen in table 9.14, perceptions of the impact of globalizing processes as enhancing globalization slipped somewhat in 2003. Of the ten issues posed as either enhancing or undermining globalization, three of them—political democracy, creation of jobs, and ecological sensitivities (each a central preoccupation of one or another faction of the antiglobalization movement)—manifest evidence of a slippage toward the respondents' viewing the processes as undermining the impact.[6] Each was significant at the most stringent statistical level.

Another possible indicator that leaders were sensitive to the antiglobalization movement to which the protests gave rise is provided by their responses to the query as to whether globalizing processes can or should be facilitated or altered. Two of the subparts of the question, each consisting of three comparisons, posited possible action ("can") to facilitate or alter globalizing processes, and another two subparts, each also comprising three comparisons, focused on value appraisals ("should") of the processes. As can be seen in table 9.15, five of the twelve comparisons were significant at the .001 level, and all of these involved the "can" alternative. Most notably, these five comparisons were all in the same direction: fewer respondents in 2003 than in 1999 indicated a conviction that globalizing processes can be facilitated or altered. No less important, all six of the "should" comparisons were not significant.

Our interpretation of these sharply discrepant findings readily follows: having experienced, witnessed, or otherwise been familiar with the intensity and breadth of the antiglobalization protests, the leaders came to appreciate in 2003 more than they had in 1999 that collective action can contribute to the transformation of globalizing processes even if they did not necessarily approve of the direction of the changes (which is probably why comparisons involving the "should" subparts did not result in significant differences). While other major developments intervened between

Table 9.13   How Would You Rank the Role the Following Can Play in World Affairs?

	Very important		Somewhat important		Not very important		Unimportant		Not sure	
	(n)	*%*	*(n)*	*%*	*(n)*	*%*	*(n)*	*%*	*(n)*	*%*
United Nations										
All 1999 respondents (n = 870)[e]	(439)	50	(312)	36	(92)	11	(23)	3	(4)	—*
All 2003 respondents (n = 808)	(472)	58	(221)	27	(80)	10	(30)	4	(5)	1
1999 Cutting Edgers (n = 185)[a]	(93)	50	(68)	37	(17)	9	(7)	4	(0)	0
2003 Cutting Edgers (n = 165)	(92)	56	(52)	32	(14)	8	(6)	4	(1)	—*
1999 Other Leaders (n = 546)[a]	(282)	52	(189)	35	(60)	11	(12)	2	(3)	1
2003 Other Leaders (n = 396)	(223)	56	(120)	30	(37)	9	(13)	3	(3)	1
World Bank										
All 1999 respondents (n = 865)[d]	(534)	62	(269)	31	(42)	5	(9)	1	(11)	1
All 2003 respondents (n = 801)	(407)	51	(325)	41	(54)	7	(7)	1	(8)	1
1999 Cutting Edgers (n = 186)[d]	(126)	68	(47)	25	(10)	5	(2)	1	(1)	—*
2003 Cutting Edgers (n = 165)	(72)	44	(74)	45	(17)	10	(2)	1	(0)	0
1999 Other Leaders (n = 542)[b]	(333)	61	(173)	32	(22)	4	(7)	1	(7)	1
2003 Other Leaders (n = 395)	(210)	53	(158)	40	(21)	5	(3)	1	(3)	1
World Trade Organization										
All 1999 respondents (n = 859)[c]	(457)	53	(328)	38	(49)	6	(10)	1	(15)	2
All 2003 respondents (n = 795)	(373)	47	(339)	43	(62)	8	(9)	1	(12)	1
1999 Cutting Edgers (n = 184)[a]	(108)	59	(65)	35	(9)	5	(0)	0	(2)	1
2003 Cutting Edgers (n = 165)	(85)	52	(68)	41	(10)	6	(2)	1	(0)	0
1999 Other Leaders (n = 538)[b]	(281)	52	(209)	39	(29)	5	(8)	1	(11)	2
2003 Other Leaders (n = 395)	(180)	46	(174)	44	(32)	8	(2)	1	(7)	2

Table 9.13 (continued)

	Very important		Somewhat important		Not very important		Unimportant		Not sure	
	(n)	%	(n)	%	(n)	%	(n)	%	(n)	%
International Monetary Fund										
All 1999 respondents (n = 836)[b]	(372)	45	(317)	38	(59)	7	(13)	2	(75)	9
All 2003 respondents (n = 769)	(282)	37	(349)	45	(74)	9	(13)	2	(51)	7
1999 Cutting Edgers (n = 184)[b]	(97)	53	(74)	40	(7)	4	(2)	1	(4)	2
2003 Cutting Edgers (n = 163)	(70)	43	(71)	44	(17)	10	(2)	1	(3)	2
1999 Other Leaders (n = 522)[a]	(218)	42	(193)	37	(42)	8	(9)	2	(60)	11
2003 Other Leaders (n = 384)	(136)	35	(174)	45	(38)	10	(7)	2	(29)	8

Note: Whenever the "not sure" category had fewer than five entries in a subpart of the question, that category was excluded when the level of significance was calculated. Likewise, whenever the "unimportant" category had fewer than five entries, it was merged with the "not very important" category in the statistical calculations. Figures may not add to 100 owing to rounding.
[*] Less than one-half of 1 percent.
[a] This comparison was not significant.
[b] This comparison was significant at the .05 level.
[c] This comparison was significant at the .01 level for the multivariate test even though it was not significant in the bivariate test.
[d] This comparison was significant at the .001 level.
[e] This comparison was not significant when subjected to the multivariate test, even though it was significant at the .001 level when subjected to the bivariate test. The multivariate analysis found that gender and political orientation are significant predictors but not the year of response.

the two surveys and may have contributed to the discrepancies evident in table 9.12, it is difficult to construct as logical an explanation of how any intervening development other than the antiglobalization protests might account for the changes.

CONCLUSIONS

Diachronic data are bound to convey mixed messages. No matter how earthshaking intervening events may be—and September 11 can reasonably be viewed as earthshaking an event as has thus far marked the twenty-first century—the changes they evoke are not likely to be all-encompassing. While leaders may be especially sensitive to the course of events and the consequences that may flow from the circumstances that alter history's path, they are not immune to habitual patterns of thought and behavior.

Table 9.14   On Balance, How Would You Assess the Impact of the Diverse Processes of Globalization on ...

	Undermining		Enhancing		Having no effect	
	(n)	*%*	*(n)*	*%*	*(n)*	*%*
...political democracy?						
All 1999 respondents (*n* = 831)[c]	(75)	9	(698)	84	(58)	7
All 2003 respondents (*n* = 780)	(121)	16	(587)	75	(72)	9
1999 Cutting-Edgers (*n* = 182)[c]	(14)	8	(159)	87	(9)	5
2003 Cutting-Edgers (*n* = 161)	(22)	14	(120)	74	(19)	12
1999 Other Leaders (*n* = 530)[b]	(48)	9	(442)	83	(40)	8
2003 Other Leaders (*n* = 385)	(64)	17	(291)	75	(30)	8
...creation of jobs?						
All 1999 respondents (*n* = 819)[c]	(82)	10	(696)	85	(41)	5
All 2003 respondents (*n* = 773)	(164)	21	(548)	71	(61)	8
1999 Cutting-Edgers (*n* = 181)[c]	(10)	6	(167)	92	(4)	2
2003 Cutting-Edgers (*n* = 159)	(22)	14	(127)	80	(10)	6
1999 Other Leaders (*n* = 529)[c]	(59)	11	(437)	83	(33)	6
2003 Other Leaders (*n* = 384)	(88)	23	(261)	68	(35)	9
...ecological sensitivities?						
All 1999 respondents (*n* = 825)[c]	(144)	17	(562)	68	(119)	14
All 2003 respondents (*n* = 775)	(211)	27	(471)	61	(93)	12
1999 Cutting-Edgers (*n* = 180)[a]	(37)	20	(122)	68	(21)	12
2003 Cutting-Edgers (*n* = 160)	(37)	23	(99)	62	(24)	15
1999 Other Leaders (*n* = 531)[c]	(88)	17	(361)	68	(82)	15
2003 Other Leaders (*n* = 381)	(120)	32	(222)	58	(39)	10

[*] Because it had fewer than five entries, the "having no effect" alternative was omitted when the significance level was calculated.
[a] This comparison was not significant.
[b] This comparison was significant at the .01 level.
[c] This comparison was significant at the .001 level.

As stressed in chapter 2, the expectations inherent in the roles they occupy reinforce their tendencies not to alter their characteristic responses to recurring situations. Viewed in this way, it is hardly surprising that the data presented in this chapter are not marked by consistent findings in which attitudinal and behavioral changes between 1999 and 2003 are pervasive. Traces of the uncertainties that marked the period were uncovered and, with few exceptions, readily interpretable. Nonetheless, the overall set of findings offer a mixed picture of change and constancy. Recall that in table 9.2, for example, more than a majority of the 138 comparisons between the responses to the two surveys proved not to be statistically significant. One of the nonsignificant comparisons brilliantly exhibits the power of constancy: as indicated in table 9.16, on the very issue of change, the

Table 9.15   On Balance Do You Believe Globalization Is ... (Check All That Apply)

	Check		No check	
	(n)	*%*	*(n)*	*%*
...a set of processes that can be facilitated?				
All 1999 respondents (*n* = 868)[b]	(362)	42	(506)	58
All 2003 respondents (*n* = 830)	(491)	59	(339)	41
1999 Cutting-Edgers (*n* = 186)[b]	(82)	44	(104)	56
2003 Cutting-Edgers (*n* = 167)	(115)	69	(52)	31
1999 Other Leaders (*n* = 547)[b]	(228)	42	(319)	58
2003 Other Leaders (*n* = 398)	(238)	60	(160)	40
...a set of processes that should be facilitated?				
All 1999 respondents (*n* = 868)[a]	(428)	49	(440)	51
All 2003 respondents (*n* = 830)	(407)	49	(423)	51
1999 Cutting-Edgers (*n* = 186)[a]	(109)	59	(77)	41
2003 Cutting-Edgers (*n* = 167)	(102)	61	(65)	39
1999 Other Leaders (*n* = 547)[a]	(261)	48	(286)	52
2003 Other Leaders (*n* = 398)	(190)	48	(208)	52
...a set of processes that can be altered, hindered, or retarded?				
All 1999 respondents (*n* = 868)[b]	(274)	32	(594)	68
All 2003 respondents (*n* = 830)	(359)	43	(471)	57
1999 Cutting-Edgers (*n* = 186)[a]	(58)	31	(128)	69
2003 Cutting-Edgers (*n* = 167)	(67)	40	(100)	60
1999 Other Leaders (*n* = 547)[b]	(174)	32	(373)	68
2003 Other Leaders (*n* = 398)	(192)	48	(206)	52
...a set of processes that should be altered, hindered, or retarded?				
All 1999 respondents (*n* = 868)[a]	(107)	12	(761)	88
All 2003 respondents (*n* = 830)	(116)	14	(714)	86
1999 Cutting-Edgers (*n* = 186)[a]	(18)	10	(168)	90
2003 Cutting-Edgers (*n* = 167)	(19)	11	(148)	89
1999 Other Leaders (*n* = 547)[a]	(65)	12	(482)	88
2003 Other Leaders (*n* = 398)	(61)	15	(337)	85

[a] This comparison was not significant.
[b] This comparison was significant at the .001 level.

leaders did not change, neither all of them nor the Cutting-Edgers nor the Other Leaders.

* * *

The Cutting-Edger and the Other Leader appear perplexed, perhaps even a bit annoyed. "That's a wishy-washy conclusion," exclaims the former. "Are you telling us that the second of your surveys was essentially unnecessary,

Table 9.16   In General, Do You Feel You That You Control Change, or Does Change Control You?

	I control change		Change controls me		Not sure	
	(n)	%	(n)	%	(n)	%
All 1999 respondents (n = 717)[a]	(295)	41	(232)	32	(190)	27
All 2003 respondents (n = 773)[a]	(283)	41	(233)	33	(182)	26
1999 Cutting-Edgers (n = 148)[a]	(69)	46	(41)	28	(38)	26
2003 Cutting-Edgers (n = 140)	(68)	49	(40)	29	(32)	23
1999 Other Leaders (n = 476)[a]	(188)	40	(162)	34	(126)	26
2003 Other Leaders (n = 335)	(141)	42	(116)	35	(78)	23

[a] This comparison was not significant.

that all the effort you put into it yielded obscure results and shed little light on how those of us on the cutting edge of globalization respond to dramatic events?"

"That's the way it seems to me, too," the Other Leader asserts. "There's no central pattern in all your comparisons across the surveys."

Not about to be pushed around, the researcher forcefully replies, "You surprise me. It would appear you weren't listening, or for some other reason you've lost your appreciation of how complex human behavior is and thus how sensitive one must be to nuance and ambiguity. It is true, as I said, that much remained constant, even as changes were uncovered. But that does not mean the absence of patterned findings. To repeat, September 11 did make a difference, and so did the battle of Seattle and subsequent skirmishes over the virtues of globalization. And it also seems clear that you and your fellow leaders were sensitive to the greater uncertainty that prevailed in 2003 than you had been in 1999. What more do you want? If significant differences had turned up in virtually all the comparisons, you would have been the first to suspect something was wrong. Perhaps you should have some coffee to clarify your perspectives."

"A good idea!" they responded in unison. "Where's the flight attendant?"

NOTES

1. It should be noted that this difficulty is partially offset by the fact that while the two samples did not exclusively comprise the same persons, to a large extent their personal attributes were undifferentiated. The differences between their genders, ages, education, occupation, income, minority statuses, languages read or spoken, parental background, number of jobs, employees supervised, and location on a

liberal-conservative scale were not significant. Only in their political party lean-
ings was the difference between them marginally significant at the .01 level, with
4 percent more in the 2003 sample reporting they were Republicans and 4 percent
less indicating that they had no party preference, even as the same proportions in
both surveys said that they were Democrats or Independents.

2. In both surveys, for example, more than three-quarters of all the respondents
reported that they "very often" or "occasionally" used "e-mail or other online
services" to interact with counterparts abroad.

3. Although they did not exceed the threshold for significant findings, it is perhaps noteworthy that in all five cases the "closely identified" percentage for 2003
was greater than that for 1999.

4. It is noteworthy that of the other five issues, four also depicted declines in 2003
even though they were not statistically significant declines. On the other hand, as
indicated in table 9.9, concern about terrorism and, to a lesser extent, globalization
also increased significantly between 1999 and 2003.

5. For an analysis contending that this pattern amounts to an institutionalization
of the bifurcation of world politics into statecentric and multicentric worlds, see
James N. Rosenau, "Building Blocks of a New Paradigm for Studying World Politics," a paper presented at the international symposium "Nonstate Actors and New
International Realities," Pantelon University, Athens, Greece, January 30, 2003.

6. Saritha Rai, "Anti-globalization Forum Adds Variety of Causes to Its Agenda,"
New York Times, January 20, 2004, A7.

10

Occupational Differences (and Similarities)

Looking at his traveling companions, the researcher senses that he needs to prepare them for his discussion of occupational distinctions. "There is no reason to be confounded by the remainder of the story I'm about to relate," he says. "Now I'm going to talk about some of the important ways in which the two of you may differ and, equally important, about the ways in which you are similar despite your different lines of work."

"You've already done that," the Cutting-Edger replies, still wary and seeming anything but relieved. "You've delineated how my new friend here, the Other Leader, and I differ and are the same. Isn't that enough?"

"No, we need to highlight data that contrasts you as a business executive as well as a Cutting-Edger from your friend, the artist, who is also an Other Leader and who we presume engages in fewer business transactions than you do."

"Are you suggesting that we've not become friends just because both of us do not fall into one of your categories?" the Other Leader interjects, a note of sarcasm in his voice.

"Not at all," the researcher responds. "We think the distinction between business and nonbusiness leaders is important enough to explore whether life on the cutting edge derives from participation in global processes or in global market processes. So there's no reason to take it personally; we're only interested in overall trends or the lack of them. I'm pleased that our project has led to friendly feelings. I feel the same way toward the two of you."

Reassured, the companions begin to relax and seem ready to put up with one last presentation of the complex data.

* * *

In compiling both our 1999 and 2003 samples, we structured them as a two-to-one ratio between, respectively, business executives and leaders whose brief biographies did not include such responsibilities.[1] The heavy emphasis in the literature on the economic dimensions of globalization was a prime reason for employing this procedure. We presumed—wrongly, it turns out—that business executives would be more active on the cutting edge of globalization than would those leaders whose concern with developments abroad does not derive from their work in the world of business.

This presumption proved to be erroneous, because the Involvement Index enabled us to test whether the sampling procedure favoring business executives resulted in their being predominant on the cutting edge of globalization. That is, if our conception of globalization had its roots in an unrecognized neoliberal economic bias—in a presumption that globalizing processes are no more than those that sustain markets—then it is reasonable to expect that the Cutting-Edgers would consist of significantly more business leaders than nonbusiness leaders. To test this presumption, we combined the responses to the two surveys and compared all business and nonbusiness leaders in the context of the distinction between Cutting-Edgers and Other Leaders. Table 10.1 presents this comparison and demonstrates that, indeed, it can reasonably be argued that our surveys measured the backgrounds, connections, and orientations of leaders who sustain diverse globalizing process rather than simply those who contribute to market liberalization. Put differently, the data in Table 10.1 serve to validate the Involvement Index as a measure of participation in a range of global processes not limited to commercial or economic processes.

This is not to imply, however, that comparisons of the business and nonbusiness leaders are of no value. They allow for an assessment of the extent to which the occupation of leaders is more relevant to their conduct and orientations than is their involvement in globalization. That is, in those instances involving significant differences between the two groups, the comparisons allow for assessing the ways in which the occupation of leaders is more reflective of their behavior and attitudes than is their participation

Table 10.1 Comparison of Cutting-Edgers and Other Leaders among Business and Nonbusiness Respondents

	Business Leaders		Nonbusiness Leaders	
	(n)	%	(n)	%
All Cutting-Edgers (n = 354)[a]	(250)	71	(104)	29
All Other Leaders (n = 952)	(631)	66	(321)	34

[a] This comparison was not significant.

in globalizing processes. On the other hand, in the case of the differences that are not significant, the comparisons highlight the circumstances under which the leaders' involvement in globalization is more relevant to their responses than is their occupation.

OCCUPATIONAL DIFFERENCES AND SIMILARITIES

Needless to say, both the business and nonbusiness categories span a variety of occupations, some of which in each category may rest on practices contrary to others in the same category. This is likely to be especially the case with the nonbusiness category, inasmuch it includes every occupation other than business, whereas the latter subsumes some practices—such as concern about profits, clients, and employment—that obtain for anyone in the world of business. Nevertheless, our findings suggest a number of ways in which leaders not in business tend to share certain values and practices as much as their counterparts in business do. The ambiguities and similarities between business and nonbusiness leaders illustrate that profession alone is a poor measure of an individual's participation in global processes.

Both the differences between and the similarities among the two occupational groupings are evident in table 10.2. It presents the responses to five reasons why the respondents maintained contacts abroad. While four of the reasons serve to explain the foreign contacts of any leaders irrespective of their occupation, only one bore directly on the distinction between business and nonbusiness leaders, and it was the only subpart of the five-part question that evoked a difference at the .001 level between the two groups. Three of the differences involved in the other four parts of the question were not significant, and the fourth was significant at the .05 level. In short, the one substantial difference in table 10.2 upholds the use of biographical summaries to distinguish between the business and nonbusiness leaders in compiling the samples used in our surveys. Since members of the business community are more likely to be located in organizations (e.g., corporations) than are leaders in other walks of life, it affirms our procedures that huge differences separated the two groups in their responses to the question of whether their "company's or organization's assignments" was a basis for their "contacts abroad." As indicated in table 10.2, the response of all the business leaders exceeded that of their counterparts by 28 percentage points. On the other hand, the other subparts of the question that yielded no difference or only a marginally significant difference focused, respectively, on the expertise, freelance work, and curiosity of the respondents as well as the continuation of globalization, all explanations relevant to any occupation and thus clear-cut support for using the Involvement Index to identify the Cutting-Edgers.

Table 10.2   What Are the Bases for Your Contacts Abroad? (Check All That Apply)

	Check		No check	
	(n)	*%*	*(n)*	*%*
Your company's or organization's assignments				
All business leaders (*n* = 1,124)[c]	(627)	56	(497)	44
All nonbusiness leaders (*n* = 571)	(162)	28	(409)	72
Your professional expertise is in demand				
All business leaders (*n* = 1,124)[a]	(577)	51	(547)	49
All nonbusiness leaders (*n* = 571)	(277)	49	(294)	51
Your freelance work involves foreign contacts				
All business leaders (*n* = 1,124)[a]	(259)	23	(865)	77
All nonbusiness leaders (*n* = 571)	(112)	20	(459)	80
Your curiosity leads you to distant places				
All business leaders (*n* = 1,124)[a]	(609)	54	(515)	46
All nonbusiness leaders (*n* = 571)	(332)	58	(239)	42
The continuing globalization of world affairs				
All business leaders (*n* = 1,124)[b]	(288)	26	(836)	74
All nonbusiness leaders (*n* = 571)	(107)	19	(464)	81

[a] This comparison was not significant.
[b] This comparison was significant at the .05 level.
[c] This comparison was significant at the .001 level.

Although less pronounced, another indicator that the surveys did differentiate between the organizational ties of business and nonbusiness leaders was uncovered through a query that probed the number of people supervised by those in each group. This significant difference is evident in table 10.3, where the proportion of business leaders who reported

Table 10.3   In Your Work, Approximately How Many People Are You Responsible for?

	None		1–10		11–50		50–500		More than 500	
	(n)	*%*	*(n)*	*%*	*(n)*	*%*	*(n)*	*%*	*(n)*	*%*
All business leaders (*n* = 1,099)[a]	(134)	12	(346)	32	(253)	23	(218)	20	(148)	13
All nonbusiness leaders (*n* = 560)	(110)	20	(197)	35	(133)	24	(91)	16	(29)	5

[a] This comparison was significant at the .001 level.

Table 10.4   Roughly Speaking, Is Your Annual Income from All Sources ...

	Less than $100,000		Between $100,000 and $999,999		More than $1,000,000	
	(n)	%	(n)	%	(n)	%
All business leaders (n = 1,096)[a]	(210)	19	(824)	75	(62)	6
All nonbusiness leaders (n = 548)	(243)	44	(294)	54	(11)	2

[a] This comparison was significant at the .001 level.

responsibility for fifty or more subordinates exceeds that of their nonbusiness counterparts by 12 percent, whereas the latter exceeds the former by 11 percent at the other end of the scale (ten or fewer employees).

Still another indicator that our procedures successfully distinguished between the business and nonbusiness samples is evident in the incomes of those in the two groups. Since members of the business community tend to be wealthier than those in other lines of work, it is reasonable that the business leaders among our respondents reported significantly higher incomes than those of their nonbusiness counterparts (table 10.4).

Another significant difference consistent with standard notions of the business community concerns the self-perceptions of the two groups. Given the prestige, or at least the salience, that attaches to corporations in the present era, it is hardly surprising that business leaders are more ready to perceive themselves as top leaders than are those whose leadership does not derive from roles in the business world. This finding is amply demonstrated by the data in table 10.5. They also allow for the inference that leaders in the business community are more likely to regard globalization as purely an economic phenomenon than are leaders in other walks of life.

Table 10.5   Do You Think of Yourself As ...

	Among the top leaders of your organization or profession		Close to the top		In the middle range		Toward the bottom	
	(n)	%	(n)	%	(n)	%	(n)	%
All business leaders (n = 1,089)[a]	(508)	47	(394)	36	(173)	16	(14)	1
All nonbusiness leaders (n = 541)	(150)	28	(189)	35	(176)	33	(26)	5

[a] This comparison was significant at the .001 level.

Table 10.6   How Would You Characterize Your Expectations for the Next Generation When Its Members Reach Your Age?

	Much better		Better		Same		Worse		Much worse	
	(n)	%	(n)	%	(n)	%	(n)	%	(n)	%
All business leaders (n = 1, 090)[b]	(124)	11	(500)	46	(219)	20	(222)	20	(25)	2
All nonbusiness leaders (n = 561)	(46)	8	(215)	38	(112)	20	(164)	29	(24)	4
All 1999 business leaders (n = 562)[a]	(72)	13	(287)	51	(106)	19	(89)	16	(8)	1
All 1999 nonbusiness leaders (n = 285)	(29)	10	(132)	46	(60)	21	(52)	18	(12)	4
All 2003 business leaders (n = 528)[b]	(52)	10	(213)	40	(113)	21	(133)	25	(17)	3
All 2003 nonbusiness leaders (n = 276)	(17)	6	(83)	30	(52)	19	(112)	41	(12)	4

[a]   This comparison was significant at the .01 level.
[b]   This comparison was significant at the .001 level.

Perhaps more surprising are the respondents' expectations for the future. Given the economic downturn and bursting of the dotcom bubble that marked the interval between the surveys, it is plausible that the business leaders would report no greater optimism than that of their nonbusiness counterparts. Table 10.6, however, indicates that this was not the case, that the business leaders were more optimistic than the nonbusiness leaders. Not only is such a pattern clearly discernible in the significant difference between the two groups combined for both surveys, but table 10.6 also reveals that most of this difference was due to the greater optimism of the business leaders in 2003, as if they anticipated the revival of economic activity. While the two groups did not record significantly different expectations in 1999, even as more than half of both groups expected the next generation to enjoy "much better" or "better" circumstances, in the second survey these expectations declined for both groups. Nonetheless, in 2003 the business leaders were significantly more optimistic than those whose leadership was not located in the business world: 50 percent of the former expected the next generation to experience "much better" or "better" conditions, whereas only 36 percent of the nonbusiness leaders recorded a comparable expectation.

The two parts of table 10.7 reveal still other ways in which business executives conformed to conventional conceptions about their line of work. Their travel and electronic contacts abroad significantly exceeded those of their nonbusiness counterparts. Differences along these lines were also

Table 10.7   Travel and Electronic Contacts Abroad

Table 10.7a Do you travel with a laptop or handheld computer?

	Yes		No	
	(n)	*%*	*(n)*	*%*
All business leaders (*n* = 1, 120)[a]	(581)	52	(539)	48
All nonbusiness leaders (*n* = 575)	(201)	35	(374)	65

Table 10.7b How often do you employ the following methods to carry forward your interactions with counterparts abroad? (check only one in each row)

	Very often		Occasionally		Seldom		Rarely		Never	
	(n)	*%*	*(n)*	*%*	*(n)*	*%*	*(n)*	*%*	*(n)*	*%*
Cellular phone										
All business leaders (*n* = 1, 037)[a]	(104)	10	(208)	20	(150)	14	(174)	17	(401)	39
All nonbusiness leaders (*n* = 501)	(24)	5	(66)	13	(52)	10	(75)	15	(284)	57
Regular telephone										
All business leaders (*n* − 1, 090)[a]	(348)	32	(409)	38	(117)	11	(115)	11	(102)	9
All nonbusiness leaders (*n* = 539)	(96)	18	(197)	37	(61)	11	(84)	16	(101)	19
Teleconferencing										
All business leaders (*n* = 1,014)[a]	(59)	6	(239)	24	(171)	17	(180)	18	(365)	36
All nonbusiness leaders (*n* = 492)	(14)	3	(67)	14	(67)	14	(70)	14	(274)	56
Fax										
All business leaders (*n* = 1,078)[a]	(338)	31	(423)	39	(80)	8	(107)	10	(130)	12
All nonbusiness leaders (*n* = 532)	(109)	20	(162)	31	(61)	11	(65)	12	(135)	25

[a] This comparison was significant at the .001 level.

uncovered in their use of laptop computers in their travels and reliance on the cellular phone, the regular phone, teleconferencing, and the fax machine.[2]

In sum, the findings presented thus far indicate that the business leaders—predictably and significantly—reported greater contacts abroad through travel and electronic communications than did their nonbusiness counterparts, thus indicating that their participation in globalizing processes was at least partially a consequence of their occupational responsibilities. The picture is much less clear-cut, however, in the case of orientations toward various aspects of globalization and American foreign policy. As the ensuing distributions show, the similarities between the groups in these respects are no less conspicuous than the differences, thus again confirming that our Involvement Index did measure participation in globalizing processes independent of any occupational obligations.

GENERAL ATTITUDES AND POLICY ORIENTATIONS

Table 10.8 highlights how leadership roles impose occupational requirements even as they allow for attitudinal variation. In response to the five-part question of the ways in which they regarded the "world" as home, the business leaders significantly exceeded the nonbusiness leaders on the two subparts that directly reflect requirements to engage in activities on the cutting edge of globalization: "I travel widely" and "I earn my living in many parts of it." However, such differences did not obtain with respect to the three subparts that focused on attitudes toward the world as

Table 10.8 In What Sense, If Any, Is the World Your Home? (Check All That Apply)

	Check		No check	
	(n)	%	(n)	%
In the sense that I have traveled widely				
All business leaders (n = 1,133)[b]	(687)	61	(446)	39
All nonbusiness leaders (n = 579)	(297)	51	(282)	49
In the sense that I earn my living in many parts of it				
All business leaders (n = 1,133)[b]	(325)	29	(808)	71
All nonbusiness leaders (n = 579)	(101)	17	(478)	83
In the sense that I am keenly aware of the large extent to which the world is interdependent				
All business leaders (n = 1,133)[a]	(902)	80	(231)	20
All nonbusiness leaders (n = 579)	(456)	79	(123)	21
No, the "world" has no special meaning for me				
All business leaders (n = 1,133)[a]	(40)	4	(1,093)	96
All nonbusiness leaders (n = 579)	(18)	3	(561)	97

[a] This comparison was not significant.
[b] This comparison was significant at the .001 level.

home. Significant differences between the two groups did not mark their responses to two of the subparts—the world as home due to an awareness of global interdependence and "the world has no special meaning"—while the remaining subpart, one that inquired into their sense of "connection with humanity everywhere," evoked a significant difference that runs counter to the general pattern of a higher proportion of the business leaders recording a positive response than that of their nonbusiness counterparts (this difference and a discussion of it are presented in connection with table 10.12e).

A similar pattern can be discerned in the orientations of both groups toward issues embedded in the processes of globalization. On the one hand, the business leaders exceeded the nonbusiness leaders on those economic matters central to their work. Not surprisingly, for example, they were significantly more favorable to free trade, more committed to facilitating processes of globalization, more inclined to perceive their work as being relevant to the economic processes of globalization, more predisposed to ascribe a minimal role to government in economic affairs and to limit its activities to a service role, and less disposed to view globalization as threatening but more ready to view professional competitors as threatening. These differences are presented in the six parts of table 10.9.

On the other hand, significant differences were not uncovered with respect to the noneconomic aspects of involvement in globalizing processes. The two groups did not differ in their views of whether globalization can be facilitated or can or should be altered; of the relevance of their work to the cultural and political processes of globalization; of whether it is a proper role for national governments to prevent potential monopolies/cartels and ensure fair and honest competition or to subsidize promising economic sectors in order to aid their competitiveness in foreign markets; and of whether social movements, religious fundamentalists, the rich–poor gap, certain individuals, certain countries, terrorist groups, and nationalism were threats to their well-being. These nonsignificant distributions are presented in the four subparts of table 10.10.

One feature of table 10.10 is perhaps especially noteworthy. The absence of a difference with respect to the threat posed by social movements is consistent with other indications (noted later) that the business leaders were not particularly disturbed by the antiglobalization protests directed at their corporate community. Two-thirds of the business respondents, both before and after the battle of Seattle in late 1999, reported that social movements were either "not a threat at all" or a "mild threat."

On the other hand, in contrast to their business counterparts, the nonbusiness leaders were significantly more prone to regard multinational corporations and environmental degradation as threatening, more ready to accord a greater role to government in protecting domestic firms and

Table 10.9   Issues Embedded in the Processes of Globalization

Table 10.9a How would you describe your views on trade issues?

	Pro–free trade		Selectively protectionist		Protectionist		Not sure	
	(n)	%	(n)	%	(n)	%	(n)	%
All business leaders (n = 1,095)[a]	(761)	70	(289)	26	(23)	2	(22)	2
All nonbusiness leaders (n = 553)	(297)	54	(204)	37	(15)	3	(37)	6

Table 10.9b On balance do you believe globalization is...(check all that apply)

	Check		No check	
	(n)	%	(n)	%
...a set of processes that should be facilitated?				
All business leaders (n = 1,124)[a]	(590)	52	(534)	48
All nonbusiness leaders (n = 574)	(245)	43	(329)	57

Table 10.9c How would you characterize the relevance of your work with respect to the processes of globalization?

	Continuously relevant		Occasionally relevant		Seldom relevant		Never relevant	
	(n)	%	(n)	%	(n)	%	(n)	%
Economic processes								
All business leaders (n = 1,099)[a]	(564)	51	(345)	31	(152)	14	(38)	4
All nonbusiness leaders (n = 554)	(222)	40	(171)	31	(116)	21	(45)	8

Table 10.9d How would you summarize your views on the proper role of government in economic matters?

	Minimum regulation		Some regulation		Maximum regulation		Not sure	
	(n)	%	(n)	%	(n)	%	(n)	%
All business leaders (n = 1,103)[a]	(333)	30	(736)	67	(25)	2	(9)	1
All nonbusiness leaders (n = 563)	(113)	20	(406)	72	(34)	6	(10)	2

Table 10.9e Do you regard a service role (providing infrastructure, police protection, health, and education, etc.) as a proper role for national governments with regard to private firms and the global economy?

	Check		No check	
	(n)	%	(n)	%
All business leaders (n = 1,126)[a]	(998)	89	(128)	11
All nonbusiness leaders (n = 574)	(449)	78	(125)	22

Table 10.9 (continued)

Table 10.9f To what extent do you consider the following a threat to your well-being?

	Not a threat at all		Mild threat		Moderate threat		Substantial threat		Not sure**	
	(n)	%	(n)	%	(n)	%	(n)	%	(n)	%
Professional competitors										
All business leaders (n = 1,085)[a]	(436)	40	(341)	31	(242)	22	(62)	6	(4)	—*
All nonbusiness leaders (n = 552)	(280)	51	(170)	31	(73)	13	(21)	4	(8)	1
Globalization										
All business leaders (n = 1,082)[a]	(728)	67	(173)	16	(99)	9	(53)	5	(29)	3
All nonbusiness leaders (n = 549)	(299)	55	(128)	23	(75)	14	(23)	4	(24)	4

* Less than one-half of 1 percent.
** Because the "not sure" category had fewer than five entries, that category was excluded from the statistical test when calculating the reported chi-square value, thus reducing the degree of freedom from 4 to 3. This change did not alter the significance level of the comparison.
[a] This comparison was significant at the .001 level.

jobs as well as to have it subsidize lagging economic sectors, more inclined to attach global causes or consequences to the Palestinian-Israeli conflict and the Enron scandal. These differences are set forth in the three subparts of table 10.11, and with the exception of the query on the Palestinian-Israeli conflict, they depict patterns that are consistent with the attitudes and orientations that might have been anticipated on occupational grounds.

In sum, the distributions set forth in the four preceding tables are hardly surprising. They further reaffirm that at the level of attitudes and orientations, in contrast to the activities that link leaders to the world abroad, the differences generated by the Involvement Index were not canceled out by the expectations inherent in occupational positions.

WORLDVIEWS

While the business and nonbusiness leaders differed on relatively few policy issues, traces of differences in their worldviews, which include matters not linked to policy questions, can be discerned in the comparative data. The nonbusiness leaders appear to be more sensitive to people and their circumstances as well as to issues that have broad implications for the welfare of individuals than is the case for their business counterparts,

Table 10.10 Noneconomic Aspects of Involvement in Globalizing Processes

Table 10.10a On balance do you believe globalization is . . . (check all that apply)

	Check		No Check	
	(n)	*%*	*(n)*	*%*
. . . a set of processes that can be facilitated?				
All business leaders (*n* = 1,124)[a]	(573)	51	(551)	49
All nonbusiness leaders (*n* = 574)	(280)	49	(294)	51
. . . a set of processes that can be altered, hindered, or retarded?				
All business leaders (*n* = 1,124)[a]	(412)	37	(712)	63
All nonbusiness leaders (*n* = 574)	(221)	39	(353)	62
. . . a set of processes that should be altered, hindered, or retarded?				
All business leaders (*n* = 1,124)[a]	(136)	12	(988)	88
All nonbusiness leaders (*n* = 574)	(87)	15	(487)	85

Table 10.10b What do you regard as the proper roles of national governments with regard to private firms and the global economy? (check all that apply)

	Check		No Check	
	(n)	*%*	*(n)*	*%*
Prevent potential monopolies/cartels and ensure fair and honest competition				
All business leaders (*n* = 1,126)[a]	(879)	78	(247)	22
All nonbusiness leaders (*n* = 574)	(449)	78	(125)	22
Subsidize promising economic sectors to aid their competition in foreign markets				
All business leaders (*n* = 1,126)[a]	(302)	27	(824)	73
All nonbusiness leaders (*n* = 574)	(194)	34	(380)	66

Table 10.10c How would you characterize the relevance of your work with respect to the diverse processes of globalization?

	Continuously relevant		Occasionally relevant		Seldom relevant		Never relevant	
	(n)	*%*	*(n)*	*%*	*(n)*	*%*	*(n)*	*%*
Cultural processes								
All business leaders (*n* = 1,096)[b]	(406)	37	(431)	39	(210)	19	(49)	5
All nonbusiness leaders (*n* = 560)	(256)	46	(206)	37	(74)	13	(24)	4
Political processes								
All business leaders (*n* = 1,124)[a]	(343)	31	(358)	33	(293)	27	(101)	9
All nonbusiness leaders (*n* = 574)	(154)	28	(196)	36	(134)	24	(68)	12

Table 10.10 (continued)

Table 10.10d To what extent do you consider the following a threat to your well-being?

	Not a threat at all		Mild threat		Moderate threat		Substantial threat		Not sure	
	(n)	%	(n)	%	(n)	%	(n)	%	(n)	%
Social movements										
All business leaders (n = 1,076)[a]	(411)	38	(325)	30	(231)	21	(82)	8	(27)	3
All nonbusiness leaders (n = 549)	(232)	42	(147)	27	(103)	19	(50)	9	(17)	3
Religious fundamentalism*										
All business leaders (n = 527)[a]	(62)	12	(80)	15	(123)	23	(254)	48	(8)	2
All nonbusiness leaders (n = 277)	(43)	16	(39)	14	(56)	20	(135)	48	(4)	1
Gap between rich and poor										
All business leaders (n = 1,100)[b]	(241)	22	(303)	28	(281)	26	(258)	23	(17)	2
All nonbusiness leaders (n = 565)	(97)	17	(144)	25	(141)	25	(173)	31	(10)	2
Certain individuals										
All business leaders (n = 1,075)[a]	(281)	26	(303)	28	(224)	21	(203)	19	(64)	6
All nonbusiness leaders (n = 540)	(124)	23	(157)	29	(118)	21	(111)	22	(30)	5
Certain countries										
All business leaders (n = 1,075)[a]	(129)	12	(251)	23	(353)	33	(326)	30	(27)	2
All nonbusiness leaders (n = 549)	(71)	13	(140)	26	(168)	31	(157)	29	(13)	2
Terrorist groups										
All business leaders (n = 1,108)[a]	(31)	3	(188)	17	(291)	26	(596)	54	(2)	—**
All nonbusiness leaders (n = 563)	(19)	3	(94)	17	(141)	25	(306)	54	(3)	1

Table 10.10 (continued)

	Not a threat at all		Mild threat		Moderate threat		Substantial threat		Not sure	
	(n)	%	(n)	%	(n)	%	(n)	%	(n)	%
Nationalism										
All business leaders (n = 1,084)[a]	(317)	2	(318)	29	(314)	30	(110)	10	(25)	2
All nonbusiness leaders (n = 551)	(145)	26	(166)	30	(148)	27	(70)	12	(22)	4

Note: Figures may not add to 100 owing to rounding.
* Not included in the 1999 survey.
** Less than one-half of 1 percent; as a consequence, the "not sure" category was excluded from the statistical test when the reported chi-square value was calculated, thus reducing the degree of freedom from 4 to 3.
[a] This comparison was not significant.
[b] This comparison was significant at the .05 level.

who reported greater concern about narrow and specific issues. In addition to the distinctions evident in table 10.11 relative to jobs and the environment, the nonbusiness leaders were more inclined than their business counterparts to regard individual altruism and ecological sensitivities as being undermined by globalization; more ready to regard Amnesty International as playing an important role in world affairs; more disposed to regard climate change, epidemics, and the disposition of nuclear materials as essential global issues; more generous in their gifts to international charities; and more possessed of a sense of "connection with humanity everywhere." Another possible indicator along this line is manifest in the importance that the two groups attached to the foreign policy goal of "combating world hunger." The nonbusiness leaders exceeded their business counterparts by 7 percent in the extent to which they perceived this issue as being "very important." This difference was especially conspicuous for the Cutting-Edgers among the nonbusiness leaders: they exceeded the business leaders by 23 percent. Taken together, and despite qualifications necessitated by two statistical tests yielding discrepant results,[3] the five parts of table 10.12 depict distinctions between the nonbusiness and business leadersthat can be interpreted as the difference between liberal and conservative approaches to world affairs.

AMBIGUITIES AND CONTRADICTIONS

If the worldviews of the two major U.S. political parties differ in ways that mirror the foregoing differences—an assumption that seems reasonable—then it is hardly surprising that the business and nonbusiness leaders

Table 10.11   Attitudes and Orientations Linked to Occupation

Table 10.11a To what extent do you consider the following a threat to your well-being?

	Not a threat at all		Mild threat		Moderate threat		Subtantial threat		Not sure	
	(n)	%	*(n)*	%	*(n)*	%	*(n)*	%	*(n)*	%
Multinational corporations										
All business leaders (n = 1,090)[b]	(556)	51	(271)	25	(165)	15	(87)	8	(11)	1
All nonbusiness leaders (n = 551)	(207)	38	(137)	25	(126)	23	(66)	12	(15)	3
Environmental degradation*										
All business leaders (n = 523)[a]	(54)	10	(155)	30	(160)	31	(150)	29	(4)	1
All nonbusiness leaders (n = 278)	(18)	6	(63)	23	(70)	25	(124)	45	(3)	1

Table 10.11b What do you regard as the proper roles of national governments with regard to private firms and the global economy? (check all that apply)

	Check		No check	
	no	%	*no*	%
Subsidize lagging economic sectors to aid their competitiveness in foreign markets				
All business leaders (n = 1,126)[a]	(127)	11	(999)	89
All nonbusiness leaders (n = 574)	(101)	18	(473)	82
Protect domestic firms and jobs from foreign competition				
All business leaders (n = 1,126)[a]	(130)	12	(996)	88
All nonbusiness leaders (n = 574)	(104)	18	(470)	82

Table 10.11c Which of the following recent events do you consider a cause or consequence of globalization? (check one item in each row)

2003 survey only	A cause of globalization		A consequence of globalization		Both a cause and a consequence		Neither a cause nor a consequence		Not sure	
	no	%	*no*	%	*no*	%	*no*	%	*no*	%
Palestinian–Israeli Conflict										
All business leaders (n = 522)[b]	(14)	3	(33)	6	(94)	18	(360)	69	(21)	4
All nonbusiness leaders (n = 276)	(10)	4	(38)	14	(59)	21	(153)	55	(16)	6

Table 10.11   (continued)

2003 survey only	A cause of globalization		A consquence of globalization		Both a cause and a consequence		Neither a cause nor a consequence		Not sure	
	no	%	no	%	no	%	no	%	no	%
2001 Enron Scandal										
All business leaders ($n = 523$)[b]	(6)	1	(51)	10	(56)	11	(386)	74	(24)	5
All nonbusiness leaders ($n = 274$)	(5)	2	(44)	16	(37)	14	(164)	60	(24)	9

* Because the "not sure" category had fewer than five entries, that category was excluded from the statistical test when the reported chi-square value was calculated, thus reducing the degree of freedom from 4 to 3. This change did not alter the significance level of the comparison.
[a] This comparison was significant at the .05 level.
[b] This comparison was significant at the .001 level.

differed significantly in their party affiliations, with the former consisting of more Republicans and the latter of more Democrats (table 10.13a). At the same time, of course, worldviews can be marked by contradictions and ambiguities. The responses to the more general question that probed political philosophies, for example, did not result in a statistically significant difference between the two groups of leaders. Although traces of such a distinction can be discerned in the distribution of their responses, both groups consisted of respondents to the left and right on the political spectrum (table 10.13b).

Similar ambiguities can be discerned in the responses to the questions that sought to probe reactions to the three major events that occurred in the interval between the 1999 and 2003 surveys—namely, the September 11 expansion of terrorism, the coalescence of the protest movement against the economic aspects of globalization, and the run-up to the war that removed Saddam Hussein from his leadership post in Iraq. Some of the responses to questions that probed reactions to these events are unclear and difficult to interpret; some are surprisingly lacking in significant differences. In the case of the terrorist attacks, for example, the business and nonbusiness respondents differed significantly, partly because the former reported that September 11 reinforced their positive orientations toward globalization and partly because the latter indicated that the attacks affirmed their negative attitudes toward globalization. On the other hand, the two groups did not differ on the question of whether September 11 was a cause or consequence of globalization. Likewise, ambiguity marked their reactions to combating terrorism as a goal, with the business leaders recording a

Table 10.12   Approaches to World Affairs: Occupational Distinctions

Table 10.12a On balance, how would you assess the impact of the diverse processes of globalization on . . .

	Undermining		Enhancing		Having no effect	
	(n)	%	(n)	%	(n)	%
. . . individual altruism						
All business leaders (n = 1,047)[a]	(169)	16	(430)	41	(448)	43
All nonbusiness leaders (n = 523)	(121)	23	(224)	43	(178)	34
. . . ecological sensitivities						
All business leaders (n = 1,059)[c]	(197)	19	(710)	67	(152)	14
All nonbusiness leaders (n = 541)	(158)	29	(323)	60	(60)	11

Table 10.12b How would you rank the role the following can play in world affairs?

	Very important		Somewhat important		Not very important		Unimportant		Not sure	
	(n)	%	(n)	%	(n)	%	(n)	%	(n)	%
Amnesty International										
All business leaders (n = 1,092)[a]	(186)	17	(388)	36	(348)	32	(121)	11	(49)	4
All nonbusiness leaders (n = 559)	(148)	26	(207)	37	(134)	24	(44)	8	(26)	5

Table 10.12c Which of the following do you regard as *essential* global issues that need to be addressed in the next decade? (check all that apply)

	Check		No check	
	no	%	no	%
Climate change				
All business leaders (n = 1,128)[b]	(559)	50	(569)	50
All nonbusiness leaders (n = 578)	(345)	60	(233)	40
Epidemics				
All business leaders (n = 1,128)[b]	(608)	54	(520)	46
All nonbusiness leaders (n = 578)	(378)	65	(200)	35
Disposition of nuclear materials				
All business leaders (n = 1,128)[b]	(789)	70	(339)	30
All nonbusiness leaders (n = 578)	(447)	77	(131)	23

Table 10.12   (continued)

Table 10.12d Approximately what proportion of your charitable donations each year goes to

	Business Leaders		Nonbusiness Leaders	
	Mean proportion	(n)	Mean proportion	(n)
2003 international charities[b]	6.70	(497)	10.17	(254)

Table 10.12e In what sense, if any, is the world your home? (check all that apply) In the sense that I feel a connection with humanity everywhere

	Check		No check	
	no	%	no	%
All business leaders (n = 1,133)[a]	(631)	56	(502)	44
All nonbusiness leaders (n = 579)	(394)	68	(185)	32

[a] This comparison was not significant.
[b] This comparison was significant at the .05 level.
[c] This comparison was significant at the .01 level.

significantly greater readiness to characterize it as a "very important" goal, even though 85 percent of the nonbusiness leaders also responded in the same way. These ambiguous findings are set forth in the three parts of table 10.14.

The two groups also differed significantly in their reactions to the protests against international institutions, with the business leaders characterizing the protests as "reinforcing" their attitudes toward globalization while their nonbusiness counterparts reported that the protests gave them "pause as to the virtues of globalization." Moreover, even though the corporate community was a prime target of the protests, 11 percent of the nonbusiness leaders reported negative attitudes toward them, and the comparable figure for the business leaders was only 7 percent, suggesting either that they ignored or were indifferent to the protests. Equally provocative were the different reactions to the question of whether the protests were a cause or a consequence of globalization. The distributions of the responses of the two groups differed significantly—even though roughly two-thirds of both groups perceived the protests as a consequence of globalization—and they suggest that the protesters have made no impression on the audience to which they are nominally directing their message. The very indifference of the business community indicates that the protesters have a long way to go before their message is heard, let alone acted on. These distributions are presented in the two parts of table 10.15.

On the other hand, a measure of partisanship can be discerned in the responses to the question of whether overthrowing Saddam Hussein was an important foreign policy goal. While half of the business leaders, who

Table 10.13 Political Affiliations and Orientations

Table 10.13a Political Affiliations of the Business and Nonbusiness Leaders

	Republican		Democrat		Independent		No preference	
	(n)	%	(n)	%	(n)	%	(n)	%
All business leaders (n = 1,092)[b]	(544)	50	(276)	25	(235)	22	(37)	3
All nonbusiness leaders (n = 558)	(170)	30	(202)	36	(135)	24	(51)	9

Table 10.13b Political Orientations of the Business and Nonbusiness Leaders

	Far right		Very Conservative		Conservative		Moderate		Somewhat liberal		Very liberal		Far left*	
	(n)	%	(n)	%	(n)	%	(n)	%	(n)	%	(n)	%	(n)	%
All business leaders (n = 1,073)[a]	(2)	—**	(117)	11	(377)	35	(316)	29	(180)	17	(75)	7	(6)	1
All nonbusiness leaders (n = 558)	(2)	—**	(49)	9	(156)	28	(176)	32	(113)	20	(50)	9	(6)	1

* The lack of a significant difference is not altered when the "far right" and "very conservative" alternatives are collapsed into a single category, and the same procedure is used for the "far left" and "very liberal" categories.
** Less than one-half of 1 percent.
a This comparison was significant at the .05 level.
b This comparison was significant at the .01 level.

Table 10.14 Perceptions of September 11 and Terrorism

Table 10.14a How would you characterize your reactions to the following recent events? (check one item in each row)

2003 survey only	Gave you pause as to the virtues of globalization		Affirmed your negative attitude toward globalization		Reinforced your positive orientations toward globalization		Had no impact on your views of globalization	
	(n)	%	(n)	%	(n)	%	(n)	%
Terrorist attacks of September 11, 2001								
All business leaders (n = 536)	(161)	30	(53)	10	(131)	24	(191)	36
All nonbusiness leaders (n = 282)	(96)	34	(51)	18	(52)	18	(83)	29

Table 10-14b Which of the following recent events do you consider a cause or consequence of globalization? (check one item in each row)

2003 survey only	A cause of globalization		A consequence of globalization		Both a cause and a consequence		Neither a cause nor a consequence		Not sure	
	(n)	%	(n)	%	(n)	%	(n)	%	(n)	%
Terrorist attacks of September 11, 2001										
All business leaders (n = 523)[a]	(18)	3	(162)	31	(87)	17	(237)	45	(19)	4
All nonbusiness leaders (n = 279)	(17)	6	(89)	32	(55)	20	(105)	38	(13)	5

Table 10.14c Turning to more general considerations, here is a list of possible foreign policy goals that the United States might have. Indicate how much importance you think should be attached to each goal.

2003 survey only	Very Important		Moderately important		Slightly important		Not at all important		Not sure[**]	
	(n)	%	(n)	%	(n)	%	(n)	%	(n)	%
Combating international terrorism										
All business leaders (n = 532)[b]	(500)	94	(26)	5	(3)	1	(1)	—[*]	(2)	—[*]
All nonbusiness leaders (n = 280)	(239)	85	(30)	11	(8)	3	(2)	—[*]	(1)	—[*]

[*] Less than one-half of 1 percent.
[**] In the case of cells with fewer than five responses, the "not sure" category was dropped from the analysis and the "not at all important" and "slightly important" categories were collapsed into the "moderately important" category when the significance level was calculated.
[a] This comparison was not significant.
[b] This comparison was significant at the .05 level.

Table 10.15   Perceptions of Protests against International Economic Institutions

Table 10.15a How would you characterize your reactions to the following recent events? (check one item in each row)

2003 survey only	Gave you pause as to the virtues of globalization		Affirmed your negative attitude toward globalization		Reinforced your positive orientations toward globalization		Had no impact on your views of globalization	
	(n)	%	(n)	%	(n)	%	(n)	%
Protests against international economic institutions								
All business leaders (n = 529)[a]	(132)	25	(40)	8	(136)	26	(221)	42
All nonbusiness leaders (n = 277)	(99)	36	(30)	11	(41)	15	(107)	39

Table 10.15b Which of the following recent events do you consider a cause or consequence of globalization? (check one item in each row)

2003 survey only	A cause of globalization		A consequence of globalization		Both a cause and a consequence		Neither a cause nor a consequence		Not sure	
	(n)	%	(n)	%	(n)	%	(n)	%	(n)	%
Protests against international economic institutions										
All business leaders (n = 525)[a]	(11)	2	(353)	67	(75)	14	(70)	13	(16)	3
All nonbusiness leaders (n = 276)	(6)	2	(174)	63	(51)	18	(20)	7	(25)	9

[a] This comparison was significant at the .001 level.

included more Republicans than did the nonbusiness leaders, viewed the overthrow as being either moderately or very important, more than half of the nonbusiness leaders, whose ranks included more Democrats, regarded the possibility of an attack on Iraq as being unimportant or only slightly important. Indeed, if the business and nonbusiness distributions are broken down by party affiliations, the partisanship factor is dramatic: while the Republican business and nonbusiness leaders recorded, respectively, 72 and 64 percent who perceived the anticipated Iraq invasion as being "very important" or "moderately important," the comparable figures for the Democrats were 21 and 16 percent, differences that yielded the highest differences of any comparisons in this book (table 10.16a).

Table 10.16   Party Affiliation and International Issues

Table 10.16a Turning to more general considerations, here is a list of possible foreign policy goals that the United States might have. Indicate how much importance you think should be attached to each goal.

2003 survey only	Very Important (n)	%	Moderately Important (n)	%	Slightly Important (n)	%	Not at all important (n)	%	Not sure (n)	%
Invading Iraq to overthrow Saddam Hussein										
All business leaders (n = 531)[a]	(137)	26	(130)	24	(98)	18	(133)	25	(33)	6
All nonbusiness leaders (n = 277)	(46)	17	(52)	19	(57)	21	(101)	36	(21)	8
Business: Republicans (n = 270)[c]	(108)	40	(85)	32	(46)	17	(17)	6	(14)	5
Business: Democrats (n = 123)	(8)	7	(17)	14	(24)	20	(67)	54	(7)	6
Nonbusiness: Republicans (n = 87)[c]	(29)	33	(27)	31	(11)	13	(11)	13	(9)	10
Nonbusiness: Democrats (n = 99)	(5)	5	(11)	11	(23)	23	(54)	55	(6)	6

Table 10.16b Which of the following do you regard as *essential* global issues that need to be addressed in the next decade? (check all that apply)

2003 survey only	Check (n)	%	No check (n)	%
Strengthening the United Nations				
All business leaders (n = 543)[b]	(250)	46	(293)	54
All nonbusiness leaders (n = 287)	(173)	60	(114)	40

[a] This comparison was significant at the .05 level.
[b] This comparison was significant at the .01 level.
[c] This comparison was significant at the .001 level.

Another indication of the convergence of the Iraq issue and party affiliations is evident in the significantly different reactions to the United Nations. Recall that the second questionnaire was administered exactly at the time that public debate focused on whether an attack on Iraq should be launched under the UN's auspices. Hence, it is not surprising that the nonbusiness leaders perceived strengthening the UN as an essential global issue when compared to their business counterparts, who ascribed significantly less essentiality to the UN's role (table 10.16b).

The differences set forth in table 10.16 are so striking that they pose the question of whether partisanship underlies all the findings relevant to the

Table 10.17   Self-Identified Political Affiliations of All Cutting-Edgers and Other Leaders

	Republicans		Democrats		Independents		No preference	
	(n)	%	(n)	%	(n)	%	(n)	%
Cutting-Edgers (n = 339)[a]	(153)	45	(97)	29	(76)	22	(13)	4
Other Leaders (n = 935)	(417)	45	(252)	27	(218)	23	(48)	5

[a] This comparison was not significant.

comparisons of the responses of the Cutting-Edgers and the Other Leaders in the previous chapters. As can be seen in table 10.17, however, the question can be answered firmly in the negative: the self-identified political affiliations of the two groups were virtually identical and the difference between them nonsignificant. Only the issues surrounding the imminence of the preemptive attack on Iraq in 2003 appear to have evoked partisan reactions traceable in the survey instrument. Put differently, the business–nonbusiness dichotomy has a partisan bias, with more business leaders describing themselves as Republicans (see table 10.13), but table 10.17 demonstrates that the Cutting-Edge–Other Leader dichotomy is free of a partisan bias, thus indicating that our Involvement Index measures participation in globalization independent of partisan affiliation.

Finally, ambiguity, if not contradiction, can be discerned in the reactions to the several questions on loyalty. The business and nonbusiness leaders did not differ significantly on the four-part question of whether patriotism is personally "of continuing major importance," "of largely symbolic or psychological significance," "an increasingly obsolete sentiment," or "no longer relevant to the course of events." The same absence of differences prevailed with respect to all four options in the context of patriotism throughout the United States. Only with respect to the "continuing major importance" option in the context of the rest of the world did the two groups differ significantly at the .001 level, with 55 percent of the business leaders having checked this alternative, compared to 43 percent of the nonbusiness leaders.[4]

Minimal differences between the two groups marked their responses to the unavoidable choices they were asked to make between their "company or organization" and their "country," between their "professional needs" and those of their "company or organization," and between their "professional responsibilities" and their "civic obligations" (these findings are presented in the three parts of table 10.18). Plainly, patriotism and loyalties were not matters on which members of the business community and those in other lines of work differed.

Table 10.18   Professional versus National and Civic Obligations

	Yes		No		Not sure		I avoid such choices	
	(n)	%	(n)	%	(n)	%	(n)	%

Table 10.18a If a vital choice involving your company or organization could not be avoided, would you put its interests ahead of those of your country?

| All business leaders (n = 1, 106)[a] | (83) | 8 | (723) | 65 | (237) | 21 | (63) | 6 |
| All nonbusiness leaders (n = 555) | (33) | 6 | (368) | 66 | (119) | 22 | (35) | 6 |

Table 10.18b If a vital choice involving your career could not be avoided, would you put your professional needs ahead of those of your company or organization?

| All business leaders (n = 1, 093)[b] | (593) | 54 | (268) | 25 | (186) | 17 | (46) | 4 |
| All nonbusiness leaders (n = 563) | (314) | 56 | (104) | 18 | (122) | 22 | (23) | 4 |

Table 10.18c If your professional responsibilities and your civic obligations come into conflict, which are likely to prevail most of the time?

	Professional obligations		Civic obligations		I avoid such conflicts		Not sure	
	(n)	%	(n)	%	(n)	%	(n)	%
All business leaders (n = 1, 088)[b]	(514)	47	(303)	28	(101)	9	(170)	16
All nonbusiness leaders (n = 560)	(240)	43	(152)	27	(49)	9	(119)	21

[a] This comparison was not significant.
[b] This comparison was significant at the .05 level.

One other set of responses in which the two groups differed only minimally is worth noting. Consistent with the greater optimism, as noted in table 10.5a, business leaders differed significantly from the nonbusiness respondents in their answers to the question of whether they controlled or were controlled by change. More accurately, the overall difference between the two groups was the product of the Cutting-Edgers being more confident than the Other Leaders that they controlled change (table 10.19).

CONCLUSIONS: SIMILARITIES BEYOND OCCUPATION

At the gross level of the distinction between members of the business community and those in other lines of work, it seems clear that the involvement of leaders in the processes of globalization is largely independent of their

Table 10.19   In General, Do You Feel You That You Control Change, or Does Change Control You?

	I control change		Change controls me		Not sure	
	(n)	%	(n)	%	(n)	%
All business leaders (n = 952)[b]	(407)	43	(301)	32	(244)	26
All nonbusiness leaders (n = 463)	(171)	37	(164)	35	(128)	28
All business Cutting-Edgers (n = 210)[a]	(97)	46	(67)	32	(46)	22
All nonbusiness Cutting-Edgers (n = 73)	(40)	51	(14)	18	(24)	31
All business Other Leaders (n = 542)[c]	(238)	44	(172)	32	(132)	24
All nonbusiness Other Leaders (n = 269)	(91)	34	(106)	39	(72)	27

[a] This comparison was not significant.
[b] This comparison was significant at the .05 level.
[c] This comparison was significant at the .001 level.

occupations, even as in some ways those in the business community can be differentiated from their counterparts elsewhere in the working world. While the data support the presumption that globalization is not only an economic phenomenon, in some respects they were marked by ambiguity. Traces of different worldviews, for example, were uncovered, with non-business leaders being more oriented toward individuals and policies that enhance the quality of life and with the business counterparts being more favorably oriented toward globalization and the viability of corporations. In addition, the business leaders engaged in more travel and relied on more varied means of electronic communication than did those whose occupations were less worldwide in scope. All in all, however, the differences between the two groups were not as conspicuous as those that marked the comparisons between the Cutting-Edgers and the Other Leaders in chapters 4 through 8, a conclusion that suggests the need for both caution in ascribing causal dynamics to occupations and in viewing globalization as being sustained primarily by economic factors.

* * *

The two travelers stare momentarily at each other. "I guess we're not so different after all," the Other Leader says, breaking the silence. "As a businessman you may travel more than I do and you may be more electronically connected to the world, but to a large extent we do not differ on a number of issues."

"It all depends on what you emphasize," replies the Cutting-Edger. "On some matters I'm more practical, even more hard-nosed, than you. And I favor globalization more than you do."

"No, that's not true. It is only the case with respect to the economic side of globalization. I do not want to deny the concerns and values that divide us, but there are a number of ways in which we see the world the same way. Equally important, I do not want the friendship we've evolved on this flight to be undermined," the Other Leader says firmly.

"Not to worry," the researcher intervenes. "As I have said more than once, quantified data only describe central tendencies. It would be erroneous to apply them to particular individuals. You guys should not take any or all of this personally."

NOTES

1. This was accomplished by using a different website on the cover page of the questionnaire in the event that the recipient wanted to respond electronically.

2. Interestingly, however, the two groups did not differ in their use of e-mail, obviously a means of communication that is no more inherent in the business field than any other.

3. When subjected to a bivariate test, all the differences between the business and nonbusiness leaders reported in table 10.12 were significant at the .001 level. However, as indicated in the table, the multivariate test yielded lesser levels of significance and in two cases, Amnesty International and "connection to humanity," the observed differences depended more on the gender and political orientations of the respondents than on their profession.

4. The precise wording of these questions is presented in tables 6.7, 6.8, and 6.9.

Conclusion

The loudspeaker is a bit faint, but the message is clear. "Ladies and gentlemen, we have begun our descent. Kindly make sure your seat belts are tightly fastened, your tray tables are stowed, and your seats are in the upright position."

"I'm kind of sorry our trip and conversation are over," the Other Leader says.

"Well, at least we've covered all the findings generated by our surveys," the researcher responds. "Our story is finished. There's no more to tell."

The Cutting-Edger is perplexed. "Is it? You haven't said what it all adds up to. Stories need a conclusion, a decisive ending that highlights the larger meaning of the tale."

"Let me put it another way," the Other Leader chimes in. "Are you satisfied with what your project has uncovered? Do you think you've made a useful contribution to understanding the dynamics that drive globalization? If you had to do it all over, what would you do differently?"

The researcher is quick to reply. "There are two ways we would do it differently—I'll come back to them—but yes, I'm satisfied we have teased all the findings we could out of our welter of data. Whether our contribution is useful depends on how the study is received and appraised by colleagues and others who focus on the underpinnings of globalization. Naturally, we hope they will ponder the patterns we have uncovered and maybe even see meaning in them that we have missed. That's the way knowledge accumulates—by different observers converging around, revising, or possibly even rejecting the products of one another's inquiries. So it remains to be seen whether we have enlarged understanding of what happens on the cutting edge of globalization. What do you think?"

The Other Leader demurs. "Look, all this is new to me. I'm not a scholar, and I've never had occasion to think systematically about the subject."

The Cutting-Edger agrees. "That goes for me too," he says. "But what about my question as to what the project adds up to? There's so much contradiction and ambiguity. Do you think you affirmed your four original hypotheses?"

The researcher looks out the window, as if to hope they were close enough to landing that he could avoid the question. They were low enough to see cars moving on the highways, and he could discern the airport runways in the distance. But clearly there was no way he could avoid attempting at least a brief assessment of the broader implications of the inquiry.

"Yes, as I said, my coinvestigators and I are satisfied with how the project turned out. At the outset we did not know whether enough of the leaders would complete our questionnaire and return it to justify writing up the results. Happily, they did, and we are grateful to them (perhaps less so to the respondent who appended this comment: 'This survey is a lot of BULL with no relevance to anything rational or reasonable; who designed it, to what end!'). It was a long and complex questionnaire, but most of the respondents filled it out carefully and fully. Then later, after we entered the responses into the database on our computer, we anxiously focused on the question of whether our Involvement Index would yield enough respondents to justify comparing you and your fellow traveler, the Cutting-Edger and the Other Leader. Again happily, it worked out, as you know. We were also nervous that the business–nonbusiness distinction would prove more powerful than the divide between Cutting-Edgers and Other Leaders, an outcome that would have reduced the question of life on the cutting edge of globalization to a matter of occupation."

"Why would that have been so regrettable?" the Cutting-Edger asks.

"Because we understand globalization to consist of diverse processes and not just those that result from trade and corporate activities. Now let me stress that the questionnaires were—"

The Other Leader interrupts. "Are you avoiding the key question? I'm not asking about your procedures. I want to know about the big picture, about how you can tell a story in the face of all the contradictions and ambiguities, about whether you feel you confirmed your original hypotheses, about whether more is known now about the dynamics of globalization than in 1999 when you launched your project?"

The researcher is quick to respond. "The ambiguities and contradictions are our story, or at least a major part of it. The world is messy, complex, lacking in any single overarching tendencies. Globalization is a composite of diverse boundary-spanning ideas and activities, and so it doesn't lend itself to a single story or big pictures. It is more like a gallery with many pictures.

"As for our four hypotheses, I'd say that to a large extent we did affirm two of them, while one proved to be ill-founded, and at best the fourth yielded murky results. We were right in anticipating that the leadership roles of the Cutting-Edgers would lead them to express more enthusiasm for globalization than that of the Other Leaders. To be sure, our findings indicate that their enthusiasm was not unbounded, but traces of it in the data are unmistakable. And we were even more impressively correct in expecting that the Cutting-Edgers would report more extensive contacts, both electronically and through travel, with the world beyond the United States than those of their counterparts among the Other Leaders. The findings along this dimension were clear and persistent.

"But our hypothesis that the leadership roles of Cutting-Edgers would shape their loyalties to a greater extent than did Other Leaders was not upheld. The expectation in the literature on cosmopolitans—one that clearly presumes that people who move widely around the world will develop a unique set of loyalties that downplay local affiliations and highlight global attachments—is faulty insofar as our data are concerned.

"As for the fourth hypothesis and its premise that Cutting-Edgers are more likely to be sensitive to changing global circumstances than Other Leaders, the findings were not clear-cut. Our analysis of changes across time revealed that, in general, both groups were consistent in their perspectives and behavior and, if anything, the Other Leaders were somewhat more sensitive than the Cutting-Edgers. The September 11 attacks and the acceleration of the antiglobalization movement, among other developments, did contribute to a sense of unease in 2003 that was not discernible in 1999, but such an impact was experienced by both groups. Apparently, the occupation of leadership positions leads to similar reactions to the state of world affairs, irrespective of the extent to which a leader is located on the cutting edge of globalization."

The Other Leader can hardly contain himself. "So would it be fair to say that in fact you are not satisfied with the results of your study?"

The researcher is taken back. "You don't understand. Negative findings can be just as useful as positive ones. They serve to clarify our comprehension. There is no reason for you to be let down by the fact that we haven't come up with grand and unqualified conclusions," he says, adding, "besides, as I've said, research into complex, nontrivial questions rarely comes up with clear-cut and unmistakable conclusions. Hypotheses that fall short serve to provoke thought and then further research. One can almost be pleased that things did not turn out perfectly."

"But I still wish your inquiry generated decisive and unequivocal results," the Cutting-Edger interjects as the Other Leader nods in agreement.

"Let me repeat," says the researcher, "perhaps I encouraged you to have exaggerated expectations, but the truth is that people are complex, that subtleties mark the ways in which people cope with challenges, that there are no blacks and whites—only grays. And that is what our findings are saying. That is the story they tell."

"It's not a very exciting story," the Other Leader comments.

"I'll not apologize for the limits of our data," the researcher replies. "We believe that we have developed a methodology for identifying those who are active on the cutting edge of globalization and the conditions under which they may sustain or temper their orientations toward globalizing phenomena. That's not a trivial accomplishment."

The researcher pauses, wondering whether he should take note of an intriguing idea that one aspect of the data provoked. To his surprise, the Other Leader anticipates his thought. "But aren't you willing to go off the deep end and speculate about some potential implications of your findings that is only hinted at in your data? Come on, give free rein to your speculative self!"

Aware that the trip is nearly over and he will not have to expound at length, the researcher abandons caution. "Okay, but remember, I'm offering an interpretation that is barely a faint trace in our data. It concerns the finding that the early years of Cutting-Edgers involve a wider exposure to the world through their parents than that of the Other Leaders. If it is the case, as the literature suggests, that such an exposure is central to cosmopolitan orientations and if it is assumed, as seems reasonable, that more and more members of upcoming generations will have childhoods marked by movement around the world, then it seems likely that cosmopolitanism, both the pure and the rooted variety, will become even more characteristic of life in modern societies. That is, more and more people will begin to sound like Esther Dyson, whom we quoted in the epigraph of the first chapter. She—"

"Wait a minute!" the Other Leader interjects. "Why is it reasonable to assume that childhoods in the future will increasingly consist of greater exposure to the world beyond the hometown and country of birth? After all, there is only one Esther Dyson!"

The researcher replies, "No, her lifestyle will soon be duplicated by many others. Why? Because people are on the move—for business, pleasure, employment, among other reasons. More and more of us are, so to speak, hybrids. One observer says we are becoming mongrels, mixtures of ethnicities, religions, nationalities, and races. Thus more and more of our children and their children are likely to evolve one or another form of cosmopolitan attitudes and loyalties."[1]

The Other Leader responds, "You are suggesting that individuals are being globalized along with societies, cultures, economies, and institutions."

"You've got it!" the research replies.

"Wow!" both of his traveling companions exclaim. Realizing that the plane is about to land, both of the travelers are disinclined to say more. But the Cutting-Edger has one more question. "Earlier you said there were two ways you would do your project differently if you had a chance. What are they?"

"One is that we would have liked to have had the questionnaire administered to elites in other countries in order to see how unique or typical the leaders in our sample are. We tried, but it proved difficult for colleagues abroad to implement the project. We're still hopeful that a comparative study can be done if we undertake a third, post-Iraq iteration of the project. And the other is that, retrospectively, we realize we didn't ask questions that would allow us trace the causal arrow that links Cutting-Edgers to globalization: Do they favor globalization because they are Cutting-Edgers (the transformation hypothesis), or do they participate in globalizing processes because they are predisposed to view globalization positively (the predisposition hypothesis)? Different aspects of our data can be read as supporting both hypotheses, but we regret that we didn't inquire more directly into the path followed by the causal arrow between the two quite different sources of action. We plan to—"

The researcher's explanation gets jolted to a halt as the plane lands hard on the runway. Warm good-byes follow, with both travelers wishing the researcher good luck with his project.

NOTE

1. See chapter 8, "Mongrel Leadership," in G. Pascal Zachary, *The Global Me: New Cosmopolitans and the Competitive Edge* (New York: PublicAffairs, 2000).

Appendix A

Procedures for Identifying Elites on the Cutting Edge of Globalization

Although we sought to construct a sample of elites who we might reasonably assume were deeply involved in the processes of globalization, from the outset we recognized that it was unlikely that all respondents could reasonably be called "Cutting-Edgers." For this reason we sought to construct a quasi-experimental group identifiable as Cutting-Edgers, with the remainder of the sample serving as a quasi-control group. To do so, we classified respondents according to six configurations of survey responses that we hypothesized might characterize an individual who is on the cutting edge of globalization. These six configurations included individual responses to three questions ("Networking with others abroad is important to me" is subsample 1; "I control change" is subsample 2; and "I am at the top of my profession" is subsample 3) and two items that combined these responses ("I control change" and "I am at the top of my profession" form subsample 4; and "Networking with others abroad is important to me," "I control change" and "I am at the top of my profession" form subsample 5).

To these five configurations of responses we added a sixth: those who scored in the top quartile of an index we constructed to measure each respondent's involvement in global processes (subsample 6). To offset the unwieldiness of respondents' answers to the 170 items in the survey, we reduced these data to six indexes that we hypothesized to measure various aspects of each respondent's attitudes toward and involvement in global processes. To construct each index, we identified survey questions that measured either a respondent's behavior or attitudes, and then we conducted a factor analysis to identify those questions to eliminate from the index. Three of our indexes proved to be statistically significant (i.e., have

Cronbach alpha scores greater than .70). We call these three indexes the Involvement in Global Processes Index (or the Involvement Index); the Positive/Negative Attitudes toward Globalization Index (Orientations Index); and the Interconnectivity in the Wired World Index, a measure of each respondent's usage of telecommunications technologies (or Interconnectivity Index). After conducting the factor analysis, we awarded points for each specific response to each question in an index. For example, one question in the Involvement Index asked, "How would you characterize the relevance of your work with respect to the diverse processes of globalization?" and offered respondents four options: continuously relevant, occasionally relevant, seldom relevant, and never relevant. Respondents indicated the relevance of their work to four options: economic processes, cultural processes, political processes, and "other processes." Each respondent received a score of +2 points for a "continuously relevant" response, a +1 for a response of "occasionally relevant," −1 for "seldom relevant" and −2 for "never relevant." We used similar scoring for each question in an index and aggregated scores for all items in each index. The factor analysis, alpha values, and scoring for the index are provided in appendix B.

We proceeded to test each of these six subsamples against six hypothesized behaviors that characterize an individual who is on the cutting edge of globalization. Since our survey asked respondents about their travel patterns, we tested the six subsamples against two hypotheses about the movements of those on the cutting edge of globalization: first, those who are Cutting-Edgers will travel abroad on business more often than will those who are not involved in globalization; and, second, those who are on the cutting edge of globalization will vacation abroad more often than those who are not. To account for the possible distorting effects of outliers in the two hypotheses, we developed a third that measures the ratio of a respondent's international to domestic travel: those who are Cutting-Edgers will undertake international travel more than domestic travel than will Other Leaders (that is to say, those on the cutting edge of globalization are more likely to travel across sovereign borders more often than they travel within them). This is simply the ratio of the number of times a respondent has traveled internationally in the last two years to the number of times the respondent has traveled domestically in the last two years.[1] Because the survey provides data for both business travel and personal travel, this third hypothesis allows us to test two separate but related questions: Do the members of the proposed subsample travel internationally more frequently for business than they travel domestically? And do the members of the proposed subsample travel internationally more frequently for personal reasons than they travel domestically?[2]

The three indexes offer three additional hypotheses against which to test our six proposed ways to identify those respondents on the cutting edge of globalization. We hypothesize that Cutting-Edgers will score higher on the Involvement Index; will score significantly differently (either positive or negative) on the Orientations Index; and will score higher on the Interconnectivity Index. We should note that it is tautological to test the top quartile of the involvement index against the index itself; for this reason, we conducted only five hypothesis tests on the top quartile of the involvement index.

We present the results of these tests in table A.1. To test each of the six samples against the six hypotheses, we started by conducting an F test to compare the variances of each subsample and the remaining respondents. When the F test failed to disconfirm the hypothesis of equal variances for the two samples, we conducted a t test to see if the hypothesized subsample scored significantly higher on each of the six tests. When the F test indicated unequal variances, we conducted a modified t test to account for the possibility of unequal variances. In table A.1, those tests significant

Table A.1   *T* Tests of Hypothesized Measures of Respondents on the Cutting Edge of Globalization in the 1999 Sample

	Subsample 1	Subsample 2	Subsample 3	Subsample 4	Subsample 5	Subsample 6
Test 1: Do those in the subsample travel internationally on business more often than those not in the sub sample?						
	Yes[b]	Yes[b]	Yes[b]	Yes[b]	Yes[b]	Yes[b]
Test 2: Do those in the subsample travel internationally for personal reasons more often than those not in the sub sample?						
	Yes[b]	No	Yes[b]	No	Yes[a]	Yes[b]
Test 3: Do those in the subsample on average travel more internationally than domestically than those not in the subsample?						
	Yes*[b]	No	No	No	Yes**[a]	Yes*[b]
Test 4: Do those in the subsample on average score higher on the involvement index?						
	Yes***[b]	No	Yes[b]	No	Yes***[b]	N/A
Test 5: Do those in the subsample on average score higher on the orientation index?						
	Yes[b]	Yes[a]	Yes[b]	Yes[b]	Yes[b]	Yes[b]
Test 6: Do those in the subsample on average score higher on the interconnectivity index?						
	Yes[b]	No	Yes[b]	Yes[b]	Yes[b]	Yes[b]

Note: Subsamples are characterized as follows:
Subsample 1: "Networking with others abroad is important" ($n = 605$)
Subsample 2: "I control change" ($n = 295$)
Subsample 3: "I am on top of my profession" ($n = 364$)
Subsample 4: "I control change" and "I am on top of my profession" ($n = 164$)
Subsample 5: "Networking with others abroad is important"; "I control change"; and "I am on top of my profession" ($n = 125$)
Subsample 6: Index 1 top quartile ($n = 187$)
[*] On both business and personal travel.
[**] On personal travel only.
[***] These hypotheses were tested against a revised Involvement Index, which excluded the question on the importance of networking with others abroad in order to eliminate autocorrelation. After excluding this question, the revised index has an alpha score of .7109.
[a] Significant at the .05 level.
[b] Significant at the .01 level.

at the .05 level are indicated by a single asterisk; those significant at the .01 level are indicated by a double asterisk.

As the table shows, three of the six proposed subsamples of cutting-edge elite generate significantly different results for each of the six hypothesis tests. One of the subsamples has weaker results, however. Recall that the third hypothesis includes two *t* tests, on the ratios of international-to-domestic business travel and international-to-domestic personal travel. Of these two ratios, subsample 5 scored significantly higher than the remainder of the sample on only the personal travel ratio. This subsample also scored at a lower level of confidence (.05) on the second hypothesis (that Cutting-Edgers vacation abroad more than Other Leaders). For these reasons, we considered the fifth proposed subsample to be inferior to the other two subsamples that met all six tests at a higher level of confidence and that passed both elements of the third hypothesis.

Given that both subsample 1 and subsample 6 scored significantly higher on all six hypotheses, the question became, which one should we use to identify those respondents on the cutting edge? We opted for the sixth subsample, which consists of those respondents in the top quartile of the Involvement Index. The top quartile offers the best quasi-experimental group for two reasons. First, because the Involvement Index purports to measure a respondent's involvement in global processes, the six hypothesis tests seem to establish the validity of the index. Second, because we constructed the Involvement Index from fifteen questions from the survey, the sixth subsample is based on more data than the first, which we constructed using responses to a single survey question. We therefore concluded that the top quartile of the Involvement Index provides a group of Cutting-Edgers with face validity as well as a more reliable representation than the other measures. To be sure, to have selected the top quartile of the Involvement Index is to have used an arbitrary value but one that yields a manageable subsample of 187 of the 741 respondents who provided enough data to receive an overall score on the Involvement Index and who are sufficiently numerous to allow for meaningful comparisons with the 554 Other Leaders.[3] That the top quartile produces a manageable subsample of 187 respondents (versus over 600 respondents from the first subsample) is an additional advantage to using this subsample as our group of Cutting-Edgers.

NOTES

1. These ratios offer a quick glimpse at the travel patterns of our respondents, since a value greater than 1 indicates that the respondent has traveled internationally more than domestically. Forty-two respondents had a business-travel ratio greater than 1, while 75 respondents had a personal-travel ratio greater than 1.

2. One possible criticism of these three hypotheses is that an individual's travel patterns—or other behaviors—may not say anything meaningful about his or her involvement in the processes of globalization. For example, the business executives we sampled, one might argue, are more likely to delegate to subordinates many of the more tedious or onerous activities we asked about in our survey, such as international travel. Fortunately, our survey allowed us to test this hypothesis using the respondents' answers to our question "Do you consider yourself among the leaders of your organization or profession; close to the top; in the middle range; or toward the bottom?" Using respondents' professional self-identification to conduct t tests, we found that respondents who identified themselves as being at the top of their profession score significantly higher on all three indexes, while those who identify themselves as being toward the bottom of their profession score significantly lower on all three indexes. Assuming that our indexes are valid measures, we believe that the presumption that Cutting-Edgers will travel more than other respondents is a reasonable one.

3. Because 148 respondents failed to answer one or more of the fifteen questions used to construct the Involvement Index, only 741 respondents received a score on it; of these, 187 were classified as cutting-edgers, while the remaining 554 become our control group. This accounts for the total number of respondents received: $554 + 187 + 148 = 889$.

Appendix B

Factor Analysis for Index on Involvement in Global Processes

Table B.1 Principal Factors (11 factors retained)

Factor	Eigenvalue	Difference	Proportion	Cumulative
1	3.52240	1.46671	0.4333	0.4333
2	2.05569	0.73707	0.2529	0.6861
3	1.31862	0.40617	0.1622	0.8483
4	0.91245	0.17661	0.1122	0.9606
5	0.73584	0.32244	0.0905	1.0511
6	0.41340	0.09290	0.0509	1.1019
7	0.32051	0.09063	0.0394	1.1414
8	0.22988	0.09056	0.0283	1.1696
9	0.13932	0.08418	0.0171	1.1868
10	0.05514	0.03852	0.0068	1.1936
11	0.01662	0.02812	0.0020	1.1956
12	−0.01150	0.01494	0.0014	1.1942
13	−0.02644	0.02465	−0.0033	1.1909
14	−0.05109	0.01002	−0.0063	1.1846
15	−0.06112	0.01936	−0.0075	1.1771
16	−0.08048	0.03470	−0.0099	1.1672
17	−0.11518	0.02473	−0.0142	1.1531
18	−0.13991	0.04240	−0.0172	1.1359
19	−0.18231	0.00711	−0.0224	1.1134
20	−0.18942	0.01304	−0.0233	1.0901
21	−0.20246	0.04422	−0.0249	1.0652
22	−0.24668	0.03688	−0.0303	1.0349
23	−0.28357	.	−0.0349	1.0000

Note: observations = 729.

Table B.2   Factor Loadings

Variable	1	2	3	4	5	6
i2econom	0.28770	0.34889	0.10058	0.38641	−0.14923	−0.00070
i2cultur	0.24254	0.37836	0.06869	0.44147	0.11389	0.06812
i2politi	0.22522	0.30913	−0.06335	0.53544	−0.06990	0.09367
ii2	0.43144	0.26408	0.30471	−0.11292	0.06495	−0.02475
*ii4busin	0.49528	0.20169	0.37598	−0.13179	−0.23209	−0.04851
ii4vacat	0.22285	0.02704	0.08178	0.01844	−0.06073	0.01611
ii7born	0.73588	−0.50235	−0.21352	0.05553	−0.09593	−0.05595
ii7citiz	0.72778	−0.52523	−0.22239	0.08472	−0.11309	−0.05695
ii7emplo	0.63198	−0.44392	−0.17479	0.09525	−0.06912	−0.02890
ii9exper	0.45582	0.14459	0.26069	−0.16631	−0.03999	0.05555
*ii9assig	0.25628	0.20815	0.24073	−0.04648	−0.32062	−0.20769
*ii9freel	0.25196	0.05676	0.07726	−0.06235	0.18955	0.14677
*ii9curio	0.16739	−0.01886	−0.03645	0.06963	0.28710	0.07021
*ii9globa	0.26090	0.07837	0.06930	0.09426	0.14633	−0.04535
iii3asso	0.54400	0.22865	0.30380	−0.14834	0.14906	−0.04302
*iii3huma	0.02838	0.11676	−0.09359	0.09867	0.35471	−0.08825
iv5yes	0.32032	0.59824	−0.58765	−0.19399	0.00409	−0.12205
*iv5nofru	−0.02875	−0.09455	0.05886	−0.01114	−0.11876	0.25379
iv5nores	−0.28231	−0.53615	0.54566	0.23531	0.18363	−0.22387
*iv5noobl	−0.10684	−0.14549	0.13711	−0.00118	−0.23357	0.36771
iv10	0.28030	0.07420	0.16849	−0.22550	0.12322	0.09212
vi3	0.40924	−0.17685	0.01524	−0.04436	0.19572	0.14020
vi9	0.45610	−0.08193	−0.01584	−0.08137	0.24307	0.11132

Variable	7	8	9	10	11	Uniqueness
i2econom	0.01678	−0.05178	0.00704	−0.01926	0.00115	0.61042
i2cultur	−0.05654	0.07943	−0.03793	−0.00561	−0.03087	0.56887
i2politi	−0.09933	−0.08756	0.00286	−0.02153	0.01110	0.53121
ii2	0.00700	0.08409	−0.07711	0.05491	−0.01619	0.61734
*ii4busin	0.09889	−0.06814	−0.03458	−0.01452	0.03398	0.48208
ii4vacat	0.36358	−0.07483	−0.09249	0.00130	−0.02856	0.79147
ii7born	−0.02841	0.01540	0.01663	−0.02317	−0.02852	0.14245
ii7citiz	−0.04831	0.05814	−0.06107	−0.01005	0.01563	0.11202
ii7emplo	−0.01748	0.07955	−0.01886	0.03967	0.02502	0.34911
ii9exper	−0.14805	−0.03863	0.04305	−0.03044	0.00325	0.64482
*ii9assig	0.09714	0.07405	0.07020	0.03169	−0.00839	0.66403
*ii9freel	−0.00883	−0.09024	−0.12597	0.01393	0.07996	0.83529
*ii9curio	0.23881	0.09970	−0.09037	−0.02038	0.00104	0.80254
*ii9globa	0.10215	0.00056	0.21972	0.04934	0.04871	0.82511
iii3asso	−0.12116	0.10381	0.00803	0.01884	−0.02292	0.48700
*iii3huma	0.03550	0.22173	0.04105	0.03634	0.01013	0.77993
iv5yes	0.00532	−0.04577	−0.00476	−0.01401	0.00162	0.13929
*iv5nofru	−0.09159	−0.02251	−0.05802	0.16252	−0.02041	0.86904
iv5nores	−0.03204	−0.07271	−0.02225	−0.02332	−0.00045	0.18854

Table B.2   (continued)

Variable	7	8	9	10	11	Uniqueness
*iv5noobl	0.10671	0.20471	0.09356	−0.06586	0.00979	0.69237
iv10	−0.14239	0.05367	−0.02604	−0.08961	−0.00373	0.78114
vi3	0.05457	−0.17445	0.14838	0.03427	−0.02144	0.68402
vi9	0.05271	−0.13363	0.03990	−0.03861	−0.03414	0.68203

* Variables dropped from index.

Appendix C

1999 Questionnaire

Foreign Policy Leadership Project

Sponsored by:

Duke University
George Washington University
Rutgers University

If you would like to respond to this survey through our website, please go to:

http://www.gwu.edu/~fplp/survey99ml.htm

Note to Respondent: The word "globalization" appears in several of the ensuing questions without being defined. If (but only if) you have a particular conception of what is meant by the term as you respond to the questions, kindly indicate here the essential meaning you bring to the concept:

If you have any additional comments you would like to make upon completion of the questionnaire, kindly indicate them here (or on the back page) before returning the questionnaire in the envelope provided:

- How would you characterize your expectations for the next generation when its members reach your age?
    - _____ much better
    - _____ better
    - _____ same
    - _____ worse
    - _____ much worse
    - _____ other (kindly specify)
- How would you characterize the relevance of your work with respect to the diverse processes of globalization? (check **only one** in **each row**)

	continuously relevant	occasionally relevant	seldom relevant	never relevant
economic processes	_____	_____	_____	_____
cultural processes	_____	_____	_____	_____
political processes	_____	_____	_____	_____
other processes (kindly specify)	_____	_____	_____	_____

- To the extent your work is relevant to the processes of globalization, do you usually
    - _____ seek to advance the processes
    - _____ seek to resist the processes
    - _____ seek to redirect the processes
    - _____ not think about its larger consequences
    - _____ my work has no relevance for globalization
    - _____ other (kindly specify)
- With respect to the course of events in world affairs, do you (check **only one** in **each row**)

	often	occasionally	never
have a sense of responsibility for them	_____	_____	_____
worry about them	_____	_____	_____
try to affect them	_____	_____	_____
feel ineffective with respect to them	_____	_____	_____
other (kindly specify)	_____	_____	_____

- What locale do you consider to be your "home"? (**check all that apply**)
    - _____ where I was raised
    - _____ where I am a citizen
    - _____ where I feel a sense of ethnic, racial, or religious community
    - _____ where I am employed
    - _____ where my immediate family or partner lives
    - _____ where I plan to retire
    - _____ wherever my professional colleagues may be
    - _____ I do not regard any particular geographic place as "home"
    - _____ other (kindly specify)

- In what sense, if any, is the "world" your home? (**check all that apply**)
  - _____ in the sense that I earn my living in many parts of it
  - _____ in the sense that I feel a connection with humanity everywhere
  - _____ in the sense that I have traveled widely
  - _____ in the sense that I am keenly aware of the large extent to which the world is interdependent
  - _____ no, the "world" has no special meaning for me
  - _____ other (kindly elaborate)

The following cluster of questions asks about your movement around the world:

- Do you travel with a laptop computer?
  yes _____   no _____
- Is networking with others abroad important to you?
  yes _____   no _____
- Have you ever thought of yourself as an expatriate?
  yes _____   no _____
- Approximately how many times have you traveled abroad in the past two years?
  on business _____   for a vacation or other personal matters _____
- Approximately how many times a year do you travel within your country but outside your city of residence?
  on business _____   for a vacation or other personal matters _____
- Approximately how many times have you traveled in the last decade to countries of
  Africa _____
  Asia _____
  Europe _____
  Middle East _____
  South America _____
  Other (kindly specify) _____
- Approximately how many times have you resided for more than six months outside the country
  in which you were born _____
  of which you are a citizen _____
  in which you are employed _____
- With respect to your country of citizenship and residence,
  Have you been a citizen of more than one country?
  yes _____   no _____
  Are you still a citizen of the country where you were born?
  yes _____   no _____
    If "no," how many years did you live in your country of birth? _____

How many years have you lived in the country of which you are
  now a resident? _____

- What are the bases for your contacts abroad? (**check all that apply**)
  _____ your professional expertise is in demand
  _____ your company's or organization's assignments
  _____ your freelance work involves foreign contacts
  _____ your curiosity leads you to distant places
  _____ the continuing globalization of world affairs
  _____ other (kindly specify)

**The following questions ask about your contacts other than
through travel:**

- How often do you employ the following methods to carry forward your
  interactions with counterparts abroad? (check **only one** in **each row**)

	very often	occasionally	seldom	rarely	never
e-mail or other online services	_____	_____	_____	_____	_____
cellular telephone	_____	_____	_____	_____	_____
regular telephone	_____	_____	_____	_____	_____
teleconferencing	_____	_____	_____	_____	_____
air mail	_____	_____	_____	_____	_____
fax	_____	_____	_____	_____	_____
other (kindly specify)	_____	_____	_____	_____	_____

- Approximately how many names do you add to your address book,
  roll-a-dex, or computer each month?
  _____ none
  _____ 1 to 5
  _____ 6 to 10
  _____ 11 to 25
  _____ 26 or more

- To what extent do you feel a sense of identity with each of the following?
  (check **only one** in **each row**)

	closely identified	somewhat identified	mildly identified	none
family and friends	_____	_____	_____	_____
neighbors	_____	_____	_____	_____
community where you reside	_____	_____	_____	_____
supervisors and/or those you supervise	_____	_____	_____	_____
professional associates abroad	_____	_____	_____	_____

professional associates
   at home   _____   _____   _____   _____
an ethnic or
   racial group   _____   _____   _____   _____
political party
   or philosophy   _____   _____   _____   _____
country of birth   _____   _____   _____   _____
a region   _____   _____   _____   _____
fellow citizens   _____   _____   _____   _____
humanity at large   _____   _____   _____   _____
other (kindly specify)   _____   _____   _____   _____

- Of the three or four persons with whom you most enjoy socializing, what are their nationalities?

_____   _____   _____   _____

The following cluster of questions asks about your orientation toward public affairs:

- In general, do you feel that you control change, or does change control you?
  - _____ I control change
  - _____ change controls me
  - _____ not sure
  - _____ other (kindly specify)
- On balance, do you regard the diverse processes of globalization as **(check all that apply)**
  - _____ making people more selfish
  - _____ sharpening the skills of individuals
  - _____ fostering political apathy
  - _____ promoting the power of corporations
  - _____ sensitizing people to other cultures
  - _____ widening the gap between rich and poor nations
  - _____ widening the gap between rich and poor individuals
  - _____ creating too much homogeneity
  - _____ other (kindly specify)
- On balance, how would you assess the impact of the diverse processes of globalization on (check **only one** in **each row**)

	Undermining	Enhancing	Having no effect
local communities	_____	_____	_____
individual altruism	_____	_____	_____
human rights	_____	_____	_____
political democracy	_____	_____	_____
economic integration	_____	_____	_____
creation of jobs	_____	_____	_____

cultural diversity	_____	_____	_____
ecological sensitivities	_____	_____	_____
ethnic identities	_____	_____	_____
capitalism	_____	_____	_____
other (kindly specify)	_____	_____	_____

- Which of the following do you regard as *essential* global issues that need to be addressed in the next decade? (**check all that apply**)
  - _____ climate change
  - _____ ethnic conflicts
  - _____ transnational organized crime
  - _____ global governance
  - _____ the stability of the world economy
  - _____ corruption
  - _____ the disposition of nuclear materials
  - _____ epidemics
  - _____ other (kindly specify)
- Are you inclined to actively promote dialogue in your home or professional community about any or all of the issues checked in the previous question? (**check all that apply**)
  - _____ yes, I feel a sense of responsibility in this regard
  - _____ no, efforts to promote dialogue are fruitless
  - _____ no, my leadership responsibilities do not encompass these issues
  - _____ I feel no obligation to participate in dialogues on these issues
  - _____ other (kindly specify)
- Would you say patriotism is (**check all that apply**)
  - _____ an increasingly obsolete sentiment
  - _____ of continuing major importance
  - _____ of largely symbolic or psychological significance
  - _____ no longer relevant to the course of events
  - _____ other (kindly specify)
- If a vital choice involving your company or organization could not be avoided, would you put its interests ahead of those of your country?
  - _____ yes _____ no _____ not sure _____ I avoid such choices
- If a vital choice involving your career could not be avoided, would you put your professional needs ahead of those of your company or organization?
  - _____ yes _____ no _____ not sure _____ I avoid such choices
- If your professional responsibilities and your civic obligations come into conflict, which are likely to prevail most of the time?
  - _____ professional obligations
  - _____ civic obligations
  - _____ not sure
  - _____ I avoid such conflicts

- To what extent do you feel you have more in common with counterparts in your profession elsewhere in the world than with your fellow citizens in different lines of work? (check **only one**)

  _____ I have more in common with my fellow citizens than distant professional counterparts

  _____ I have more in common with professional counterparts abroad than with my fellow citizens

  _____ I feel equal commonality with both my fellow citizens and my professional counterparts abroad

  _____ other (kindly specify)

- On balance, do you believe globalization is (**check all that apply**)

  _____ a "good" set of processes?

  _____ a "bad" set of processes?

  _____ a "good" set of processes for some and a "bad" set for others?

  _____ a set of processes that can be facilitated?

  _____ a set of processes that should be facilitated?

  _____ a set of processes that can be altered, hindered, or retarded?

  _____ a set of processes that should be altered, hindered, or retarded?

  _____ other (kindly amplify)

- Do you believe an organization with a workforce that shares the same background is more productive than one that has diverse backgrounds?

  _____ same background   _____ diverse backgrounds

  _____ other (kindly specify)

- How would you rank the role the following can play in world affairs? (check **only one** in **each row**)

	very important	somewhat important	not very important	not unimportant	not sure
United Nations	___	___	___	___	___
World Bank	___	___	___	___	___
World Trade Organization	___	___	___	___	___
Amnesty International	___	___	___	___	___
IMF	___	___	___	___	___
G-7	___	___	___	___	___
NATO	___	___	___	___	___
NAFTA	___	___	___	___	___
European Union	___	___	___	___	___
United States	___	___	___	___	___
ASEAN	___	___	___	___	___
Greenpeace	___	___	___	___	___
other (kindly specify)	___	___	___	___	___

- How would you describe your views on trade issues?
  _____ pro–free trade
  _____ selectively protectionist
  _____ protectionist
  _____ not sure
  _____ other (kindly elaborate)
- To what extent do you consider the following a threat to your well-being? (check **only one** in **each row**)

	substantial threat	moderate threat	mild threat	not a threat at all	not sure
social movements	____	____	____	____	____
professional competitors	____	____	____	____	____
multinational corporations	____	____	____	____	____
gap between rich and poor	____	____	____	____	____
certain individuals	____	____	____	____	____
certain countries	____	____	____	____	____
terrorist groups	____	____	____	____	____
nationalism	____	____	____	____	____
globalization	____	____	____	____	____
other (kindly specify)	____	____	____	____	____

- Do you regard the efforts to bail out countries in economic trouble like Russia and Brazil as (check **only one**)
  _____ futile
  _____ questionable
  _____ worthwhile
  _____ necessary
  _____ unsure
  _____ other (kindly elaborate)
- Did the advent of the financial crises that began in Thailand in 1997 and then spread around the world (**check all that apply**)
  _____ give you pause as to the virtues of globalization
  _____ affirm your negative orientations toward globalization
  _____ reinforce your positive orientations toward globalization
  _____ had no impact on your views of globalization
  _____ other (kindly elaborate)
- How would you summarize your views on the proper role of government in economic matters? (check **only one**)
  _____ minimum regulation
  _____ some regulation
  _____ maximum regulation

_____ not sure

_____ other (kindly elaborate)

- What do you regard as proper roles of national governments with regard to private firms and the global economy? (**check all that apply**)

    _____ a service role (providing infrastructure, police protection, health and education, etc.)

    _____ prevent potential monopolies/cartels and ensure fair and honest competition

    _____ protect domestic firms and jobs from foreign competition

    _____ subsidize lagging economic sectors to aid their competitiveness in foreign markets

    _____ subsidize promising economic sectors to aid their competitiveness in foreign markets

    _____ other (kindly elaborate)

The following questions ask about the ends and means of American foreign policy:

- This question asks you to indicate your position on certain propositions that are sometimes described as lessons that the United States should have learned from past experiences abroad. Please indicate how strongly you agree or disagree with each statement by checking **only one check** in **each** row.

	Agree Strongly	Agree Somewhat	Disagree Somewhat	Disagree Strongly	No Opinion
There is considerable validity in the "domino theory" that when one nation falls to aggressor nations, others nearby will soon follow a similar path	_____	_____	_____	_____	_____
Any communist victory is a defeat for America's national interest	_____	_____	_____	_____	_____
It is vital to enlist the cooperation of the UN in settling international disputes	_____	_____	_____	_____	_____
Russia is generally expansionist rather than defensive in its foreign policy goals	_____	_____	_____	_____	_____

There is nothing wrong
   with using the CIA to
   try to undermine
   hostile governments   _____   _____   _____   _____   _____

The U.S. should give
   economic aid to
   poorer countries even
   if it means high prices
   at home   _____   _____   _____   _____   _____

The U.S. should take all
   steps including the
   use of force to prevent
   aggression by any
   expansionist power   _____   _____   _____   _____   _____

Rather than simply
   countering our
   opponent's thrusts, it
   is necessary to strike
   at the heart of the
   opponent's power   _____   _____   _____   _____   _____

- Turning to more general considerations, here is a list of possible foreign policy goals that the United States might have. Please indicate how much importance you think should be attached to each goal. (check **only one** box in **each** row)

	Very Important	Moderately Important	Slightly Important	Not at all Important	Not sure
Containing communism	_____	_____	_____	_____	_____
Helping to improve the standard of living in less developed countries	_____	_____	_____	_____	_____
Worldwide arms control	_____	_____	_____	_____	_____
Combating world hunger	_____	_____	_____	_____	_____
Strengthening the United Nations	_____	_____	_____	_____	_____
Fostering international cooperation to solve common problems, such as food, inflation and energy	_____	_____	_____	_____	_____

The following questions ask about your personal background:

- _____ male _____ female   year of birth _____
- What is the highest educational degree you have obtained? _____
- Did you ever study abroad? _____ yes _____ no
- What do you regard as your primary occupation? _____ secondary? _____
- Roughly speaking, is your annual dollar income from all sources
    _____ less than $100,000
    _____ between 100,000 and $999,999
    _____ $1,000,000 or more
- Approximately what proportion of your charitable donations each year goes to
    local charities?   _____
    national charities?   _____
    international charities? _____
    Total   100%
- Are you a member of an ethnic, racial, or religious minority in the country in which you live?
    _____ yes _____ no
- Do you think of yourself as
    _____ among the top leaders of your organization or profession
    _____ close to the top
    _____ in the middle range
    _____ toward the bottom
    _____ other (kindly elaborate)
- How many languages do you read and/or speak?
    _____ one
    _____ two
    _____ three
    _____ four
    _____ five or more
- Do you regard one country as "home"?
    _____ yes _____ no   If yes, which one? _____
- Did either or both of your parents (**check all that apply**)
    _____ come from a country other than the U.S.?
    _____ speak other languages in addition to English?
    _____ travel extensively?
    _____ take you on their travels when you were young?
- Roughly, how many employers have you worked for since completing your education?
    _____ none _____ one _____ two _____ three
    _____ four _____ five or more

- How many years have you been with your present employer?
  - _____ one or less
  - _____ two to five
  - _____ six to ten
  - _____ eleven to twenty
  - _____ twenty-one plus
- In your work, approximately how many people are you responsible for?
  - _____ none   _____ 1 to 10   _____ 11 to 50
  - _____ 51 to 500   _____ more than 500
- How would you describe your views on political matters?
  - _____ Far left   _____ Moderate   _____ Far right
  - _____ Very liberal   _____ Somewhat conservative   _____ Other
  - _____ Somewhat liberal   _____ Very conservative   _____ Not sure
- Generally speaking, do you think of yourself as a Republican, a Democrat, an Independent, or what?
  - _____ Republican   _____ Independent   _____ Other
  - _____ Democrat   _____ No preference
- If there are any other aspects of your life relevant to the processes of globalization you want to note, please feel free to do so here:

Thank you very much for sharing your ideas.

Kindly return to Foreign Policy Leadership Project
The George Washington University
2130 H Street, NW, Suite 709G
Washington, DC 20052

Appendix D

2003 Questionnaire

Foreign Policy Leadership Project

Sponsored by:

Duke University
George Washington University
Rutgers University

If you would like to respond to this survey through our website, please go to:

http://www.gwu.edu/~fplp2002/survey02ms.htm

NOTE TO RESPONDENT: The word "globalization" appears in several of the ensuing questions without being defined. If (but only if) you have a particular conception of what is meant by the term as you respond to the questions, kindly indicate here the essential meaning you bring to the concept:

- On balance, what have been the consequences of globalization for the United States?

   _____ _____ _____ _____ _____

   _____ mostly good
   _____ both good and bad
   _____ mostly bad

_____ neither good nor bad
_____ other (kindly specify)

- How would you characterize your expectations for the next generation when its members reach your age?

_____ much better
_____ better
_____ same
_____ worse
_____ much worse
_____ other (kindly specify)

- How would you characterize the relevance of your work with respect to the diverse processes of globalization? (check **only one** in **each row**)

	continuously relevant	occasionally relevant	seldom relevant	never relevant
economic processes	_____	_____	_____	_____
cultural processes	_____	_____	_____	_____
political processes	_____	_____	_____	_____
other processes (kindly specify)	_____	_____	_____	_____

- To the extent your work is relevant to the processes of globalization, do you usually (check **only one**)

_____ seek to advance the processes
_____ seek to resist the processes
_____ seek to redirect the processes
_____ not think about its larger consequences
_____ my work has no relevance for globalization
_____ other (kindly specify)

- With respect to the course of events in world affairs, do you (check **only one** in **each row**)

	often	occasionally	never
have a sense of responsibility for them	_____		_____
worry about them	_____	_____	_____
try to affect them	_____	_____	_____
feel ineffective with respect to them	_____	_____	_____
other (kindly specify)	_____	_____	_____

- How would you characterize your reaction to the following recent events? (check **one item** in **each row**)

	Gave you pause as to the virtues of globalization	Affirmed your negative attitude toward globalization	Reinforced your positive orientations toward globalization	Had no impact on your views of globalization
The '97-'99 Asian financial crisis	_____	_____	_____	_____

Protests against international economic institutions	_____	_____	_____	_____
The terrorist attacks of Sept. 11, 2001	_____	_____	_____	_____
The contested presidential election in 2000	_____	_____	_____	_____
The Israel-Palestine conflict	_____	_____	_____	_____
The 2001 Enron scandal	_____	_____	_____	_____

- What locale do you consider to be your "home"? (**check all that apply**)
  - _____ where I feel a sense of ethnic, racial, or religious community
  - _____ where I am employed
  - _____ where I plan to retire
  - _____ wherever my professional colleagues may be
  - _____ I do not regard any particular geographic place as "home"
  - _____ other (kindly specify)
- In what sense, if any, is the "world" your home? (**check all that apply**)
  - _____ in the sense that I earn my living in many parts of it
  - _____ in the sense that I feel a connection with humanity everywhere
  - _____ in the sense that I have traveled widely
  - _____ in the sense that I am keenly aware of the large extent to which the world is interdependent
  - _____ no, the "world" has no special meaning for me
  - _____ other (kindly elaborate)

The following cluster of questions asks about your movement around the world:

- Do you travel with a laptop or handheld computer?
  yes _____   no _____
- Is networking with others abroad important to you?
  yes _____   no _____
- Approximately how many times have you traveled abroad in the past two years?
  on business _____ for a vacation or other personal matters _____
- Approximately how many times a year do you travel within your country but outside your city of residence?
  on business _____ for a vacation or other personal matters _____
- Approximately how many times have you resided for more than six months outside the country
  in which you were born   _____

of which you are a citizen   _____

in which you are employed _____

* With respect to your country of citizenship and residence,

                                 _____   _____

                                 _____   _____

                                 _____

Have you been a citizen of more than one country?

    _____ yes   _____ no

Are you still a citizen of the country where you were born?

    _____ yes   _____ no

How many years have you lived in the country of which you are now a resident? _____

* What are the bases for your contacts abroad? (**check all that apply**)
  _____ your professional expertise is in demand
  _____ your company's or organization's assignments
  _____ your freelance work involves foreign contacts
  _____ your curiosity leads you to distant places
  _____ the continuing globalization of world affairs
  _____ other (kindly specify)

The following questions ask about your contacts other than through travel:

* How often do you employ the following methods to carry forward your interactions with counterparts abroad? (check **only one** in **each row**)

	very often	occasionally	seldom	rarely	never
e-mail or other online services	_____	_____	_____	_____	_____
cellular telephone	_____	_____	_____	_____	_____
regular telephone	_____	_____	_____	_____	_____
teleconferencing	_____	_____	_____	_____	_____
air mail	_____	_____	_____	_____	_____
fax	_____	_____	_____	_____	_____
other (kindly specify)	_____	_____	_____	_____	_____

* Approximately how many names do you add to your address book, Rolodex, or computer each month?
  _____ none
  _____ 1 to 5
  _____ 6 to 10
  _____ 11 to 25
  _____ 26 or more

- To what extent do you feel a sense of identity with each of the following? (check **only one** in **each row**)

	closely identified	somewhat identified	mildly identified	none
neighbors	___	___	___	___
community where you reside	___	___	___	___
supervisors and/or those you supervise	___	___	___	___
professional associates abroad	___	___	___	___
professional associates at home	___	___	___	___
an ethnic or racial group	___	___	___	___
religious organizations	___	___	___	___
political party or philosophy	___	___	___	___
fellow citizens	___	___	___	___
humanity at large other (kindly specify)	___	___	___	___

The following cluster of questions asks about your orientation toward public affairs:

- In general, do you feel that you control change, or does change control you?
  - ___ I control change
  - ___ change controls me
  - ___ not sure
  - ___ other (kindly specify)
- On balance, do you regard the diverse processes of globalization as (**check all that apply**)
  - ___ making people more selfish
  - ___ sharpening the skills of individuals
  - ___ fostering political apathy
  - ___ promoting the power of corporations
  - ___ sensitizing people to other cultures
  - ___ widening the gap between rich and poor nations
  - ___ widening the gap between rich and poor individuals
  - ___ creating too much homogeneity
  - ___ other (kindly specify)
- On balance, how would you assess the impact of the diverse processes of globalization on (check **only one** in **each row**)

	Undermining	Enhancing	Having no effect
local communities	___	___	___
individual altruism	___	___	___
human rights	___	___	___
political democracy	___	___	___

economic integration	_____	_____	_____
creation of jobs	_____	_____	_____
cultural diversity	_____	_____	_____
ecological sensitivities	_____	_____	_____
ethnic identities	_____	_____	_____
capitalism	_____	_____	_____
religion	_____	_____	_____
other (kindly specify)	_____	_____	_____

- Which of the following do you regard as *essential* global issues that need to be addressed in the next decade? (**check all that apply**)

  _____ strengthening the United Nations

  _____ climate change

  _____ ethnic conflicts

  _____ transnational organized crime

  _____ promoting democracy

  _____ global governance

  _____ terrorism

  _____ the stability of the world economy

  _____ worldwide arms control

  _____ corruption

  _____ the disposition of nuclear materials

  _____ epidemics

  _____ international drug trafficking

  _____ other (kindly specify)

- Are you inclined to actively promote dialogue in your home or professional community about any or all of the issues checked in the previous question? (**check all that apply**)

  _____ yes, I feel a sense of responsibility in this regard

  _____ no, efforts to promote dialogue are fruitless

  _____ no, my leadership responsibilities do not encompass these issues

  _____ I feel no obligation to participate in dialogues on these issues

  _____ other (kindly specify)

- Would you say patriotism (**check all that apply in each row**)

	of continuing major importance	of largely symbolic or psychological significance	an increasingly obsolete sentiment	no longer relevant to the course of events	other (kindly specify)
for you personally is ...	_____	_____	_____	_____	_____
for the United States is ...	_____	_____	_____	_____	_____
for most of the world is ...	_____	_____	_____	_____	_____

- If a vital choice involving your company or organization could not be avoided, would you put its interests ahead of those of your country?

  _____ yes _____ no _____ not sure _____ I avoid such choices

- If a vital choice involving your career could not be avoided, would you put your professional needs ahead of those of your company or organization?

  _____ yes _____ no _____ not sure _____ I avoid such choices

- If your professional responsibilities and your civic obligations come into conflict, which are likely to prevail most of the time?

  _____ professional obligations   _____ civic obligations

  _____ not sure   _____ I avoid such conflicts

- To what extent do you feel you have more in common with counterparts in your profession elsewhere in the world than with your fellow citizens in different lines of work? (check **only one**)

  _____ I have more in common with my fellow citizens than distant professional counterparts

  _____ I have more in common with professional counterparts abroad than with my fellow citizens

  _____ I feel equal commonality with both my fellow citizens and my professional counterparts abroad

  _____ other (kindly specify)

- How would you rate the role the following can play in world affairs? (check **only one** in **each row**)

	very important	somewhat important	not very important	not unimportant	not sure
United Nations					
World Bank					
World Trade Organization					
Amnesty International					
IMF					
NATO					
European Union					
United States					
other (kindly specify)					

- How would you describe your views on trade issues?

  _____ pro–free trade

  _____ selectively protectionist

  _____ protectionist

  _____ not sure

  _____ other (kindly elaborate)

- To what extent do you consider the following a threat to your well-being? (check **only one** in **each row**)

	substantial threat	moderate threat	mild threat	not a threat at all	not sure
social movements	___	___	___	___	___
professional competitors	___	___	___	___	___
religious fundamentalism	___	___	___	___	___
multinational corporations	___	___	___	___	___
gap between rich and poor	___	___	___	___	___
certain individuals	___	___	___	___	___
certain countries	___	___	___	___	___
terrorist groups	___	___	___	___	___
nationalism	___	___	___	___	___
globalization	___	___	___	___	___
environmental degradation	___	___	___	___	___
other (kindly specify)	___	___	___	___	___

- Do you regard efforts to bail out countries in economic trouble like Russia as (check **only one**)
  - _____ futile
  - _____ questionable
  - _____ worthwhile
  - _____ necessary
  - _____ unsure
  - _____ other (kindly elaborate)

- Which of the following recent events do you consider a cause or consequence of globalization? (check **only one** in **each row**)

	a cause of globalization	a consequence of globalization	both a cause and a consequence	neither a cause nor a consequence	not sure
The '97-'99 Asian economic crisis	___	___	___	___	___
Protests against international economic institutions (battle of Seattle, etc.)	___	___	___	___	___
The terrorist attacks of Sept. 11, 2001	___	___	___	___	___
The contested presidential election of 2000	___	___	___	___	___

The Palestinian-
Israeli conflict   _____   _____   _____   _____   _____
The 2001 Enron
scandal   _____   _____   _____   _____   _____

- How would you summarize your views on the proper role of government in economic matters? (check **only one**)
  - _____ minimum regulation
  - _____ some regulation
  - _____ maximum regulation
  - _____ not sure
  - _____ other (kindly elaborate)
- What do you regard as proper roles of national governments with regard
  to private firms and the global economy? (**check all that apply**)
  - _____ a service role (providing infrastructure, police protection, health
    and education, etc.)
  - _____ prevent potential monopolies/cartels and ensure fair and honest
    competition
  - _____ protect domestic firms and jobs from foreign competition
  - _____ subsidize lagging economic sectors to aid their competitiveness
    in foreign markets
  - _____ subsidize promising economic sectors to aid their competitive-
    ness in foreign markets
  - _____ other (kindly elaborate)
- Would you say patriotism (**check only one** in **each row**)

	temporarily increased since September 11th	permanently increased since September 11th	is unchanged since September 11th	other (kindly specify)
for you personally has...	_____	_____	_____	_____
for the United States has...	_____	_____	_____	_____
for most of the world has...	_____	_____	_____	_____

- On balance, do you believe globalization is a set of processes that (**check
  all that apply**)
  - _____ can be facilitated?
  - _____ should be facilitated?
  - _____ can be altered, hindered, or retarded?
  - _____ should be altered, hindered, or retarded?
  - _____ other (kindly amplify)

The following question asks about the goals of American foreign policy:

- Turning to more general considerations, here is a list of possible foreign policy goals that the United States might have. Please indicate how much importance you think should be attached to each goal. (Check **only one** in **each row**)

	Very important	Moderately important	Slightly important	Not at all important	Not sure
Preventing the spread of nuclear weapons	_____	_____	_____	_____	_____
Combating international terrorism	_____	_____	_____	_____	_____
Combating world hunger	_____	_____	_____	_____	_____
Improving the global environment	_____	_____	_____	_____	_____
Strengthening the United Nations	_____	_____	_____	_____	_____
Invading Iraq to overthrow Saddam Hussein	_____	_____	_____	_____	_____
Promoting and defending human rights in other countries	_____	_____	_____	_____	_____
Protecting weaker nations against aggression	_____	_____	_____	_____	_____
Helping to bring a democratic form of government to other nations	_____	_____	_____	_____	_____
Helping to improve the standard of living in less developed nations	_____	_____	_____	_____	_____
Controlling and reducing illegal immigration	_____	_____	_____	_____	_____
Stopping the flow of illegal drugs	_____	_____	_____	_____	_____

The following questions ask about your personal background:

- _____ male   _____ female   year of birth _____
- What is the highest educational degree you have obtained? _____
- Did you ever study abroad?   _____ yes   _____ no
- What do you regard as your primary occupation? _____ secondary? _____

- Roughly speaking, is your annual dollar income from all sources
  _____ less than $100,000
  _____ between 100,000 and $999,999
  _____ $1,000,000 or more
- Approximately what proportion of your charitable donations each year goes to
  local charities?   _____
  national charities?   _____
  international charities? _____
  Total   100%
- Are you a member of an ethnic, racial, or religious minority in the country in which you live? _____ yes _____ no
- Do you think of yourself as
  _____ among the top leaders of your organization or profession
  _____ close to the top
  _____ in the middle range
  _____ toward the bottom
  _____ other (kindly elaborate)
- How many languages do you read and/or speak?
  _____ one _____ two _____ three _____ four _____ five or more
- Do you regard one country as "home"?   _____ yes   _____ no If yes, which one?_____
- Did either or both of your parents (**check all that apply**)
  _____ come from a country other than the U.S.?
  _____ speak other languages in addition to English?
  _____ travel extensively?
  _____ take you on their travels when you were young?
- Roughly, how many employers have you worked for since completing your education?
  _____ none
  _____ one
  _____ two
  _____ three
  _____ four
  _____ five or more
- In your work, approximately how many people are you responsible for?
  _____ none _____ 1 to 10 _____ 11 to 50 _____ 51 to 500
  _____ more than 500

- How would you describe your views on political matters?

_____ Far left	_____ Moderate	_____ Far right
_____ Very liberal	_____ Somewhat conservative	_____ Other
_____ Somewhat liberal	_____ Very conservative	_____ Not sure

- Generally speaking, do you think of yourself as a Republican, a Democrat, an Independent, or what?

_____ Republican	_____ Independent	_____ Other
_____ Democrat	_____ No preference	

- How would you characterize your recollection of receiving the 1999 version of this questionnaire?

  _____ I clearly remember receiving it

  _____ I vaguely remember receiving it

  _____ I do not remember receiving it

  _____ other (kindly specify)

- If you did receive it, did you complete and return it?

  _____ yes   _____ no   _____ not sure

- If there are any other aspects of your life relevant to the processes of globalization you want to note, please feel free to do so here:

Thank you very much for sharing your ideas.

Kindly return to Foreign Policy Leadership Project
The George Washington University
2130 H Street, NW, Suite 709G
Washington, DC 20052

Index

About the Authors

David C. Earnest is assistant professor of political science and international studies at Old Dominion University (Norfolk, Virginia). His substantive research focuses on the political incorporation of migrants in democratic societies, while his methodology interests are in the application of agent-based models to problems of domestic and international politics. At Old Dominion, Dr. Earnest teaches courses in international political economy, international relations theory, and political methodology. He has held an appointment as a fellow in political-military studies at the Center for Strategic and International Studies in Washington, D.C., where he was a specialist in military technology, the defense industrial base, and transatlantic security relations.

Yale H. Ferguson is professor of political science at Rutgers University (Newark, New Jersey); a codirector at the Center for Global Change and Governance, Rutgers University; and an honorary professor of the University of Salzburg, Austria. Professor Ferguson's recent books include *Remapping Global Politics: History's Revenge and Future Shock* (2004) and *The Elusive Quest: Theory and Global Politics* (2003), both with Richard W. Mansbach; and *Political Space: Frontiers of Change and Governance in a Globalizing World* (2002), edited with R. J. Barry Jones.

Ole R. Holsti is the George V. Allen Professor of International Affairs at Duke University (Durham, North Carolina), where he has been on the faculty since 1974. He served as president of the International Studies Association (1979–1980) and has received lifetime achievement awards from the International Society for Political Psychology and the American Political

Science Association. He has also received two university-wide teaching awards. His most recent book is *Public Opinion and American Foreign Policy* (revised edition, 2004).

James N. Rosenau is University Professor of International Affairs at The George Washington University (Washington, D.C.), having been affiliated with three other universities. He is a former president of the International Studies Association (1984–1985) and a holder of a Guggenheim Fellowship (1987–1988). His books include *Turbulence in World Politics: A Theory of Change and Continuity* (1990), *Along the Domestic-Foreign Frontier: Exploring Governance in a Turbulent World* (1997), and *Distant Proximities: Dynamics beyond Globalization* (2003).